Eyewitness to Hell

Eyewitness to Hell

With the Waffen SS
on the Eastern Front in W.W. II

by
Erich Stahl
translated by Robert J. Edwards

THE WAR YEARS

Ryton Publications

Published in the United States by Ryton Publications

RYTON PUBLICATIONS
P.O. BOX 2306
BELLINGHAM, WA. 98227
U.S.A

Printed in the United States
by Applied Digital Imaging

FOREWARD

Eyewitness to Hell represents the first in a Series of exciting titles to be released by Ryton Publications. These titles will concentrate on operations conducted during World War II – a subject already well covered, to be sure – but with a new and exciting twist: The focus will be on warfare from the German soldier's perspective, the so-called "other side of the hill."

Unlike many of the books, which attempt to interpret this perspective, "*The War Years*" will present it in the soldier's own words. These narratives and memoirs will present the reader accustomed to reading Allied accounts with a totally new outlook on operations, tactics, training, doctrine and fighting. In short, an entirely new way to perceive the war. The emphasis will be on the Eastern Front – an area that has commanded considerable fascination over the years, but which still suffers from a dearth of First-hand accounts – until now.

We chose **Eyewitness to Hell** as our inaugural title since it was one of the first books to be written after the conclusion of world-wide and tragic conflict, which attempted to offer a glimpse into the mindset of the average soldier behind the gun at the front, who represented the *Wehrmacht*, nation and people. It was an effort to counter the "conventional wisdom" of the day, and which continues to this day to a large extent, that the Allies were fighting a nation of criminals, who had nothing but disdain for their opponents and human life in general. Stahl not only sets the record straight. He offers a rebuttal to all that – and more. While he was and, to a large extent, continued to be an ardent National Socialist in the post-war years, he was no unblinking adherent of that regime. Indeed, he was deeply critical. While the conclusions he draws and the comments he makes may seem shocking to some, they do show the German opponent as more than an unthinking automaton, executing orders, whatever they might have been.

Stahl posses that are rare ability to captivate his audience through a vivid writing style that captures the ferocity of the fighting on the Eastern Front, while serving in a variety of positions among several different famous and not-so-famous *Waffen SS* formations: *Leibstandarte SS Adolf Hitler,* the *Wiking* Division, Dutch and Ukranian volunteer SS elements. He puts a human face on the combat and the often-tragic events that occurred behind the lines. He makes the war understandable from the German viewpoint and demonstrates convincingly why the German Armed Forces continued to fight long after the war was in sight and defeat inevitable.

While some of his viewpoints on the Soviet Bolshevism may seem anachronistic in today's world, they do serve to vividly demonstrate the complete and utter conviction of the average man in the trenches, when it came to combating Soviet Russia. In the discussion of the fighting in the East, the ideological framework is sometimes forgotten. This book draws the reader in and helps to make the seemingly inexplicable understandable.

Contents

PRELUDE

The afternoon was quiet and very still. I lay on the narrow peasant bed, looking out on the yellow glory of the lemon tree in front of my window. From away in the distance came the fading song of a company on the march.

They were over, the days of Klidi Pass and Kastoria, of the passage across the Gulf of Corinth, of the great victory parade in Athens. We had stormed our way through the pages of history: Corinth, Delphi, Thebes, the Pass of Thermopylae — the radiant Acropolis.

Everywhere, cheering, elated crowds. We had felt the sigh of relief which went up from men and women, even from children, because we had come and not the Italians. We had been swept up in a hot wave of happiness as so many times before — as in Hungary, in Rumania, in Bulgaria. Our tanks had rolled over a carpet of Bulgarian roses; we had drunk wine with Macedonian peasants and shared their bread and salt.

The Balkan campaign was over. Once again, we had been the faster and tougher ones. Yet even so, for all our pride, we could not escape a shadow of' discontent. We knew by now only too well that the Italians were no more than a few days' march behind us, their army communiqués proudly proclaiming the capture of towns and villages that we had handed over to them.

I could not forget the eyes of that old woman in Monsoglion who, gazing in horror at the waving plumes of the Bersaglieri, had said to me in a uncomprehending voice: "So that's it: This is a bad thing you've done, you Germans."

Suddenly, I was jolted from my dream. The ceiling was rocking. With a leap I was out of the window and wedged in the broad branches of the lemon tree. An earthquake, an earthquake in Larissa!

But it did not last long. A few short tremors and then the earth settled down and became quiet, whereupon the peasant family came rushing up to my tree, crossing themselves in wild excitement and shouting to me, heedless of the fact that I did not understand a word.

Shaking my head, I left my involuntary perch—which reminded me of happy days in my youth—climbed down to earth and ran off to the company orderly room, where I found an uproar, our alpine troops crowding round the first sergeant, all talking at once. It was a moment before I realized that it was not all about the earthquake. The men had been listening to an enemy broadcast and had come to ask if it were true what they were saying: That Rudolf Hess, the deputy of the *Führer*, had parachuted into Britain.

That, of course, seemed to be the wildest nonsense. We scoffed at those terrific light infantrymen from Styria and the Bavarian Alps. They departed unconvinced.

Evening brought confirmation. Rudolf Hess had jumped into enemy country. He wanted to bring about peace—all in vain, needless to say! We were stunned, touched by the breath of an unknown terror. Everyone talked without listening; in the end, we fell into an uneasy silence.

Next morning the commander sent for me, to receive a highly secret order. He hesitated a moment and cleared his throat. Finally, he said: "Get all the information you can on Soviet Russia and the part of Poland occupied by Russia in 1939."

I looked at him in blank incomprehension.

He said abruptly: "We're moving east. We're going to finish this everlasting threat."

My first reaction was sheer horror. I remembered Hitler's words in *Mein Kampf* about a war on two fronts. Then the statement that had been issued after the signing of the pact with Russia—a pact that had come as such a shock, especially to National Socialists—but which had in fact simply taken account of the real facts of the situation.

Now this was all to be thrown overboard. A threat? Indeed it was. One of the gravest threats, not only to Germany but to the whole world. But did it have to be then, before we were through with the other guys? Another damned war on two fronts?

Most of my friends had been horrified by the pact with the Kremlin, but I had felt relief. That had been a feat worthy of the Iron Chancellor himself. It was what he would have done: Grasped the bull by the horns, smashed the encirclement. If there were no other choice, if it had to be war, then let it at least wait until we had cleared our backs.

Now, all at once, it was all being swept away. And then I thought: "But this is sheer nonsense, he's putting on an act. It isn't true. It can't be true."

But it was true enough. And it was unavoidable. When there had been only a few German divisions securing on the eastern frontier, the Red Army was concentrating with all of its strength.

The men were completely unconcerned. It was all the same to them, they were used to marching, to fighting, to dying, if need be—but always as victors. It was not often that any man stopped to think about things.

**

Back in Vienna, I ran into a friend, a man closely connected with the Foreign Office Information Service. "He refused to see him!" he spluttered. "He wouldn't even see him one time!"

"Who, what, damn it?" I asked.

"The *Führer*! He refused to see old Count Schulenburg, the ambassador in Moscow, you know. He caught Hitler at the Hotel Imperial. He had all the documents in his briefcase concerning the true status of the Red Army. It's said that Molotov himself had seen to it that he got them—probably in the hope of stalling off the decision. Schulenburg brought his own intelligence reports as well. But Ribbentrop stopped him in the corridor and told him the *Führer's* mind was made up, that his decision was irrevocable and that he couldn't even be received. Schulenburg was livid. He said it wasn't as though he'd committed a crime, his information was of the highest importance. But Ribbentrop would hardly let him speak. It just wasn't going to happen. No matter what he may have, the *Führer* had already decided."

I was silent. After a while, I said angrily: "This is all nonsense. You journalists let your imagination run away with you. It'd do you good to get out and see us for a bit. You'd soon forget all about it."

He gave a nod. "I'm going to as soon as I can. I wish to God you were right and it was only a shithouse rumor. But it's gone beyond that, it's damn near an official story."

***

I said good-bye to my mother and then used the rest of my short leave to pay a quick visit to my former boss, *Gauleiter* Josef Bürckel.[1]

He was in excellent spirits and radiated confidence. "Send me a postcard from Moscow," was his cheerful parting. " Your guys won't waste any time...and then look out, England!"

My brigade, the *"Leibstandarte Adolf Hitler"*,[2] was in Brünn[3] when the news broke that war against the Soviet Union had begun. There was very nearly mutiny in the ranks.

---

1   Translator's Note: Bürckel was an influential member of the National Socialist Party, who was a key player in the integration of the annexed Austria into the greater *Reich*. In 1944, he received the highest NS award that could be given to a civilian, the German Order, First Class, With Swords, for his work for the party. He and his wife died under somewhat mysterious circumstances in the fall of 1944. *Gauleiter* was the NS term for a high-ranking district leader.

2   Although the *Leibstandarte*, Hitler's elite bodyguard formation, is commonly considered a division, it did not officially gain that status until after the invasion of the Soviet Union in 1941. As it underwent a number of designations throughout the war years, ending with the *1. SS-Panzer-Division "Leibstandarte SS Adolf Hitler"*, it will simply be referred to as the *Leibstandarte* throughout the text.

3   Brünn is the German name for the current town of Brno in the Czech Republic. At the time it was heavily populated with ethic Germans, the *Sudentendeutsche*.

"Where do we fit in? You can bet your ass we're going to miss the whole show."

"Shit! Didn't the *Führer* promise we'd be in on everything? We're stuck here, while the others'll soon be entering Moscow."

We spent the night drinking, and after I had had a few drinks more than I could really handle, I was soon swept up in the general wave of confidence. We passed round newspaper articles. Their authors, White-Russian refugees, predicted the immediate break-up of the Soviet Union. We listened in breathless excitement to the first Armed Forces Daily Reports and passed on their contents to the others.

At last, on the third day, our convoys moved out and began to roll toward the east. In Silesia, we found cheering and waving people everywhere. Crowds almost frantic with delight. Old men, veterans from the first Russian campaign, spent hours by our resting columns, showering them with advice on how to eliminate the Cossacks and the Russian infantry. Women stuffed us with food and cigarettes, too much to take with us, let alone to consume on the spot. Happy, shouting children followed us everywhere; girls we didn't know hugged us and covered us with kisses.

But soon, our nostrils were filled with the stench of burning villages. The air trembled with the distant rumble of guns. Our hearts beat faster, seasoned though we were to war. Tomorrow's battle never fails to put a clamp round the heart. We hastily wrote our first postcards home.

Then the curtain rose on the great drama which was to hold us all in its spell for so many long years.

Whenever there are differing place names, they will be indicated in the text with square brackets.

TIME OF VICTORY

Chapter One:
The Northern Route of Advance

The division had been on the march since dawn. For hours it had rumbled past smoldering, reeking houses. We saw the first dead lying beside the road. The troops looked at them closely, curiously, and with mounting excitement. They were the bodies of men from Siberian and Mongolian regiments, men whom the reeling giant of a nation had torn from their homes in the east and thrown in to defend its threatened frontier in the west.

The thunder of the battle rolled close ahead of us. Waves of Kleist's armor[4] had pushed deep into enemy country; thrusting far ahead on the northern route of advance. Where they had come in sight of Kiev. Once the enemy had recovered from the shock of our first onslaught, his forces had advanced in waves in front of, behind and on both sides of our armor, which stood like a huge porcupine in the surrounding chaos, short of fuel and out of ammunition—supplies had not arrived.

Our division's mission was to clear the northern route of the enemy and allow fuel to get through to the armored spearheads. So far, we had seen nothing of the Red Air Force. In the woods we were moving through, the first rounds of Soviet artillery were impacting, but they stopped almost as quickly as they had come.

---

4   Translator's Note: This was *Panzergruppe von Kleist*, which had a total of four mechanized divisions allocated to it, including the author's *Leibstandarte*.

The battalion commander called up his liaison officer: "I want you to reconnoiter the approaches to the northern route. Take a couple of men with you."

The young *SS-Untersturmführer*[5] turned and pointed to his driver and me. We moved out over hilly country, past waving grain fields, past apparently deserted hovels with brown and blue washed walls and golden yellow thatched roofs. Every now and then the officer looked at his map. Suddenly, he turned to me, squatting in the back of the vehicle, and said in a strained voice: "The map's wrong."

I looked up at him, astonished, and saw how beads of sweat were standing on his forehead. We had long since lost all sight and sound of the battalion and had moved forward a good 10 kilometers miles into enemy country. Everything was calm and peaceful, like a quiet Sunday morning. Even the sound of the distant tank fighting had ceased. It seemed like the church bells had to toll at any second. We raced up a steep hill from which we could see deep into the terrain, where far away, almost on the horizon, there was a broad, grey ribbon. Dust clouds rose and vanished. The northern avenue of advance!

"Convoys," the officer said, his poise returned. "Ivan's bringing up reinforcements." He had the vehicle turn around and we started back. In the mean time, the battalion had been slowly following along, and we met it about half way. The officer made his report, and our vehicle remained at the head of the column. By the time we reached the hill again, the dust clouds had vanished. In the meantime, it had turned dark. We moved on and on. There was no sign of the enemy.

The men were cheerful and in high spirits. I heard an NCO say: "We'll be in Moscow in six weeks, if only Ivan will move fast enough." I sat in the vehicle looking out over the tranquil countryside, trying desperately to fight down my feverish mood. I felt like a stranger in my own skin. I was certainly no stranger to war and knew what was going on. It was our task to avert the danger from the east, to smash it and be done with it, once and for all. And yet, faced with this vast

---

5   Translator's Note: For those not familiar with German ranks, a rank chart is included at the back of the book. An *SS-Untersturmführer* was the equivalent of a 2nd Lieutenant.

expanse of land, I found myself gripped by a feeling of hopeless abandonment and fear, fear of falling into a trap. It was, of course, ridiculous. Our armies had been triumphant everywhere they had been; the furious onslaught of our tanks had smashed the enemy wherever he had been found and had driven all before it.

Gradually, the air became clearer and visibility improved. The day's haze was gone. Evening came down over the wide plain, and in the fathomless forests and marshes that we passed were the first deep shadows of the night.

A shout went up through the battalion: We had reached the main route of advance. Right and left of us towered the walls of the Ukrainian forests. All talking and singing had long since died. Still not a shot. We drove on.

Our vehicle was second in the column by then and the CO waved it up. I could hear him ordering the *Untersturmführer* to reconnoiter a crossroads. "Take a sidecar motorcycle...it'll be more maneuverable."

The *Untersturmführer* nodded to me. We mounted the machine and rode out into the darkness of the night, far ahead of the battalion. I was feeling more myself again. We drove on...one kilometers... two...three...four. Behind us we could hear the comforting rattle of the battalion coming up fast. Suddenly, the officer had the motorcycle stop. The crossroads was just in front and to our right. Halfway in the roadside ditch was an armored car—a Russian one.

The *Untersturmführer* lit a cigarette in a leisurely fashion. "The tanks have made a good job of that one," he said, smiling. He went up to the vehicle, one door of which was open. "Ivan's bailed," he added. He ran his hand over the roughly riveted sides of the vehicle and said: "It's a shoddy looking job."

In the meantime, I had joined him beside the vehicle. I put my head into the open door and withdrew it again. "Gives you a strange feeling all the same, *Untersturmführer*." He tried to suppress a loud laugh and stuck his head inquisitively into the car. While that was happening, I walked off to see if the old man was following up with

17

the rest of the unit. At that moment, a shot rang out. The officer turned in surprise and dropped. A second later, the armored car started to move and headed out on to the road. The driver and I were already in the ditch, almost by instinct. A burst of machine-gun fire whipped over our heads and, before we had time to grasp what was happening, the car vanished into the night.

The driver shook the officer. "You all right, *Untersturmführer*? "

There was no answer. Upset, I tried to raise him up; when I supported his head, however, my hand became moist. Despite the risk, I switched on my pocket lamp for a second and then extinguished it. Right in the middle of the young officer's forehead was a neat round hole.

"He's had it," the driver whispered, and cursed to himself.

Just as we were getting ready to start up the motorcycle, there was a wild flurry of noise from the direction of the battalion. Shots whipped through the night. We looked at each other, not sure what to do. "The best thing we can do is to stay where we are," the driver said.

The noise stopped as abruptly as it had begun. There was no doubt that the battalion was getting closer. A few minutes later, the commander's vehicle came to a halt beside me. Somewhat shakily, I reported what had happened. The CO shouted at me at the top of his voice; I have no idea to this day what he said. He probably doesn't either.

Shortly afterwards, the battalion moved on again.

By that time, it had grown pitch dark, and you couldn't see your hand in front of your face. According to the map, we weren't to far from Shitomir, west of the village of Klewan.

Suddenly, a few more rounds went crashing through the night. Wild confusion was the result. Orders were bawled. The young liaison officer ran past me shouting: "Get moving, all company vehicles to move up the side road and set up 360 security! "

I ran on to find the first company commander I could. A few moments later, the heavy vehicles were clanking and clattering nose to tail up the side road away from that fatal crossroads. Machine-gun rounds tore into our midst, and the first wounded cried out. Self-propelled 3.7cm *Flak* at the head of the column heaved their way like gigantic ploughs through the nighttime grain field. Short bursts of fire rattled through the night. Machine-gun sections formed the continuous links between the self-propelled guns. Men crouched among the huge vehicles trying to locate the enemy. Tanks clattered through it all; light Soviet tanks. One of our vehicles caught fire but, miraculously, it was put out immediately. It was an ammunition truck. The enemy fire grew heavier, bursting and crashing round our ears from all sides. There was no longer any doubt—we were surrounded.

Together with a few other men unknown to me, I crouched in the ditch beside the road, firing wildly into the night. I dug in as well I could. Tracers whipped across the sighing grain sheaves. A hand touched my shoulder. It was Kaul.

"This is it," he said hoarsely. "Maybe…"

I tried to pass it off. "Let's find the bastards first. And then wait till morning."

Kaul looked me in the face, his eyes shining white in the flashes of impacting shells. "Are you afraid?" I asked, worried. He smiled. "If you'd been through what I have, then you wouldn't be afraid. Of course, I also want to live."

"Don't be an idiot," I interrupted. "You're not going to die that easily…"

Kaul laughed softly. "Easier than you think."

I stood up, keeping my head low, and said: "I'm going to take a leak."

He tried to force me down. "Stay here."

But I tore myself away and walked a couple of steps into the grain, which was tall enough to reach my shoulder. As I was standing there taking a leak, a figure detached itself from the darkness a few yards away. "Watch out," I said, "there's a hell of a lot of iron in the air...supposed to be good for lung problems, iron in the air." Then I saw him unmistakably pull out a grenade.

"Ivan," I yelled as loudly as I could, throwing myself on the ground. I had hardly reached the ground before the first bursts from Kaul's submachine gun hissed across inches away from me. I saw the Russian collapse without a sound. As quickly as I could, I jumped back into the ditch. I was unable to speak.

"I joined up in '39," he went on, as if nothing had happened. "SS leader in a small town, you know; it was meant to be. But I was on the old side and my heart a bit suspect so, after basic training, I went off to the *Totenkopf* guard units."[6]

"Well?" I said, still rattled by what had happened.

"Well, you say. That's what I said at the time. I was disappointed of course, but still quite hopeful of getting into action. Instead, I found myself on concentration camp guard duty. I haven't slept properly since then...Guard at a concentration camp for a whole year...You know, a lot of what's said isn't true, or, at any rate, is exaggerated, but what is true is bad enough. People herded together, cooped up for years in a tiny space. I got quite friendly with one of them in time—a Polish university professor. Then one day, he was at work as usual with the others, when he suddenly walked towards the camp limits. 'Shoot!' he implored me, in a quiet manner. 'Please shoot. I can't stand it any longer.' 'Stay where you are,' I shouted in horror, bringing my rifle up—those were our orders—only that the desperate man no longer saw me or heard me. He was already in another world. I was shaking all over. 'Stay where you are, for God's sake, stay where you are...you know the orders. He crossed the line with his eyes shut. I couldn't shoot. I was incapable of it. Then the neighboring guard opened fire.

---

6   Translator's Note: The soldier is referring to the *Totenkopfverbände*—Death's Head Formations—which were responsible for guarding concentration camps.

"I wrote to the *Reichsführer*;[7] I wrote to everyone I knew who had any sort of pull. I wanted to get to the front...to the front line forces. I didn't want to be a jailer. Finally...finally...it worked.

"All this," he gazed vacantly out into the fire-studded night. "This is heaven after that."

"You've got nerves," I said uncomfortably. "You don't know what you're saying!"

He just smiled.

Gradually, the Russians drew their ring of death tighter, and their fire became heavier. "Come on," cried an *Untersturmführer*, who was unknown to me. "A few men can be pulled out here without any problem." He took Kaul and me and another man by the sleeve. "Ammunition for the infantry guns!"

An Untersturmführer stood on a truck and intensely observed the muzzle flashes of the nearby enemy battery. He didn't pay any attention to the raging fires around us. He was the platoon leader of the infantry guns. Besides the *Flak* platoon, they were our salvation. The *Untersturmführer*—Waldemar Schütz—had identified the firing position of the Russians and issued brief orders. Round after round howled through the night and impacted with a screech into the nearby enemy firing position. We breathed easier.

We humped crate after crate of ammunition through the enemy fire to where the guns had taken up position in the deep ditch to our right. There was a heavy machine gun close by at the edge of the road and, whenever it fired, the enemy rifle fire stopped. An *Oberscharführer* was directing the fire. I exchanged a few casual words with him when he praised us on how quickly we had brought up the ammunition. After we had crossed that stretch of hell for perhaps the tenth time, I crouched down at his feet and lit a cigarette. Suddenly, an invisible hand struck him behind the knees and he sank soundlessly to the ground.

---

7   Translator's Note: He is referring to the *Reichsführer SS*, Heinrich Himmler, the leader of the *SS*.

"Shot in the head," Kaul whispered when we turned him over. "That's the kind of death you want."

The next noncommissioned officer in command jumped up and continued to direct the fires. By the time we had staggered up with the next load of ammunition, he was also lying stretched out beside his comrade.

"You see," Kaul said, lost in thought, his words cutting into my horror, "this is what I always dreamt it would be; this is the real *SS*—not the concentration camps, not the *Gestapo* or the *Sicherheitsdienst*[8]—but soldiers who fight and die when they're told." He paused. "Not barbed-wire fences and security zones."

I was too bewildered to answer. A moment later, shells from a Soviet battery crashed into our defensive positions. But only once or twice. Then they were silenced by the salvoes from our self-propelled *Flak* and infantry guns. Towards morning, a rumor went round that all units of the division had been surrounded and that radio contact had been lost. Shortly afterwards, the battalion commander's orders came down the line: "Enemy attack expected at dawn. No one can come to our aid. The battalion will hold the crossroads in accordance with orders. Quarter will neither be asked nor given. You saw the mutilated bodies of your comrades yesterday afternoon and know what to expect."

Towards morning, the enemy fire suddenly ceased. Everyone sat up in his makeshift trench or in the shelter of a vehicle. I piled up ammo clips beside me to have everything within reach. They would probably be enough for two hours. After that—but it was no use thinking about that.

For half an hour there was no firing. Our nerves were stretched to the breaking point. If only something would happen. If only they would come. But nothing happened. An hour passed and morning claimed its due in the skies.

"Good light for firing," Kaul said, elaborately lighting his pipe.

---

8   Translator's Note: = Security Service (of the *SS*).

I looked in the direction of the broad road to the west. I narrowed my eyes to see better. What...that was impossible! I feverishly tore across to the commanding officer's dug-out.

"German bicycle forces coming up from the west," I reported breathlessly.

He looked at me without a word. Then he raised his field glasses. "Come on," he roared, and we leapt on the sidecar motorcycle and raced off along the line of surprised riflemen.

A slow-moving and portly Army *Major* dismounted awkwardly from his bicycle, a laugh across his face. "It's crazy," he said. "I was told in the last village that they'd heard firing over here all night; but I see it's all quiet!"

My commander cleared his throat. "Pretty quiet," he said in a strangely thick voice, "I've only got about 40 dead."

The friendly face of the *Major* turned to stone.

"But," my commander went on, "it seems that the enemy has withdrawn."

Shortly afterwards we climbed on the motorcycle again and rode away to the east.

***

Soon the sky darkened, and a soft rain began. The men were tired out after their sleepless night and sat, wet and shivering, in their combat vehicles. Above us came the sound of engines. One of theirs? No, it was ours. But then bombs began to fall over to our right. They had been unable to identify us in the light fog and took us for retreating Soviets. The men all stood up and gestured. More bombs fell, but no one attempted to take cover. Instead, there was general shouting, cursing and waving. Finally, the good man figured it out. Thoroughly ashamed of himself, he climbed steeply and disappeared. We didn't take a single casualty; our respect for the *Luftwaffe* had not increased.

Towards afternoon we realized that the narrow lane we were following led into our objective, the northern route of advance. We were now close behind the divisional armored assault battalion, which showed that there was something afoot. We moved on and on. Occasionally, we heard sniping, but nobody bothered to stop, it would have cost too much time and by now every man knew what our mission was. The armor had advanced to within a few miles of Kiev, where they were stuck, out of fuel and with little food and ammunition. Behind them the Russians were closing their ranks and had our tanks nicely in the trap. Supply columns could not get through as the main supply was enemy held. It was our mission to free it and allow the armor some breathing room. We moved on and on. At four in the morning we crossed the old Russian frontier. Later the same morning, we experienced our first Russian air raid—30 to 40 machines at a time. We suffered two dead and several wounded. Towards evening we were attacking outside the village of Romanovka against stubborn Russian resistance. The enemy was thrown back. I did not see any action.

***

That evening, we took up quarters in a large collective farm. Most of the cattle belonging to it had been shot by the retreating Russians. It was there that I talked for the first time to ethnic Germans.

A young woman brought us milk and honey. "Are any of your men from the Palatinate?" she asked.

We were sorry to say there were not. She told us that her family originally came from the Rhine Palatinate.

We asked what sort of a life they had had. Life? Oh! They got by until 1928.

After that?

Her father had been shot; he had been against the collective farm.

"Perhaps he should have thought more of his family," she said in a tired voice. "But he was always saying, we paid for this plot of ground with our own sweat and money, and nobody was going to take it away from us. So he was shot for sabotaging the revolution. Two of my brothers were given ten years; we've never heard from them since. Georg, the younger one, wrote once from Irkutsk. But nothing since then. Mother left us; her mind gave way and she hanged herself. Hans, my husband was taken off a month ago to dig defenses. I wonder if I'll ever see him again? I doubt it. And so I'm left alone with three children."

The three little ones, two girls and a boy, clung shyly to their mother's skirt.

We looked at each other. What amazed us was the matter-of-fact way in which this young woman told her story, as though it were no more than trivial village gossip. We listened incredulously.

An old Ukrainian spoke up; he had been a prisoner in Austria during the first war and knew a few words of German.

"You must think not that only ethic Germans in Hell," he said with some difficulty. "Five years in prison for being late for work twice. I have no watch and live a long way from the collective farm. My brother shot."

He said it in the same matter-of-fact, almost indifferent voice.

"But you all talk as if you were talking about a bad harvest," I said. " You tell us these horrible stories and don't seem the least bit upset."

The Ukrainian smiled. "Do you know what it's like to live close to death? Nothing is as big as it first looked."

We had no reply. There was no more to be said.

***

On again next morning. Through huge pine forests, over fertile hills, across enormous marshes, deeper and ever deeper into the endless land. Demolished bridges forced us to detour, but we held our course for the northern route. At last, on the 11th of July, we reached our desired objective, the main road. The lead companies rested in the dense vegetation and groups of hills; immediately in front of us were the assault guns. .

At about nine, a German sergeant appeared on the road, without cap or belt, an pistole P08 in his hand. While wiping the blood off his face, he rendered a report. An Army motorcycle battalion had been encircled for three days in the village of Sokoloff, three kilometers north of the main road. He had been sent out in a last attempt to get help and had spent all night infiltrating through the Soviet lines; in the end, he'd been seen and fired on, but he had got through by a miracle.

A few minutes later, assault guns loaded with infantry were headed towards Sokoloff. The sergeant was on the first gun.

We had gone some way down the road when an antitank gun fired. Before the first gun could reply, it was on fire. The second gun moved up. It was luckier, and silenced the enemy antitank gun at pointblank range. We moved the few meters into the village and immediately ran into enemy fire. The infantry scrambled off the guns and took up positions in the ditch by the side of the road. I pressed myself close to the ground, staring in the direction from which the enemy fire must have come. The assault guns were firing indiscriminately into the open country. Suddenly, I saw a head move in the window of the roof of the building opposite. I found myself looking straight into the eyes of a Russian who was setting up a machine gun to fire against comrades in a defile 30 meters or so behind me. I raised my rifle and took aim. The building was not 10 meters way.

As he brought up his machine gun, I pressed the trigger. The man staggered, and I distinctly saw blood trickle down his forehead. I remained where I was, motionless, incapable of moving. The men around me leaped out of the ditch and ran across the road into the building. One nudged me as he went: "You all right?"

I stood up, trembling, and wiped the sweat off my forehead. My knees were weak. I had killed a man for the first time in my life, coldly and deliberately.

The next few minutes had the quality of a dream. I saw myself running through the village street with the others; to our right, an assault gun was firing its main gun and machine gun as it went. Then I was looking into sweaty, grimy faces, faces filled with joy. Dozens of hands stretched out towards me; a slim and elegant officer, his immaculate uniform making a strange contrast with his surroundings, pulled me head over heels towards him into cover.

"I've killed one," I gasped, then pulled myself together. The *Oberstleutnant*, a man considerably beyond 50, gave me a sharp look and then smiled. "Shoot faster, son, you'll have longer to live."

I settled down beside him. He brought up his rifle and fired into a patch of open ground across which brown figures were running back and forth. I followed his example. I heard the officer say: "You did well. We were practically finished. I won't forget your division any time soon."

In the meantime, the platoon leader of the assault guns had taken a look at the situation and radioed for reinforcements. Soon, the whole assault gun battery was rolling into Sokoloff. The Russians fell back before the pressure; the pocket grew.

"Have you eaten?" The *Oberstleutnant* suddenly asked me. Eaten? I said no. "Then you'll be my guest."

I looked at him, speechless, and then tried to straighten my mud-covered uniform. A soldier served the *Oberstleutnant* and his adjutant, a corpulent *Major*, with gleaming white paper napkins and proper, white soup bowls with beef soup, meat and vegetables. It was like a fairy tale. During the meal, the *Oberstleutnant* was continually receiving company reports and issuing orders.

The meal over, I stood up and asked permission to take leave to go to my comrades who were in a defile about a hundred meters away.

In turning, I glanced back in the direction from which we had come that morning and saw several dozen yellowish-brown steel helmets at the edge of the grain field near the narrow sandy road.

"Ivan's behind us," I said quickly. The *Oberstleutnant* smiled incredulously. "Those are probably your reinforcements."

I looked closer: "Our camo helmet covers don't shine in the sun."

He stiffened and stood up. "Engineer platoon, drivers, messengers, clerks, cooks—everybody out! Ivan's behind us!"

The men came scrambling out of the command post dugouts and were assembled. At that moment, the Russians attacked in company strength from the rear. I stood up with the others and fired blindly into the grain field. Machine-gun fire forced us to the ground. Lying there, firing magazine after magazine into the field, I became aware of a shadow falling across me. I looked round and saw, three paces from where I was lying, the *Oberstleutnant* standing upright in the open, a small pistol in his belt, white leather gloves.

"More to the right, men. A lot more to the right. And take better aim. Silence that machine gun, Franz. Give it a few bursts," he directed the machine gunner. Hesitantly, I also got to my feet. From there I could see something. In a flash, all the men were up, and then came the immediate counterattack, whereupon the Russians stood up and ran straight into the well-aimed fires of the reinforcements coming up to help us.

In the meantime, the whole battalion had closed up and joined in. A German aerial artillery observer began to circle over our heads. Artillery support at last! But we were also in a hail of Russian shells bursting about our ears. The command posts received particular attention. Again, the aircraft circled low overhead. And again enemy shells screamed down with an uncanny precision. The men became worried. Heavy artillery joined in as well—28cm. The earth thundered and heaved.

"This is stupid," cried Kaul beside me. "The guy's got to be a Russian!"

He pointed to the German aircraft. True enough, as if to confirm his words, enemy shells started falling again with withering accuracy. The wounded could no longer be taken back. The command posts were shifted and we combed through the village houses again. Radio messages flew back and forth between battalion and division. At last, we received permission to fire on the German aircraft, and the next time it approached it was immediately ringed with bursting shells. He went higher and circled. Once again, enemy shells came down on our positions. Only then did the aircraft take off. A *Fieseler Storch* must have fallen into Ivan's hands at some point, and he was now using it against us—complete with its German markings. By evening, the enemy had been beaten and forced back towards the Rokitno Marshes.

As if to counterbalance that, the whole division then became involved in a violent defensive action along 10 kilometers of the main road.

The 1st Battalion was on the right, with the reconnaissance battalion next to it. To the left were the 2nd and 4th Battalions, with the latter battalion seeing action for the first time there. Over and over again, the Russians charged the lines of the division in seemingly endless waves and, without any regard for casualties, attempted to penetrate our positions. Things got ugly in the sector of the reconnaissance battalion at first light on the second day, even though the men of the battalion were performing like heroes. When another gigantic massing of Red Army men advanced out of the woods to the north of the road and through a grain field when it turned day, Schütz' infantry gun platoon fired ricochet rounds into them[9]. The results were horrific. Working with the platoons from the reconnaissance battalion, the Russian thrust could be stopped and then eliminated. The Russians that had penetrated in the sector of the 1st battalion were defeated.

---

9   Translator's Note: These were rounds intentionally fired short, so as to skip upwards and explode, thus causing greater casualties among their targets.

The casualties that the Red Army had to take were so heavy that their offensive efforts were derailed and the division was able to gain more and more terrain. The plan of Marshall Budenny—to roll up our entire right flank—had failed.

At last, there came a day's rest in the village of Motyshin, where I met the first Ukrainian industrial workers I had seen, employees from a neighboring pottery. One of them, a Pole, spoke German well. I was desperately eager to talk to people from what one might expect to be the elite class within this workers' paradise.

"How do we live? That's not difficult to tell you," he said in answer to my question. "We get about 400 rubles a month. A pair of shoes costs 500 to 600, a suit at least 600. Bread is 9 rubles a loaf; meat, 15 rubles."

"But no one can live on that," I said, astonished.

The Pole shrugged his shoulders. "They don't let that worry them. The director gets 3,000, of course, and the engineers at least 1,500."

I began to wonder if I was hearing right.

"And not only that," he said, "our shops have different prices and goods from those used by the engineers, directors and party men. As a worker you can't just buy where you want to, but only in the cooperative that has been assigned to you. And you can't buy what you like either, only what you're allocated."

"The NKVD, Red Army officers and party leaders have other co-ops, other shops. We don't even know what they get there. But they look all right and dress well enough—unlike us," said an old ethnic German woman who had elbowed her way up. "And if you're allowed to buy a dress once in a year—and that often costs more than 400 rubles—maybe you want a green one, size 2—the salesman takes a red one, size 4, off the hook because there's nothing else there. And you're happy just to have anything, something for which you've saved an entire year."

"But," I said, "you've got your proletarian democracy...why don't you do something about it at the elections?"

There was general silence for a moment, and then the little crowd that had gathered around rocked with laughter. The Pole had tears running down his cheeks, he thought my comment was so funny.

"The voting lists have always got Joseph Stalin and Molotov at the top; then comes Zhdanov, Beria and the rest of the Central Committee. After that you get the local candidates of the Communists and non-aligned block—all on one list, the only one allowed. It was all laid down in the election laws of 1936, drawn up by Stalin himself. There's no other list of candidates to vote on. And not voting is more than a little dangerous. It's called high treason. So, if you value your life and freedom, you give your vote along with the rest. That's what's called proletarian democracy."

The ethnic German women went on: "The 'freely' elected deputies represent the 16 Soviet Republics, and 631 paid yes-men sit in the Supreme Soviet, 650 more in the Soviet of the Nationalities. The 53 ministers and 33 members of government are nothing more than departmental bureaucrats. All decisions are taken by the 14 men of the Politburo, the Central Committee, and these men decide the fate of 200 million. Yet they are not appointed to their posts by the millions whom they rule, nor by the six million party members, but solely and exclusively by the order of Joseph Stalin. His is the most absolute dictatorship history has known. Next to him, the Czar, even Napoleon, were babes in arms. What those Caesars tried to do, he has accomplished: He has established his dictatorship over doing and being, over sleeping and waking, over the bearing of children, over children and families themselves, over thought and speech, even over silence—and over life and death. He alone is master, accountable to none; not even to his own conscience—because he has none.

"And this," continued the old woman, "is what the world outside calls 'proletarian democracy.' How far the fraud has succeeded is obvious from your question, German soldier. But within Russia itself, it has come to the point where men and women starve and want, thinking all is well, that that is what life is. They cherish their chains, never having known anything different!"

Our conversation was cut short by the order to move.

***

That evening we stopped in a fair-sized village. As soon as the locals saw that I was trying to make contact with them, hundreds of men and women clustered round me.

An intelligent-looking youth caught me by the arm. "For years, we Ukrainians have been suffering and dying," he said. "Now it's our turn. We want nothing from you Germans; we are ready to do anything. Just give us rifles, give us ammunition."

In his excitement, his last words poured out in Ukrainian, whereupon the crowd fell into a frenzy.

"*Pushka! Pushka!*"[10] the shout went up.

"I'm just an ordinary soldier," I replied, deeply affected by their emotion, "but I hope your wish comes to pass."

"You see, *Pan*," the boy went on, "my father was an old Bolshevik who was sent to Siberia by the Czar, because he believed in liberty, equality and fraternity. Later on, he fought as a partisan, and we were very proud of him. But when he raised his voice in factory meetings against the senseless terror and the class distinctions in distributing food and goods, he disappeared and hasn't been seen since. The same happened to all the old guard; they suddenly became Trotskyites, saboteurs and traitors. These men who'd won power for the revolution and the workers' councils with their blood. You'll be lucky to find a dozen of them left in all of the Ukraine. The rest of them have been purged, branded as 'traitors' and shot or simply disappeared. They brought us liberty, the liberty to die if you don't knuckle under; they brought us equality, an equality with class distinctions which couldn't be more rigid under the worst capitalist regime. The man who doesn't belong to the party doesn't get a special identity card,

---

10   Translator's Note: = rifles.

and the man without the card barely gets enough to live on. Fraternity they brought us too, the fraternity of the commissars and the bullet in the back of the head."

At the word commissar, the crowd went nearly frantic. "The commissar," cried a crippled old man, pointing to his deformed back.

"The commissar," cried a young woman, pointing to her missing eye.

Two younger women carried an older Ukrainian out to us on a primitive stretcher. She grasped my hands tightly with her skinny fingers and, in a passionate whisper, repeated again and again a few sentences that I could not understand.

"She was the wife of our village priest," the boy said in a soft voice. "When the Red Army pulled out, the commissars rounded up all the 'unreliable' peasants...and shot them." The woman's eyes held me in a fixed stare. "Our priest and his two sons were among them, the youngest eight years old. She was prostrate with the shock and now she's paralyzed. She wants you Germans to revenge her; she wants you to revenge each of her children a hundredfold."

"Puschka! Puschka!" they all cried, men and women alike. Overcome by the intensity of their passion, I pressed the many hands stretched out to me and turned away wordlessly.

Chapter Two:
Advance to the South

We moved all that night, noting that we were heading the south. Infantry units had already arrived by forced marches to within sight of Kiev. We moved through Zhitomir—still smoldering—and went on as far as Justynbrad. The enemy was resisting desperately with everything he had, and concentrations of his artillery and air force made our lives a misery for the next few days. One day, in the midst of a ticklish situation, I came to know a side of myself that was quite new to me. Enemy bombs were falling among us again, accurately for once, and a fountain of earth spouted up beside me. As the splinters whistled their hard, metallic tune, I heard a voice crying, "Field dressing!" My hand went instinctively to my pocket. The last one! We had been dressing the wounds of comrades all day and although I had drawn three that morning, I had only one left. My hand came out—empty. What if I needed one? Then I got a hold of myself, crawled out and held out the dressing to the wounded man. I was unable to look him in the face, I was so ashamed of my hesitation.

In quick succession, we took Popofgrad, Medovada and Zipananovka, in the last of which I heard that Max Amon, a friend from my recruit days, had been killed in action. The first of our old unit.

At Zipananovka, it was brought home to us just how bitter the fighting in the east had become. We lost the place again for a time and, on recapturing it, found that our war graves had been rooted up and fouled by human excrement. We continued the attack and cleaned up Novo Archangelsk.

The enemy was well dug in on the hills nearby and proving very difficult. He was apparently determined to hold these hills at all costs as the focal point for a full-scale defense line. There was one light battery in particular, located just behind a slight depression in the ground a few hundred yards in front of our infantry line, which refused to budge and fired salvo after salvo against our advancing infantry, inflicting heavy casualties. The commander of 6th *Flak* Battery, which had been attached in support to us, made a snap decision and brought up one of his guns—*Anton*[11]—to the infantry lines and an exciting duel began between old *Anton* and the Russian battery.

Round after round screamed out of the hot barrel at pointblank range. When the Soviet battery commander saw our *Untersturmführer* standing upright on a limber, directing *Anton's* fire through his glasses, he also stood up and walked back and forth on a low wall directing his battery's fire, heedless of the hail of metal about his ears. *Anton's* first round fell short. The second was over. That depression was not easy to hit. We were fearful of the fate of our gun, which enemy shells were wreathing in a spraying fountain of earth and splinters. But the third round was on the spot and the fourth must have been a hit, because the battery fell silent for a moment, only to resume firing with redoubled fury shortly thereafter. But then *Anton* struck home, plumb in the center of the depression. Wheels, gun parts and men whirled into the air. Another hit, and yet another. The Soviet commander had finished his fight for world revolution. Our infantry resumed their advance and, by evening, were securely dug in on the hills.

Back in the village, darkness fell over the sunflower fields, and the tapping of the Morse keys by the signalmen was the only thing alive. We had again lost contact on both flanks. Just as I was getting ready to lie down, the liaison officer called out: "Runner!"

I was to go to 17th Company and tell it to move back 500 meters to prevent Ivan from infiltrating between the companies. The motorcycle whirred through the night. We rode without lights and, every now and then, lurched into a crater left behind by the previous day's shelling. Then the driver stopped: "The 17th should be right in front of us, now." Unfortunately, the messenger from the 17th Company's runner had been wounded that afternoon, and I did not know the position of any other company but my own. So, exhausted by fatigue, I

---

11   Translator's Note: Battery guns were usually designated alphabetically which, in the phonetic military alphabet in use by the German military at the time, was *Anton*.

stumbled straight ahead over furrows and dead Russians, tripped and pulled myself up again, trying all the time to steer a straight course. For safety's sake, I put the cigarette I had been going to light back into my pocket. All around me it was dead, but I felt that something might start at any moment.

It did. All at once, I knew I was lost and felt the cold touch of panic. I had been wandering through the pitch-black night for at least half an hour, and there was no sound to be heard far and wide. Off to the left, a few bursts of fire echoed through the night, but everything all deadly quiet where I was. I dropped to the ground and pressed my ear to the soil. I remembered reading way back in some Karl May book[12] that the ground carries sound better than the air. But that earth carried nothing. When I stood up, I had to admit to myself that I had completely lost my bearings. Suddenly, I heard a noise in front of me. I listened tensely in the darkness. I heard it again, clearer; some men were coming towards me.

I started off to meet them and was about to call out when I heard clearly and distinctly through the silence: *"Njet, na pravo..."* I stopped, frozen with terror, and then dropped noiselessly into the nearest furrow. A Soviet combat patrol was out looking for the German lines. In the meantime, they had come even closer. I could distinctly hear the clink of their weapons. They were even with me. Their boots crunched past on either side, barely a couple of feet away. My heart beat so violently I was afraid they would hear it. I only realized they were past me when their leader again ordered: *"Na pravo...*to the right!" I stood up again with an effort and crept quietly after them. Judging from the noise, there were no more than 20 men in the patrol. Minutes passed, but there were no incidents.

Suddenly, a young soldier's high voice rung out straight ahead, "Halt, who goes there?"

"Look out, it's Ivan!" I yelled and fired off my entire clip. Then I dropped. Almost simultaneously with my last round there came the

---

12   Translator's Note: Karl May was a German writer of westerns, who was extremely popular among German youth during the pre-war period. He produced hundreds of westerns, although he had never once set foot in North America.

first machine-gun burst. Almost the entire patrol was wiped out; only a few men got away in the darkness. I had found the 17th.

***

The next morning brought more fighting and more victories. Towards midday, enemy resistance stiffened considerably. We had thrust through Olgopol and reached Pullakovka, where we found a huge tank abandoned by its crew for lack of fuel. We opened up the hatches and looked inside. Ammunition was stacked high up to the top. A Vodka bottle was positioned beside the main gun sights. A thick book lay open by the gunner's telescope—*Das Kapital* by Karl Marx.

I slowly paged through the large work. For years the doctrine of surplus value and its uses had brought destruction and disaster to the peoples of the world. Strikes, penal servitude and death were the concomitants of this pseudo-science. In the few decades of its existence, it had destroyed hundreds of thousands of human beings, uprooted millions, brought endless misery over the world. Here, in its Mecca, it had for years been driving people by their millions from life into death; in this land of Russia, the world's greatest laboratory, it had handled living human beings—individuals and the masses—as just so many guinea pigs.

We often wondered at the almost inhuman tenacity with which the Red Army was fighting, the terrible obstinacy with which even the youngest *Komosol* youths, boys of 15, defended their pillboxes, their tanks and their own selves, until one day a Caucasian prisoner lifted the veil from the secret. As soon as any situation became completely untenable, the commissar would leave his pillbox or tank on some pretext, barricade it from the outside and take off to where new resistance was being formed. The simple Siberians and Kalmucks left inside had been taught all their lives that Europeans were fascists and capitalists who murdered their prisoners with horrible gruesomeness. And so they went on fighting with the desperation of hunted, cornered animals until overcome by the superior strength of our arms.

***

That evening an Uzbek deserter, an old man, gave himself up to the company's outposts, and I was ordered to take him back. He interested me, and I asked permission to be present at the interrogation.

"I'm not going back," he said. "I want to fight the Bolsheviks."

"But the Uzbek regiments are fighting like fanatics for Stalin," the interpreter replied.

The old man shrugged his shoulders. "Young men who know nothing of the world...but me, I've been a sailor. I've seen America and I've seen German sailors. And I saw the great revolution when they cheated us first time."

The interpreter asked the old Asian man to tell his tale. He took a deep breath...

Limitless and immense the Russian soil stretches down from Archangel, out from the tundras and steppes, out to the granaries of the Ukraine in the south, to the Volga and the vast plains of Siberia.

Limitless and immense, like the sufferings of the Russian people.

In the morning, the Mongolian regiments of the Red Guard rode out to meet the squadrons of the White Brigades; again in the evening and again next morning. Time was ticking away like the clapper of the prayer wheel at home. Shooting, riding, dying. And the freedom they had been promised never came; nor the land of one's own, the promise of which had lifted these men of the Far East into the saddle.

Cautious whispers went quietly round the ranks of the yellow Cossacks as they rode to the attack on Kolchak or formed skirmish lines to stop the soldiers of General Wrangel.

And when at last, the longed-for rest brought a brief respite, an aching yearning would grow for home. Home, where, far away in the east, the women were crying in their lonely villages. And when the Uzbek sentries were alone at night in the complete, lurking silence, they heard the beckoning call of the fallow earth.

In September 1918, it was known all along the Red Army's line from Perm to Ekaterinburg that there was mutiny in the Uzbek regiments.

"Do you believe it?" Comrade Yakoff, the chief commissar of the Cheka, asked. "You've got to make them more promises again...offer them what they want: Plunder, white women..."

The Bolshevik political officer attached to the Uzbek regiment screwed up his wide mouth: "Do you know what homesickness is? The Uzbeks aren't cowards and they're not looking for loot. They're homesick."

The commissar hammered on the table with his fist.

"You're not up to this job, comrade. We've got ways and means of dealing with these people."

A knock came at the flimsy door.

"Comrade commissar," the Caucasian said, "there's a delegation of Uzbeks outside. They demand in no uncertain terms to talk to you."

"Well, my dear comrade and political adviser...what now?" The commissar was smiling. "Let them in."

"But commissar..."

"Let them in, I say!"

"But there's at least 200 of them."

The commissar stood up.

"Papa commissar," the old Uzbek said submissively, "you're the big man in this district. You've promised us land, freedom and peace. We beg of you—we know you won't mind—allow us to ride home."

The commissar put on a smile.

"Not just now, comrade, we can't do it yet. But we'll soon deal with those white dogs, and then you'll get land freedom and peace."

We didn't want to go without telling you," the old man went on, undeterred. "We're the elected representatives of the regiments," he said slowly, " and we've come to say good-bye, beloved commissar."

The commissar gripped the plaited whip that always hung from his belt. But his glance fell in time on the brand-new rifles of the Uzbek soldiers.

"You wouldn't...Get back to the front!" he roared.

"Good-bye, beloved commissar." The old Uzbek bowed. "You've been our master for a long time. We've had all we wanted, food, horses and rifles. But now the soil is calling us. And our soil, great commissar, is stronger."

"You're breaking our agreement," the Cheka officer said slowly. "But let us part without hard feelings. You've fought very bravely."

The faces of the Uzbeks shone with pride.

"That's right," said the old man with joy, "that's how we wanted it to be; To depart in peace."

"You've had food," the commissar continued, "and you've earned it. You've had good pay, and you've earned that too."

The Uzbek's mouth twitched. He wanted to speak, but courtesy restrained him.

"You've been given horses. They're yours, because of your courage. But," he paused, "you've also been given rifles, brand new, unused rifles. We need rifles to continue our fight against the Whites, we need them for victory, to protect our towns and villages. Your villages, too, comrades. You must let us have the rifles back."

The rifles," the old man said with uncertainty, "the rifles, yes, you're right, commissar, the rifles are yours. We'll get our old guns out of the depot. The rifles are his," he said firmly in the direction of the rebellious murmur which had started behind his back. "We'll bring them in tonight."

"No need for the trouble," said the commissar. He shouted across the yard to the Cheka guardroom. "Two platoons saddle up, bring my horse. Leave your rifles here, and we'll come along to protect you and fetch the other weapons."

Trumpets sounded shrill. With a clatter, the rifles fell in a circle, followed by sabers and revolvers.

The Uzbeks turned their horses. In front, in two long files, rode the Red soldiers of the first platoon of the Perm Cheka. And the second platoon followed closely at their rear.

Almost unnoticeably, the commissar moved his tightly shut lips. A Cheka officer saluted and galloped off to the head of the column.

Fields began to appear on either side of the road. Behind them, a sparse scrubby wood grew out of the steppe.

The commissar lit a cigarette.

"Here," he said loudly and moved away from the column. The forward platoon came to a sudden halt and in an instant the Uzbeks were surrounded and dragged from their saddles.

"Get the horses away." The commissar straightened himself in the saddle. "Hurry. We have no time to lose."

The Uzbeks huddled together like cattle.

"But, commissar" The old man fixed his dark, oriental eyes on him uncomprehendingly.

Then the rifle bolts clanged; silently, the Uzbeks stared into the dark muzzles. From far back, at the rear, the sound of a slow, monotone song rose from the doomed men. It ceased when the first volleys sounded across the wide field.

"Just cover them up. Don't make a fuss about it. A little earth, and then back in the saddle!"

"You, you and you." The commissar detailed his political trusties. "The Uzbeks are to be divided up among the Caucasian and Ukrainian regiments. Tell them their delegates were ambushed and wiped out by the Whites."

"Mount up!" He bellowed out across the area. "Long live the Soviets!"

A small cloud of dust swept along, past the edge of the village. One of the clouds headed to the right, one to the left and one right though the middle. They headed toward the areas in the large camp where the Uzbek regiments were bivouacked and waiting for their spokesmen.

"And one of those old men was my father," the Uzbek said, finishing his story. "Two of my brothers were also there. We didn't hear what had actually happened till much later, when it was too late. But we haven't forgotten. We've been waiting for the hour of revenge. Give me leaflets with your promises written on them and let me go back to the regiments, and we'll bring back more than two-thirds of the Asiatic regiments. You can believe me on that, sir!"

The interpreter looked embarrassed. "I'm not responsible for that. I'll write down everything and make a report."

The old Uzbek was led off to the nearest prisoner-of-war camp.

***

Next evening, I met Kaul again. The front was quieter by then. I told him what I'd seen in the Ukrainian villages and about the old Uzbek.

"If only we use this God-given opportunity," Kaul said heavily. "We at least need to pray that that happens."

I looked at him in amazement. "You don't think we'd ignore it, do you? The Ukrainians, even the Russians, are ready for an uprising. We can't overlook it as if there were nothing there?"

"You forget, old friend, that we're already sitting in our own trap. They're all *Untermenschen*."

He continued: "Jesus, if I ever hear that damn word again...ask yourself: *Untermenschen* in German uniform?

"But, Kaul," I stammered, "you're becoming too much of a cynic. You've let that damned concentration camp take hold of you...maybe experiences you took too personally. Here it's not a question of dogma, good or bad, right or wrong—I haven't even thought about that. Theories don't hold water here. It's a question of life. Everything is at stake—our future and the future shape of the whole world...and not least of which are these miserable people, who, after the hell they've been through, have approached us in good faith and look to us for freedom and equality..."

Kaul cut me short: "Fine, we'll see which is the stronger: Party doctrine or life."

I took off in a sullen mood. That man had a perfect genius for souring your whole existence. But I was frightened all the same. Supposing he was right?

Tired and depressed, I spread my blanket.

***

The morning brought more fighting, more attacking. Progress was rapid all day. I was surprised when I found that daylight was nearly gone. It was only in the distance that a glow was still hanging above the flat hilltop,where the Soviets had placed their *Ratschbumm* battery[13]. Down in the village, which the enemy had given up to the lead platoon without a shot only a few hours previously, dusk was spinning its first threads.

A tiny mud hovel beside the road, facing the enemy, looked like the right place for us. We knocked, and a narrow gap opened.

---

13   Translator's Note: the Soviet 7.62cm antitank gun was referred to in soldier slang as the *Ratschbumm*, because the sound of its report seemed to be virtually simultaneous with the impact of its round, due to its high muzzle velocity.

"There, there," pointed a brown-haired, slim Ukrainian girl. "There's room over there." We went in. As usual, a big living room that served as both kitchen and bedroom. We drug in straw across from a nearby stack, the two small children following our every movement. The girl, who was about 16—half-child, half-woman—smiled when we spread our blankets and threw ourselves on the floor, dressed as we had come in.

"Your father?" I asked.

"Shot...dead."

"What for?"

"Who knows?"

"Your mother? "

"Died...a year ago."

"And what do you live on? You and the two children?" She shrugged her shoulders and then laughed, showing her white teeth. *"Sjemitchki!"* she said, taking a handful of sunflower seeds from a big heap she had been roasting on the stove.

We had been hard on the enemy's heels all day, and I did not wake until well on in the night. Were none of us supposed to pull guard, or had we been forgotten? From the village street came the sound of the sentries" footsteps; they had been doubled up. Away in the distance, a wounded cow was screeching and, occasionally, a single round echoed through the night. Otherwise, all was still. By the restless light of the oil lamp on the table, I could see the girl in her narrow bed. She had let her blanket slip, and her tender boyish shape was indistinctly revealed in the dim light. Moving quietly, I went across to her and carefully pulled the blanket straight, but she woke up in alarm. *"Nitchewo,"* I said softly, to avoid waking the others. "What's your name?" It was Tekle, not a very common name in the Ukraine; more common for girls in Latvia and Lithuania. But then she was probably an uncommon girl, one who had not run away but had taken up the burden her mother could no longer carry. "Tomorrow, Tekle," I said with a smile, "you must tell me your story."

A pale flush crept up from her neck to her face as she replied, "Yes, German man, tomorrow."

But a soldier's life seldom works out the way things are planned. We attacked at dawn, ousted the enemy from his hilltop in hard and bitter fighting and drove him before us towards the town whose towers and factory chimneys we could see gleaming through the misty distance.

The alert had come suddenly; we barely had time to pack our personal gear, none at all to eat. "Tekle," I said, but the platoon leader shouted then and I ran out. She stood at the door for a moment, as if paralyzed, and then ran back into the house. She caught us up just as we were leaving the village and thrust something into the pocket of my tunic. I only had time to press her hand and then the heavy Russian Maxim machine guns started their rattle.

It was a nasty mess. The air was thick with lead, and our heads seemed far too big. My right tunic pocket was bulging and I rolled irritably on one side from the firing position in which I was lying. A dull thud hit the moist earth close beside me. But by that time my hand had already withdrawn some of the contents of my pocket: *Sjemitchki!* I pushed the first sunflower seed into my mouth. "What've you got there?" the man next to me asked. Cautiously, I passed over a handful of seeds. He looked surprised, and then, with a grin, crushed the first seed between his teeth. His neighbor also asked for some, and my pocket was soon empty. Meanwhile, things were warming up nicely, and the splinters were singing their eternal, discordant song of death close over our heads.

Toward evening, we entered the contested town and, in a few minutes, were deep in a death-like sleep.

***

That morning bad news came in from the companies, one after the other. The engineer company had been attacked in the flank from the woods. It had only been by the energetic action of one of guns of the 3rd Platoon of the 2nd Battery of *Flak* that the situation had been saved and the massed attack broken up. Up front, the 16th, 18th and also the 17th Companies were having to withstand the pressure of massed enemy forces.

Then an SOS came over the air: "Ammo running out. Send up all calibers immediately; otherwise cannot hold."

To top everything off, heavy rain had been falling all the morning, and the ground had become bottomless and slippery with that vicious sliminess we hated so much, in which vehicles simply slid out of control. Feverishly, we loaded the big prime mover belonging to the heavy detachment; it was the only thing that always got through. Box after box went up. Then orders came to me: "You know the way. Take two men and get through. The ammunition has to get forward."

We roared off in our huge crate. A first-class dust up was going on on either side of us but we had no time to look. No ammo! The company had no ammo!

We reached the hill, which had been the scene of yesterday's fighting, and then turned off to the small, half-collapsed bridge. I took the prime mover up to the ridge through a broad depression, which offered us concealment from enemy observation. The driver looked at the marshy ground with some concern, but we got through and came out at a stretch of road that had only just fallen into our hands. We held up at a small patch of vegetation for the time being.

A man raced across the field towards us.

"The 16th? Yes, it was here; but God only knows where it is now. Contact is shot...everything's advancing."

Up on the ridge something whistled just over the top of our prime mover, which must have stood out like a sore thumb for kilometers on end. What if antitank guns start on us? The driver echoed my thoughts. "The ammo," he said, "supposing it's lost?" We forgot about ourselves. We were needed up front!

Voices called to us from out of the clover. Two wounded men.

"Take us with you! Don't leave us here!"

The ammunition had to get forward.

"Can't," I shouted, avoiding their eyes. "We'll be back, comrades."

Far ahead, over to the right, we saw a few figures in the grain field. Friend or foe? It was the contact I had been looking for—not actually the 16th Company but the 18th, nonetheless. I reported to the *Obersturmführer*.

"You're just in time," he said, greeting me. "Start unloading. I have to get up this hill first with my men and then I'll have it picked up."

Twenty or thirty prisoners came shuffling back through the high grain. Soon they were beside the prime mover and, in a few minutes the boxes, were stacked in rows, all carefully covered with straw. The prisoners squatted obstinately in the ditch. Two Russian aircraft came droning across the sky—an unusual sight in the recent past... very, very unusual. But unusual or not, those two flipped over and swooped over our heads, spewing death and destruction from their weapons. But their aim was bad.

The whole expanse of the broad field was full of dead Soviet soldiers. I started to walk across to where the 16th Company should be. A *Rottenführer* caught up with me, and we walked along together. He was equally uncertain of the 16th's location. Suddenly I froze—a dead Russian had moved.

"Just take it easy," the *Rottenführer* said, pulling out his pistol. In a flash, the" dead man" straightened up to throw the grenade he had ready in his hand. But our pistols were quicker.

We looked suspiciously over the other bodies lying in heaps and rows on the field. Old man Hein[14] had been very busy.

---

14   Translator's Note: Soldier jargon for the grim reaper.

We had seen them die so often, those victims of the Kremlin. Expressionless, their dull eyes fixed into the distance as if mesmerized by the rattle of our guns, they would run into our hail of fire. Frequently, not even the moment of death brought any flash of realization or shock into their expressionless faces. Again and again they would come, soulless, like puppets in a dreadful marionette, with the same short and jerky movements: Everything about them was mechanical, without soul. That was perhaps the most horrible of our experiences on the Eastern Front: Mechanical dying.

We found the 16th: "Ammunition next to the road."

A man ran up to me. "Where is it?" I showed him, and he dashed off with the news to his company headquarters. Then another approached me. He was going to the 17th, and he was also told where to find the ammunition.

After that we made our way back, down into the depression with its edge dotted with enemy shell craters; up the road.

At the headquarters, we found a beehive of activity. The radio operators were already bringing traffic for the commander: "Progress good all along the line!" The battalion commander snatched the paper out of the radio operator's hand. It was the first time for days that we'd seen him smile.

**

That evening, an Austrian NCO said to me: "Did you hear...The captain has been killed in action!"

"What captain?" I asked, surprised.

"Leopold[15]...it just came over the radio."

---

15   Translator's Note: *Hauptmann* Joseph Leopold was a relatively minor figure on the stage of Austrian pre-annexation politics. An ardent National Socialist, he was brushed aside later and lost importance after the *Anschluß* in 1938. Among the former Austrians in the German Army, and, in particular, in the *SS*, he was a well-known figure at the time.

I couldn't shake the news. The eternal opponent of Dollfuß and Schuschnigg had fallen unjustifiably into Hitler's disfavor just at the moment when things were happening in Austria. His rivals, on the other hand, rose in power.

But he had quietly gone where the arch enemy was. And died.

He was thereby rewarded with that which had been denied to his opponents: The death of an honest and brave soldier, which he had been his entire life. But with him had also dies revolutionary National Socialism in Austria with all of its lofty illusions.

**

By the time evening came, the companies had dug in again, and a noose had been drawn round the town of Uman. The evening sky was aflame with the staccato light of heavy guns. My company had an excellent field of fire from the steep bank of the small river we were holding, but there was nothing stirring. The prisoners we had taken during the day, a lieutenant and 60 men, huddled silent and exhausted in a small depression just behind our line.

A runner came up to me: "Company commander's orders. You're to get the prisoners to the rear. Pick one man to go with you." I stood up wearily, beckoned to Rudi, and called to the prisoners: *"Davai!"* They roused themselves stiffly and stood up. I kept the lieutenant beside me and the remainder marching in a column behind us, with Rudi bringing up the rear, a submachine gun at the ready under his arm.

We marched westwards into the vanishing day, past dead and badly wounded. Here and there we saw medics at work, but then they stopped as well. The rapidly gathering darkness swallowed all of us up. "If the prisoners want to," the thought went quickly racing through my head, "then both of us will be heaven-bound in a flash. We'll be standing in front of St. Peter faster than we ever thought possible...60 against the two of us..."

The Russian lieutenant stumbled along beside me.

"Papirossi?" I asked him. His mud encrusted eyes lit up and he nodded. I gave him a *Juno*[16] and, in the light of the match, looked closely at his impassive face, cursing my ignorance of the language. What was going on behind that countenance?

Back at the rear, I could hear Rudi's voice, cursing to himself. Every so often, a man stepped out of the loose formation. We had been going through the deserted night for a good hour and I began to wish we would encounter an ammunition column. I had not realized it was quite so far back to battalion.

Suddenly, we heard firing away to our left, and I halted in alarm. The prisoners clustered round me like a herd of frightened cattle.

"You idiots," I screamed. "Column of prisoners."

The firing grew more intense, and the slow bark of a machine gun sounded in between.

"Hey!" Rudi called out, running towards me. "It's Ivan!"

The Russians must have broken through somewhere farther along the line and were trying to get through to the road we were marching on.

Bullets were flying only a few inches over our heads. I dropped to the ground instinctively and started to low crawl towards the ditch, pulling out my pistol as I went. "Any moment now there'll be one of them on my back," I thought, but nothing happened.

I heard the lieutenant panting close beside me and glanced nervously over my shoulder. Judging by the noise, the attacking Russians were barely 200 meters in front of us. When I looked round, I saw the whole column of prisoners crawling behind me in a bunch, not a flicker on their indifferent, impassive faces. Suddenly, I felt a sense of security and gratitude. Every now and then we could hear the entreaties of the attacking Russians. But my prisoners did not answer; they crawled on behind me, pressed close against the Ukrainian soil. The road fell away into a wide defile.

---

16   Translator's Notes: A brand of cigarettes.

Then I leapt to my feet, gasping with relief. From off to one side, I had heard the German battle cry—*Hurra!*—the cheer of attacking German infantry, who were thwarting the enemy's advance. It came none too soon for us.

It was pitch dark by the time we arrived at battalion headquarters, where I received orders from an officer to take the prisoners on back to the military police.

We trudged on, tired and beat, until at last we reached the prisoner-of-war cage, where I made my report. A fat NCO took charge of the column. He kicked one of them who had not understood fast enough back into line.

"Hold on a minute," I said harshly. "These poor guys could have made short work of us two." I briefly told him the story. He looked at me in amazement.

Then I emptied my pockets and gave all the tobacco I had to the prisoners. Rudi did the same. It was the only thing I had and there was nothing more that I, a *Rottenführer*, could do for them.

"You know," Rudi said, measuring his words when we were on our way back to the front. "I'd made up my mind to wade into them with my submachine gun. I thought we'd had it, and I wasn't going to be the only one to go. But you were right, your way was better."

I said nothing; this 19-year-old from Kassel had not been at the front very long and, in any case, would not have understood me.

But, at the time, I also did not understand what had actually gone on in the prisoners' minds: Over there—their own men—freedom—a chance to join up with one of their own units—and over here, two German soldiers.

Why hadn't they run for it? We could not have stopped them, nor would we have tried. In the position we were in, we would have been glad enough to get away with our own skins.

But the explanation was not really so difficult. In the eyes of the Soviets, the captured Red Army man was written off. He died politically, before he died physically. He had come in contact with the enemy. He had made it through the glass wall, and it was uncertain how he would react. He may have seen through the whole gigantic swindle even in the short time he was held; in any case, he was contaminated—an unreliable element.

He would be questioned for days on end—questioned, questioned, questioned. What did the enemy do? What did he ask you? What did you say? What impression did you get of the enemy? Woe be to him if anyone of his replies were suspect. Woe be to him if, in the first shock of captivity, he let fall a single unguarded word. The penalty was death.

The Red Army man—no matter how great the fear of the enemy engendered in him by the commissar's hate campaign—once finding himself a prisoner and still alive, had no less fear of returning to the Red Army. For the very fact that he was still alive, that he has not returned wounded or broken, made him living proof of the fraud of the entire fabric of Bolshevik propaganda and, in the nature of things, a traitor. For, in the words of the Bolsheviks, who but a traitor could succeed in returning whole from the enemy?

***

At first light next morning, a hail of enemy artillery fire screamed over us, but it was 100 meters beyond us. All hell had broken loose in the next battalion's sector to our right, at the point where the enemy had been trying to break out the evening before.

Their lead tanks were attempting to smash their way through our blocking positions. Soviet infantry mounted on them, Red Cossacks close behind, regiment after regiment; in between, horse artillery and regiment upon regiment of infantry. Two of our 88mm batteries had moved up to the line and were firing over open sights. Blazing tanks, neighing horses rearing and falling, men shouting. And between it all the hard and rhythmic bark of our 88's and the hammer of machine guns.

We crouched wide-eyed in our holes and watched the whole terrible spectacle as if from an expensive seat in the theater. Within an hour, the outcome was decided. The breakthrough attempt had been smashed; our ring round Uman was impenetrable.

We were relieved by an infantry unit around noon and resumed our advance—towards the Black Sea.

Morning found us once again fighting hard against a desperately struggling enemy, who had dug himself in along a high railway embankment. Four times we attacked, four times we were thrown back. The battalion commander cursed a blue streak. The company commanders were about to give up. Artillery support—which had been urgently requested over and over again—did not come. Instead, a regiment of Hungarian Hussars came in its place. We smiled. What the hell did those Magyars think they were going to do here? It was going to be rough on their handsome, elegant horses.

Suddenly we stood aghast: Those bastards had gone stark, raving crazy. Troop after troop[17] moved up towards us. An order was shouted and, in a flash, the bronzed, slim cavalrymen were in the saddle; a tall colonel, his collar glittering with gold, actually drew his saber. Four or five light armored cars barked from the flank, and they were off, the whole regiment, careering across the wide plain, their sabers flashing in the afternoon sun. That was the way Seydlitz must have attacked. All caution forgotten, we scrambled out of our holes. It was like a close-up in a cavalry film. The first shots whipped across the embankment, strangely thin and sparse.

Then, astonished and laughing, we saw the Soviet regiment, which had so fiercely and fanatically resisted all our assaults, turn tail and run in panic, the triumphant Hungarians driving the Reds before them and their shining blades making a very rich harvest. The glitter of steel had been too much for the nerves of the *Muschiks*. Their primitive hearts had been shattered and defeated by primitive weapons.

---

17   Translator's Note: A troop is a company or battery equivalent.

We mounted up again to pursue the routed enemy, but all contact had been lost by evening.

Shortly before dusk, the news went round that during the pursuit two German Army companies operating on the right flank had advanced too far ahead and there was no news from them in spite of the fact that they were equipped with radios. We were given the mission of finding them and, if necessary, to relieve them.

We moved until almost midnight, clashing several times on the way with minor enemy forces, which were beginning to make their appearance again. But there was no sign of the two missing companies. Finally, the commander called a halt just as we were passing the edge of an enormous plantation of apricot trees. The companies deployed around the command post and took up improvised positions.

"I don't know," I said to another runner, as we were going off to sleep, "but there's a really strong smell of corpses round here."

"What's that?" barked a sharp voice which, to my dismay, I recognized as the commander's. "What kind of nonsense is that? Where would the corpses come from? Go to sleep, that's the best thing for you."

I rolled myself up in my shelter half and sank into a deep and dreamless slumber.

A rough hand woke me. I could see a faint touch of dawn.

"The old man wants you. Quick!"

I ran off. The commander looked at me strangely. "You and your stupid nose were right, damn you...go and have a look at the shit."

Close to the command post, in a small depression covered with apricot trees, was a small group of men whispering together. I pushed my way through them and shrank back in horror at what I saw. The small trees were bearing fruit, very strange fruit—German soldiers. They were not a pretty sight, with their arms tied high behind them to the weak branches, their jackboots off and their legs burnt and carbonized up to their knees. So distorted were their faces that even seasoned soldiers had to look away.

"Stalin Socks," was the thought that came into my mind. We had heard of them several times, but had not really believed the stories. Fuel had been poured over their feet and then lit, and they had died in the most terrible agony: 2 lieutenants, three senior NCO's and 98 other ranks.

The crowd stood silent. Farther ahead, in the middle of the small village, a few prisoners we had taken the day before were beginning to dig a mass grave. The crowd grew, as more of our officers and men clustered round. When the digging was finished, the prisoners were ordered to untie the bodies from the trees and carry them to the grave. This they did, impassively, indifferently, as they did everything they were ordered to do.

They shouldered the stiffened corpses which, with their strangely bent and contorted arms and tortured faces looked like the medieval figures of Christ created by Tilman Riemenschneider, and carried them through the rigid ranks of the cordon that the men had formed. In the meantime, a number of officers and men had arrived from the battalion to which the two companies had belonged.

"Christ!" said a junior NCO next to me. "It's Karl, my brother Karl."

White as a sheet, he drew his pistol. As the sound of the shot died away, the prisoner carrying his mutilated brother slowly collapsed. Then the next one, his face impassive and unmoved, picked up the corpse and shuffled off.

A *Hauptsturmführer* placed himself in front of the sergeant. "Take it easy, comrade. I know how you feel, but it's not only your affair now."

Dazed and bewildered, the sergeant put back his pistol. "What am I supposed to write Mother?" he said, as if to himself. "I should have looked after him. He was the youngest."

We heard the story of events from the villagers in Gejgowa. When the two young lieutenants, boys barely out of their teens and newly arrived at the front, had realized that their men had fired off all their ammunition and that they could expect no outside help, they had surrendered, thinking that those opposing them under the hammer and sickle were also soldiers. We saw what then happened.

***

We began the pursuit at noon. The enemy accepted battle in the afternoon, and there was a bitter fight, but the enemy regiment was shattered by the overwhelming fury of our assault. It did not last long.

Over by the golden sunflower field a few desultory shots still echoed through the late summer afternoon, and a few bursts of fire dropped in the plain from high up on the hill, but it was all just show. The drama was over.

Once again a superior enemy had been driven before us, and a decision forced by the reckless dash of our men. At that point, I was quietly walking down the long street of the ethnic-German village of Nowa Danzia. It was always the same picture, whether up by Kiev, over on the Dnieper or down here by the Black Sea: Villages without men.

I talked to the tall, blonde woman of the house where I was billeted. "My husband?" she said in a surprised voice. "He was taken by the Reds one night four years ago. I've heard nothing from him since."

"My son is in a forced labor camp in Siberia," said a haggard old woman from next door.

"And my brother," the tall blonde took up the story again, "him they took as a spy. Whom he spied for nobody ever discovered, nor to what end. But they picked him up at the same time as my husband and sentenced him to 10 years of forced labor. And I sit here with six children, and haven't had a single line from either of them. Have they been shot? I don't know, I don't know anything. Oh God! What a life..." She began to cry. The other women around me looked at the ground.

Sometimes the impact of events and experience seemed almost too much to bear. And yet the very horror of this front had done one thing: It had kicked us out of our rut and cured us of being the least bit jaded. It had restored to us the ideals with which we had started. The great was again great and had lost its tarnish; every simplest, humblest thing brought confirmation of our ideas.

"Good-evening," a little girl's voice broke into my thoughts, "What's time is it, German soldier?"

I replied mechanically. Then I stopped with a jerk. How many thousands of German peasants were being liquidated in the forced labor camps and prisons of the "workers paradise"? How many villages without men might there be in the Ukraine and along the Volga? Yet, after 20 years of unimaginable horror, there was still a child in a grassy lane to ask: "What time is it, German soldier?"

Only that morning I had been puffed up with pride at our quick victory. But then I suddenly saw that our victories were no more than milestones along the great march of mankind, which sweeps up all along its path. Into eternity.

***

I went on my way down the village street, which was then wrapped in evening twilight. Over by the ramshackle school, Uzbek prisoners were humming a plaintive, nostalgic song of distant mountain and steppe. Soft giggling emanated from the dark corners of the barns of the collective farms barns. Only the footsteps of our sentries echoed lonely through the early night. In my pocket I could feel the photograph of a woman I did not know, which to-morrow I would hand over to the first sergeant, who in turn would send it to the unit from which the six dead men had come.

In the first few minutes of our entry into the village, while we were still combing out the houses, a trembling old man had come directly up to me and taken me by the arm.

56

"Over there," he whispered. "That's where they are." Before I could ask any more questions, he led me through a small garden to a couple of disused chalk pits located on the boundary of the "Lenin" Collective Farm.

"Here," he said hoarsely, tears rolling down his wrinkled face. We brought prisoners with spades. They lifted the big stones and shoveled the earth away. A German army boot appeared, attached to it—a dead man. There were six of them, six men, who had been cut off from their unit and taken prisoner after a gallant fight.

They were interrogated by commissars of the Red General Staff.

They did not speak.

They were threatened.

They did not speak.

Then they were led to the edge of the chalk pits, which served as a dump for refuse. The Soviet general stood close by. They knew what was coming, and looked the general straight in the face.

One of them pulled out a small photograph, a picture of his wife. He held it in front of him. He did not feel the first blow. As he collapsed, the woman of his longing stood radiantly in the gateway and helped him past the torment of the moment into the peace of eternity.

In the distance, the women of New Danzig stood and wept.

Stones and earth were heaped over their bodies, these victims of Bolshevist bloodthirstiness, even before their limbs had stopped quivering. They hurried, because the first assault troops of the *Waffen-SS* were moving on the village at the edge of the woods.

We stood there for a long time in front of our dead comrades. In front of us was a freshly filled canteen, a few dog tags and the photograph. I picked it up. Suddenly, the man to my left moved away, as did the one on my right. I walked quickly off down along the street, hearing the clink of shovels behind me, as some prisoners prepared a worthy grave for our dead brothers.

It was late when I arrived back at my billet, but they were all still awake. One of them asked, a little embarrassed: "Do you still have the photo?"

I nodded. They passed it from hand to hand, quietly and reverently.

It is not in the soldier's nature to be noisy in his emotions. We were all too closely acquainted with death to talk about heroism and bestiality. But our weapons had a very thorough cleaning that night.

We attacked again at dawn, defeated the powerful enemy, smashed his last line of defense and threw him back to the shores of the Black Sea.

**

At noon next day an order was received by Division to the effect that all prisoners captured during the last three days were to be shot as a reprisal for the inhuman atrocities which the Red Army had committed in our sector.

It so happened that we had taken very many prisoners during those fatal days, and so the lives of 4,000 men fell forfeit. They scarcely looked up when our interpreter told them in a cold voice of their fate.

They lined up eight at a time at the side of a large antitank ditch. As the first volley crashed, eight men were hurled forward into the depths of the ditch, as if hit by a giant fist. Already the next row was lining up. It was strange and incomprehensible to us how these men used their last minutes in this world, a world which had treated them so unmercifully. One took off his greatcoat and folded it neatly before laying it sadly on the ground; then he rose for his last walk. Textiles were rare in the workers' paradise, and he may have thought that it might still serve to warm someone who was cold. Or perhaps it was only the automatic respect for the deity of material things that had been instilled in them for so long. Others greedily smoked a last ciga-rette, which they had clumsily rolled from a filthy scrap of newspaper. Nobody wrote a last message home; there were no tears.

Then suddenly one of them, a tall Georgian or Ossetian, seized a shovel lying beside him, and brought it down like lightning on the skull—not of the German guard who was standing next to him—but of a Red commissar. *"Sabak Bolshevik"* he mouthed, breathing heav-ily.

The officer in charge of the execution walked across to him. "Of-ficer?"

"Da!" answered the Caucasian.

The German hesitated. "Come with me," he said and hurriedly tried to pull the Caucasian behind his car. We all looked away. We would have like to have saved the handsome, tall man as well.

But the man knew at once what was in the officer's mind and shook his narrow head proudly, pointing to the row of his dead com-rades. *"Nasha fronta,"* he said slowly "Our front." Then he tossed away his cigarette and walked impassively forward to join the file at the edge of the ditch.

Chapter Three:
Along the Black Sea
to Mariupol

The retreat of the Red Army's "Southwest Front" was growing to the dimensions of a panic-stricken rout. Stalin's Marshal Budyonny, whom the Bolsheviks had showered with glory for his exploits in the civil war, was showing himself to be amateurish and incompetent, a bungler and loser of battles, like his colleague in the north, Marshal Timoshenko, Commander of the Russian Central Army Group.

Next morning found us already on the outskirts of Cherson. A tremendous enemy artillery barrage was in progress, supported by naval guns of the Black Sea Fleet, but they were dropping their shells too far to the left and doing us little or no damage.

A train was in the station laden with Soviet T-34 tanks, destined never to go into action. Our commander was still undecided whether to attack. Several fires were raging in the town, and we heard the frequent roar of exploding ammunition dumps. Finally, the young liaison officer from Styria[18] received orders to reconnoiter the portion of the town nearest to us. He called me on the field phone. "I want you to come along," he said.

Our sidecar motorcycle roared through the empty streets. There was no trace of the enemy. A few buildings stood in flames. Swinging around a corner, we encountered a frightened civilian making a beeline for the nearest house.

"Stoj! Stoj!" He stopped, frozen in his tracks. I walked to him and tried to question him in my primitive soldier's Russian. No, there were no more Reds left in this quarter. Shops? Wine? *Schnaps*? He grinned broadly. "Oh yes. Over there, first right and round the cor-

---

18   Translator's Note: A province of Austria, which had been incorporated into the *Reich* and renamed the *Ostmark*.

ner, the big red house. You'll find the NKVD supply room for the entire city."

The young *Untersturmführer* did not hesitate. "If we can't take the old man any prisoners, at least let's get him a bottle of wine. Come on, let's go."

We saw the building immediately. Its driveway was open and we rode straight in, and our hearts almost stopped. The small courtyard was jammed full of Red Army men, 40 or 50 of them, all fully armed. And the driveway was too narrow for our driver to turn. The *Untersturmführer* raised his submachine gun; the Red Army men stood motionless. I slid down from my seat and, mustering all the Russian I knew, walked up to the man nearest to me and said: "You want cigarettes? German cigarettes?" Then I held out a full pack.

Their faces beamed. *"Da, da."*

We lit our cigarettes. Out of the corner of my eye, I could just see the *Untersturmführer*, submachine gun at the ready, directing the driver to turn the motorcycle around.

My heart still thumping, I said, "The war *kaputt*...Stalin no good for Russia."

The men around me nodded their heads and grinned. One of them brought me a battered mess tin full of red wine. I drank some and took the rest to the *Untersturmführer*, who sampled it. "Good God! " he said laughing, now quite calm. "Where the devil did that come from?" I asked my Russian friends, who grinned and pointed to the dark entrance of the basement. After a glance back at my comrades, I followed three or four Red Army men into the blackness of the cellar with very mixed feelings. A whole mob of them crowded in behind. They struck matches, barely lighting the roomy cellar, which was already knee deep with wine. I pointed to the smallest of the barrels, whereupon my Russian helpers delightedly rolled it up and out into the daylight. We heaved it on the motorcycle, which creaked and groaned beneath the weight. I barely had time to signal the Red Army men to lay down their arms and to say that we'd be back shortly, when we were racing off again back through the burning streets.

The commander barely had time to take the wine when the general order to attack came. A short while later, our men were busily engaged in the happy task of rolling out the NKVD barrels; the Russians who lent them a hand were later attached to our companies and the battalion trains as volunteers[19]. That wine had brought them luck.

***

Cherson was the first real port we had come across in the Soviet Union. All we had seen so far were the villages and small towns we had hurriedly crossed or fought through in the course of operations. A different Russia revealed itself before our eyes there. The population was at first reserved though invariably friendly, freed from the unbearable pressure of the political commissars who, during the recent past, as their defeat became more obvious, had behaved like raving madmen in the town.

It was the many small children who forged the first links between us and the frightened populace. Sugar especially, which even here in the fertile south was almost out of reach of the ordinary citizen, very quickly brought us friends. The girls were friendly, but very proper in their approach. My own first acquaintance was with an old woman who, to my surprise, spoke fluent German. She came from one of the German settlements on the Volga. Happy to have found someone with whom I could talk freely, I invited her to come to our billets that evening. She hesitantly agreed. My quarters, which I shared with two other men, was an empty room, the previous occupants of which had fled across the Dnieper before our advance.

"What should I tell you?" the old woman began with some ceremony after her first cup of tea. "You wouldn't understand anyway.

---

19   Translator's Note: On the Eastern Front, surrendering Red Army men were often afforded the opportunity to work for the Germans. They were referred to as *Hiwis*, which stands for *Hilfs-Freiwillige* or Volunteers. They were usually outfitted with German uniforms and received the same rations and front-line benefits as other German soldiers. Oftentimes, these *Hiwis* formed up to 10 percent of the on-hand strength of the divisions. They were used strictly in a combat-support capacity and not as front-line forces, however.

The Russians have always been subject to quite different laws from other people. Nothing is ever left unsaid or unsolved as far as it is in anybody's power to solve it. The Russian must always get to the bottom of everything, get right down to its roots; it was true under the Czar and it's true now, if not more so since Lenin translated the dream of liberty, equality and fraternity into Russian. But, since you're so insistent, perhaps the best thing I can do is to tell you a story...

As a young girl I was great friends with a family from Marseilles; its name was Lavalle. Pierre Lavalle had an import-export business in Odessa, where it was intended that I be brought up in the best finishing school. By chance, I made the acquaintance of his young wife, Marguerite Lavalle, a woman 10 years my senior, and we became close friends. Then came the summer of 1919...

The disintegrating Cossack squadrons and the last remnants of the Czarist regiments of the line were being forced back in a disorderly scramble toward Odessa. Around them, a circle of Budyonny's Red Cavalry was flinging itself in an unstoppable assault against the beaten detachments of the "White Army".

The officers of the international force, the French in particular, were frantically requisitioning every ship in the harbor, from old battleships to the most modern motor launches. They took coal, fuel and all the food they could lay their hands on and then put their men aboard as fast as they could clamber up the gangways.

Behind them the Red artillery was already dropping its shells into Odessa's streets, spurring on the vast horde of White Russians to ever more hasty flight.

Soon the men of the Red Army had overcome what little resistance remained and were storming the last houses of the defeated and desolate city. At that moment, the *Cheka* terror began its bloody work, and the shootings of the unfortunate victims started. They went on for several days, but the number of counterrevolutionaries who had fled into the city was so vast that even the commissars of the *Cheka* were helpless in face of the enormous mass of condemned people.

Quick to action, the *Chekas* loaded their victims into three old merchant ships, which had been left in the harbor as unseaworthy, and took them a few miles out to sea. Without trial and without mercy, "White" officers, priests, Menshevik officials and anti-Red workmen and peasants were tied together in pairs and thrown overboard alive.

But the dead bodies remained on the surface and came drifting back to harbor with the tide. So, on the next trip, iron weights were tied to the human bundles before they were pushed in the water.

In the general upheaval, Pierre Lavalle had been left behind in Odessa with his wife and children and had fallen into the hands of the terrorists during the indiscriminate arrests. Lavalle swore in vain that he had distanced himself from all political affairs and pointed in vain to his French citizenship. Before his family had had time to penetrate to the appropriate commissar, Pierre Lavalle had been taken on board one of the three death ships and tumbled into the sea with the rest.

His unhappy wife, Marguerite, did not rest until she was received at the Red Police Commissariat. The Soviet Government was embarrassed by the blunder that had been made, and Marguerite Lavalle quickly received permission from the senior *Cheka* officers to recover her husband's body. This was made easier by the fact that Lavalle had been wearing a white linen suit at the time of his murder.

It was a brilliant late summer morning. *Madame* Lavalle stood in silence beside the diver, Gregor Ivanovitch, as the small motor launch made for the death ships still lying at anchor in the harbor. It was eleven o'clock before the sea was calm enough for the diver to let himself down to the shallow sea bottom.

The pumps worked rhythmically. Marguerite stared tensely towards the spot where the diver had disappeared, while the Red police officer watched the hand of his wristwatch. After exactly three minutes had passed, two quick distress signals were received, whereupon the crew immediately hauled the diver back into the launch. Outwardly, Gregor Ivanovitch appeared unharmed but, when his helmet was unscrewed, he was dead.

The crew of the boat stood speechless round his body.

"*Madame*," said the Cheka officer in command, after all attempts to bring the man back to life had failed. "An unforeseen accident, you see. We have complied with your request, and there is no more I can do."

"But isn't there another diver on board?"

The Cheka officer looked inquiringly around the circle of sailors, who shrank back.

"Men!" *Madame* Lavalle said, "There's 10,000 rubles for the man who brings me back my husband's body."

"Ten thousand rubles!" the whisper went round. "Ten thousand rubles."

"Quick," said the Cheka officer. "The French woman keeps her promises."

The fireman watched with a rigid face as the diving suit was being dragged off the dead man's body. Then, without a word, he had it slipped on himself and went overboard.

The ripples receded in widening circles, and the line of air bubbles showed plainly the firm course that the new diver was taking towards the spot where the previous day's bodies were known to be. Again, the French woman fastened her gaze on the sea and, again, the *Cheka* officer checked the passing minutes.

A desperate pull on the alarm rope broke the tension. All hands grasped the rope and pulled in the fireman, whose arms beat the air crazily as he was hauled aboard. When, after some difficulty, his helmet was unbuckled, blood and saliva were seen to be running from his mouth and nose. He looked wildly around.

"What's the matter?" the *Cheka* man shouted angrily. "Have you gone mad?"

"Ten thousand rubles!" the Georgian screamed. "There are 10,000 bodies walking across the sea bottom. Priests, bourgeois, generals, soldiers." He began to scream and rave and beat the air. It took a long time to calm him down.

***

"Have you heard, comrade? There's a man in the hospital who's seen them."

"Seen whom? "

"The dead men," said the woman as she emerged from the bread distribution point, clutching the loaf she had secured in the scramble ever closer to her chest.

"And the priest is standing upright among them, with his hair on end and his arms held high, cursing us and the city. Standing, did you hear, the dead are coming upright across the sea bottom."

The news of the assembly of the dead flew from house to house, leaked into the Red Army barracks, into the cells of those condemned to die, out into the narrow crooked lanes and hunger slums of Odessa's proletariat.

By the evening, the first threats against the Red leaders were flying through the town. Next morning, a strike and mutiny broke out in the port. Comrade General Commissar of the *Cheka* rushed down in his car.

"Dead is dead, you fools," he shouted in a fury at the excited crowds. "The bodies are standing up because the iron is holding their feet down, and because all bodies try to come to the surface after three days. Get back to work, comrades."

"The dead are cursing you," screamed the high voice of a woman.

"The dead have bewitched our city and us and our children."

"And you, you bastards," the crowd roared.

Comrade General Commissar disappeared behind the rifle barrels of the *Cheka.*

"Clear the street! Or..."

Stones were thrown and the crowd showed no sign of going away.

He lifted his leather-gloved hand.

When the smoke had drifted away into the narrow, high-walled sharp-angled streets of the harbor, the square was empty. Comrade General Commissar stepped hurriedly over the bodies on the pavement towards his car.

We were silent.

The old woman emptied her cup, also remaining silent.

"We are going to liberate the Russian people," I said quickly, "liberate them from the Red slavery and the senselessness of the life they're leading now."

The old woman smiled enigmatically. "My last husband was a Menshevik before we married. He also dreamt that one day the Russian people would be saved. Every Russian dreams it, whatever his opinions or feelings. Yet in his troubled days my husband went through the same events as we had seen around us, the same shootings, hangings and deportations. And now, after 20 long years of forced labor, he too has died without having seen his dream realized, while the shooting, hanging and deporting goes on."

"We shall save the Russian people," I repeated stubbornly and with some agitation. The old woman stood up. "Allow me to thank you, young soldiers, for being kind to an old woman. And now, before I go, I shall tell you a great truth: The Russian people will not be saved by the man with the bigger cannons and gun, but by the man with the greater soul."

The rest of us sat on round the big samovar into the night.

***

Next morning, it became clear that there was an enemy observation post somewhere in the city. Shells rained down accurately from the Black Sea Fleet and from artillery batteries on the big islands in the Dnieper on the buildings housing German headquarters elements.

Houses were divided into groups and searched. It was striking how foodstuffs and lots of textiles had been stockpiled in the apartments along the harbor, especially in the apartments of Jewish families. All of it was in crass contrast to the lack of items and poverty found in the proletarian apartments. Nothing was confiscated by the combat soldiers, in accordance with strict orders. There were no arrests. A town militia recruited from anti-communist elements proved very useful in the search and it was, in fact, due to this militia that the man was later interrogated and arrested. He had been using carrier pigeons to direct the enemy fire.

The next day, I came across a strange procession in the harbor area. Five German policemen and several men of the town militia were marching a handcuffed man round the town; the man, who was walking with the other had a carefree attitude. He had a large placard round his neck saying in both German and Russian: "I am the man who has been directing the Soviet artillery fire on Cherson, and I am responsible for the death of 63 Russian women and children together with a number of German soldiers. For this I am to be hanged today." Wherever the little procession went, men, women and children crowded to read the words on the placard, then stepped back to allow others to come forward and read. When an old peasant came along who had some difficulty in spelling out the words, the condemned man readily and with obvious pleasure read them out for him.

"So you're the one," the peasant said. The man answered coolly and affirmatively.

"Serves you right," the peasant replied, equally coolly. "I'm glad those damned commissars have been packed off to the devil at last."

The man's expression did not change. "They'll be back," he said. The peasant looked frightened and made the sign of the cross. A few women followed his example. "Well, may God grant you a quick death," said the peasant, offering the man a cigarette, which he took with his fettered hands. "When do you have to die?"

"This evening," replied the communist, quite ready with the information. Then he was moved on.

We looked at each other, not understanding. Was the old German woman from the Volga region right: Were the Russians subject to different laws from other people?

***

The next day, we returned to the area around Bobrinetz and Komanyelka to rest and refit. New recruits had arrived from Germany to fill the heavy gaps in our ranks. And with them, almost overnight, came dysentery.

The hospitals were soon full and overcrowded. The first of my friends to catch it was Kaul, whom I hadn't seen for some time, since he had been transferred to another battalion. He complained of severe internal disorders, and he looked terribly pale and thin. We told war stories, and I told him about my conversation with the German woman in Cherson.

"Maybe she's right," Kaul said slowly, "maybe she's right. One thing is quite certain; whatever the Reds start, they finish. They are as consistent and ruthless in their lying as in their killing. Whatever they undertake, they carry through with a ruthless and steely resolve, the likes of which we only talk about. In fact they're the real thing, while we, in so many things, are only half steppers."

I looked at Kaul furtively. He seemed to have changed somehow.

The next few days passed in sleeping, eating and drinking. The *Wehrmacht* Daily Reports reported a dizzying array of victory after victory.

More and more cases of dysentery were reported. Some were discharged from the hospital after a day and came back to us full of ghastly stories about its horrors. Many of the sick had nothing but straw to lie on; there were no bed pans, and they had to make do with old steel helmets.

One morning, I caught myself looking affectionately at my normal excrement. There was obviously nothing wrong with me, I was fit enough. An order arrived forbidding us to drink unboiled water or to eat melons.

Our rest period was broken off abruptly. The new offensive had begun and we were to move towards the Dnjepr. As we approached the river on the first evening, I suddenly realized I was feeling ill and got down from my vehicle. It was with some difficulty that I managed to rejoin it in the long column that had piled up at the military bridge at Berislaw. After that, I had to go three or four times in quick succession. My forehead was covered with sweat, and I was shivering.

Our *Spieß*[20] was standing at the entrance to the bridge.

"Have you heard the news?" he asked. "We just buried Kaul."

My heart skipped a beat. He'd been sent to hospital for a follow-up, and the following day he was dead. Apparently his heart had given out.

"Here today, gone tomorrow," the first sergeant said laconically. "Watch yourself, we're in for a hell of a barrage."

At last we moved onto the bridge; it was a pitch-black night, but after we had crawled along for a kilometer or so the sky became bril-

---

20   Translator's Note: German soldier slang for the company first sergeant. A *Spieß* is a spear or a pike. It can also mean the spit used for cooking meat over a grill. In that sense, it has a double meaning in German, which is appropriate for the function the *"Spieß"* has to perform in maintaining law, order and discipline among the enlisted personnel of the unit.

liant with flares. Then came the first bombs, thick and fast. Down they rained, right, left and all round us, while we sat motionless in our vehicles on the bridge. *Flak* batteries on either bank belched and roared into the night sky, but still the bombs came. But none found the bridge that night.

***

Next day I was losing blood. But I could just imagine that horrible hospital and tried to pull myself together. I ate nothing, and suffered all the time from a raging thirst. During rests, the battalion physician gave me charcoal, then tannalbin and, finally, opium, but it made no difference.

Fortunately, there was practically no fighting, as the enemy was in wild flight before us. By the end of the week I was so limp that I could barely stand. Then, in the midst of my daze, I received orders: "Take a squad of men in a *Kübelwagen*[21] and two dispatch riders and reconnoiter the road ahead." It was all I could do to follow the officer's hand on the map. "You're to get as far as these two villages."

We moved out into a sunshine-filled day. Moved and moved. The road led through fertile countryside, with vineyards climbing up the sides of the sandy dunes on the right. The men peered uncomfortably around them into the tall fields of grain in which whole companies could have hidden themselves. I couldn't have cared less. If only those damned villages would come, and then, at last, rest again and sleep.

Then the first thatched roofs of Bolshe Kopani showed through the green foliage of the fruit trees. We approached the village with utmost caution. My knees weak and trembling, I dismounted and spoke to a young girl, who was standing there. Not saying a word, she shook her head, no matter what I asked. Obviously, a Young Communist. I turned away in a fury and left her where she stood. The woman, who had appeared at the door of the house across the way in the meantime, readily supplied information. The last Red Army men

---

21   Translator's Note: The *Kübelwagen* was the ubiquitous military version of what would become the *Volkswagen*.

had moved through the village three hours earlier. "They went that way," she said, her hand pointing to the horizon.

We moved slowly through the village. Men and women brought us milk and melons. I looked away. It was more than I could bear to see people drink.

The ripening harvest received us again: Vineyards, orchards, fields of tall grain. And then the second village appeared. When we rode in—more precipitously than I should have permitted—we found the place swarming with Red Army men. The dispatch rider behind heard the screech of our brakes, saw the first batch of brown uniforms, turned like a flash and was gone. The second followed close behind him. In a cold fear, I dismounted, and the machine gunner beside me slowly raised the barrel of his weapon. At that moment a tall Ukrainian walked up to us. *Wujna kaput* —the war's over." Then he complained that the peasants were refusing to provide food for his hungry men. I had all rifles, machine guns and mortars collected into a pile and then sent for the village elder. There was none. "Alright then, you're it," and I pointed to an old man. He was flattered and smiled. As it happened, I had picked the right man; he had done five years' forced labor for refusing to join the collective farm and had a very healthy hatred of the Bolsheviks. There was soon food for our hungry prisoners. Before very much longer the whole battalion came racing up, expecting to find nothing but our bodies. Everyone was happy to discover that we had come to no harm.

***

On the next day, it had been two weeks since my amoebic dysentery had started.

"Now I'm going to try something really special," the battalion physician said. "Castor oil, and in good-sized doses. That'll do the trick."

"You'll be all right if you can stand it, chum," the *Unterscharführer* whispered. He was the battalion's senior medic. "If you can't, you've had it. Come and see me afterwards. I'll give you something."

And give me something he did, a whole bottle of "gin, but not too rough!" On his advice, I drank the whole lot at one go, promptly sinking into a stupor-like sleep which lasted many hours. When I awoke, I was already feeling much better.

For a few days, I ate nothing but dry bread and biscuits, and then I was all right again. A horse cure perhaps, but apparently the amoeba found the gin less to their liking than I did.

***

In front of Tschulakowka, Ivan had dug himself in again along an extended swell in the ground. We attacked, but since the artillery had not come up and there were no signs of any armor, we had to call it off after a few hours. Towards evening, four women came in and asked to see the commander. They told him that in their village a woman had suddenly reappeared who was not only a commissar herself but had always cooked for the higher ranking commissars.

The woman was picked up and questioned. She would not talk except to say that she had only done the cooking because she had been asked to. Apart from that, she knew nothing. The other women were brought in and they were put face-to-face, the result being uproar. The commander was furious and finally had the female commissar put behind bars for the night.

That evening, a couple of deserters came in, two fully armed Russian seamen, hailing from Odessa. They had had enough. Just to be sure, the commander decided to lock them away as well, and he had them put in with the woman commissar. Next morning, the two sailors reported. One of them, who was an unpleasant type, tattooed all over and obviously a skirt chaser, protested that he was not going to be insulted by the likes of this woman. She had been giving him hell for going over to the enemy and betraying his country. "Does your country mean so little to you that you would betray it?" she had asked. I heard the whole story afterwards from the interpreter.

So the woman was brought in and questioned again. She guessed what she was in for and became insolent. That finally settled her fate. The execution squad was to be formed by the company runners, but we had all vanished in a flash. Willing volunteers were found from some supply personnel who had just come up with ammunition and rations.

Later, the Ukrainian peasant women came to the commander again and asked if they could have the fine clothes that the woman had been wearing, but he turned his back on them. A short while later they reappeared bringing a hundred thousand rubles and two detailed maps on which our positions were accurately pinpointed. They had found it all in the dead woman's undergarments.

***

Next morning, nine *Stukas* raced in and bombed the enemy positions. Nobody stirred in the enemy positions. However, the moment the *Stukas* had gone, a well-placed artillery barrage fell on our lines. A battery of 105's finally arrived in the afternoon, after which we resumed our attack and ejected the enemy. At that point, we were off again along the great Dnjepr Peninsula, heading for the sea.

Once again, my vehicle was out in front, reconnoitering. But I was not alone this time; the party had been joined by the liaison officer and an interpreter. As before, there were two dispatch riders spaced out behind our *Kübelwagen*. The vegetation grew dense. Low sand hills came in sight, somewhat similar to the dunes on the North Sea coast. Between them, narrow hedgerows came right up to the sandy road. Elsewhere there were tall fields of millet and grain and even small woods. Death could have been hidden anywhere, and each moment could have been our last. Our rifles had been loaded and ready to fire for some time. Then the first houses appeared and we asked an old woman if there were enemy forces there. She shook her head: "*Nema, nema*...gone long ago...a good four hours...Red devils."

The village was clear of the enemy. One of the dispatch riders rode off back to report, while we moved on, deeper into the unknown. The country turned even denser, and the woods came right up to the road. Suddenly, we came across a railway line that was not marked on any of our maps. We stood on the running boards, rifles at the ready, expecting to be fired on at any moment. Our second dispatch rider was 100 meters behind. At least one of us would get back.

But nothing happened. We moved on and on through more villages that were clear of the enemy; the villagers, men and women alike, clad in their Sunday best. For hours on end these southern Ukrainian women and children stood in front of their mud huts or lined the road, waving and calling to us. One old woman with trembling hands brought a huge loaf of bread to our vehicle, and was overcome when, with a smile, we accepted it.

All along the road, armfuls of autumn flowers were showered in on us, asters of all colors: Red, white, yellow, blue. Nobody had prompted these people to garland our vehicles, nobody had asked them, and yet they risked their lives to do it. They would have had short shrift if a stray detachment of Reds had heard of it. Many a life had already been forfeited because of a single flower. Great mountains of melons were brought to us. Soon, we could take no more, not even the eggs and grapes.

Then the battalion closed up after us. Towards evening, bursts of fire began to whistle around our ears again, and on each side we heard the metallic welcome of the *Ratschbumm*. The parade of flowers was over, and we were back in the grim dance. But our men were full of the offensive spirit. They felt the sea in front of them.

There was already a sharp sea breeze blowing over the steppe and, far in the distance, a white haze gleamed on the horizon. We had reached the Black Sea.

The 1st Platoon of the 16th Company advanced to the small harbor where the Russians were making frantic efforts to get the remnants of their shattered army away by sea. We moved out across the steppe. The first buildings appeared, and we approached them slowly. At any moment, the first shot might come and release an inferno of fire. The men in their vehicles; the antitank gun and *Flak* crews observed intently to the front. But nothing stirred. Only few pitiable creatures, who happily surrendered to our first scouts. The poor wretches had only been called up a few weeks before and had been without food for days.

We dismounted our vehicles with pistols and rifles at the ready and combed through the houses of the fishing village. From away in the distance came the low rumble of heavy explosions, which at first we thought came from coastal artillery. Soon we realized it was the work of our own *Stukas*.

And then they were there. In a moment, they were over our heads and circling far out at sea. The first one dipped down into its dive and a fountain of water rose steeply up from the sea. Then we caught our breath. There was a roar like thunder, and iron plates, planks, machines and men were hurled in the air. A direct hit on a Soviet warship. Slowly the crackle of ammunition died away, and it was all over. The *Stuka* swooped twice. Twice, and death remained the victor over men, science and machines.

Hard by the gutted landing drifted the smoldering remains of a wrecked sailing craft; a few hundred meters further out the red-hot hulk of a steamer spewed a rain of sparks into the evening sky. From still further out on the high sea we heard the recurrent boom of heavy explosions.

"They tried time and again," a villager told us, "to get their troops away to the open sea, but," he waved his hand at the many masts and the burning hulks, "none of them got through."

The beach down to the water's edge was littered with abandoned trucks, and there were even a few guns. Without wasting any time, our forces started securing the coastline. Artillery came up and patrols cleaned up the whole area.

The last scattered Soviets who had "missed the bus" gave themselves up without resistance.

Some time later, I strolled through the village with one of our young recruits to take a look at the primitive nets and fishing tackle. On our way, we came across an abandoned Russian gun concealed in the yard of a small fisherman's hut. Inquisitive as all soldiers are when they get strange weapons in their hands, the recruit fumbled round the gun, which was completely intact, even down to the breech-block.

A big command car was just coming up the road into the village. I looked closer and saw that it was the battalion commander. At that moment there was an ear-splitting crash beside me. The Russians had left a round in the chamber, which the young comrade had managed to fire in his fumbling.

But the noise from the road was worse, much worse. The shell had landed a few meters in front of the commander's car and showered it with earth and shrapnel. It was nothing short of a miracle that nobody was hurt.

In less time than it takes to tell, the two of us were round the next corner and had disappeared into the excited throng. The investigations initiated by the commander lasted two whole days, but both of us kept our traps shut. It was only when we saw each other that we would wink knowingly.

In the meantime, night had come. Dusk had slowly crept out across the steppe and overtaken us here by the sea. All was silence and peace where we were, save for the fiery glare which came in from the sea.

Our mission in this area had been accomplished and word came round that we were to move to the Crimea, where some of the division's armored elements were already said to be fighting hard at Perekop among the Tartar Ditch. Nothing came of it, however, and we pushed on instead along the Black Sea, past the weakly defended town of Melitopol, on to Mariupol.

Chapter Four:
To Taganrog

The next day, a bitter struggle raged for the possession of an end-less field of sunflowers.

The sunflowers were all aglow with the rich yellow of early ripe-ness. Now it was over, and the sun, grown gentler in the thunder of battle, was spinning its misty threads out from the blackthorn hedge, where we had moved out that morning, out to the golden sea of sun-flowers. The glare of burning villages was deepening; it was almost evening.

The first crimson rays of sunset broke on the tawny seed shields over our heads. A bird took a last quick peck at nature's rich bounty. Then its fluttering wings faded in the distance, and we were left alone with the wind and the waving sunflowers. We were glad it was quiet. Whenever we heard the first shots of battle whip across the field, the first shells begin to burst, the same old fever still gripped at our senses. Long forgotten was the terror of our first baptism of fire; things had to be bad indeed to worry us. Yet the first shot never failed to cast its spell, a spell that opened for us the gates into darkness and brought the last revelation to tangible reality. And just as we desired that first shot in the upcoming fight, the quiet of the evening embraced us with its secrets and shelter.

The day was over.

Nothing was heard but the rustle of foliage, bending in the wind all over the huge field—here, there, and far below, in fact, as far as the vast field that we had taken went. We had found shelter in the enemy's holes and trenches, folded deep in the maternal care of the heavy Ukrainian soil. Around us, on every side, was the forgotten debris of battle, a litter of hand grenades, steel helmets and gas masks. The enemy dead were curled up in holes and swells in the ground, wherever our assault had reached them. This heavy Maxim had been silenced. Its crew had surrendered, despite the threats and pistols of the commissars. That mortar that had given us so much trouble and had been so well concealed by the giant sunflowers was orphaned near our foxholes, its crew of Kalmucks beside it. Our machine-gun burst had sat well. Wherever you looked, at every meter, death was to be seen among the sunflowers. On the edge of the field, our listening posts were secure in Russian trenches, covered from the side, from above, from the front, by the great yellow blooms. Even the anti-tank guns and the 2cm *Flak* had vanished below the yellow sea. It was as though Death himself held court there among the sunflowers.

Yesterday, he had worn a Red Star on his pointed Moscow helmet. Today he had joined our ranks. The yellow roof over our heads, we lay on the edge of our trenches and awaited the Red counterattack. Thin smoke rose from a nearby hill, where a small village was burning. But the enemy was taking his time.

Sunflowers. As a child I had already loved them—slim and graceful and yet so strong. Later on, when I had my first room of my own, my unskilled boy's hand had cut the picture out of an illustrated magazine, put it under glass and hung it as a beloved decoration above my bed: Sunflowers. I dreamt the first dreams of my life under it. The first good picture I had from an artist's hand was a small study: blooming sunflowers. To me, they were an eloquent expression of youth and maturity. Everything was unified in them: Delicate playfulness, unique beauty and maternal generosity, which gives of itself in teeming abundance.

Thus the first Ukrainian sunflower fields came like a greeting from home and childhood. They fascinated us still more when we saw what an important part they played in the harvest of those wide plains and hills, and the many ways in which their seeds served the *Muschik*. It was no wonder then that they were an endless delight for us.

Until the day when death first sprang out from behind their tall stems and tore great gaps in our ranks. It seemed like a friend's treachery, until bitter experience taught us that sunflowers spelt death.

One day, the field would be the enemy's, the next day ours. Today the enemy would find shelter beneath the yellow roof; tomorrow it would be our turn. It was a true struggle that had erupted around this flower. The question arose: Would we ever see sunflowers again without seeing the death in their midst?

But all was now peaceful in our field. A pale moon was rising, pouring her lifeless, waxen light over the yellow flood, and a deep, almost alien calm drifted over us, bringing a strange sense of sanctuary in the sunflower field.

Hours passed before morning greeted the new day. It greeted our outposts up front and us in the lines. The glint of its first light on our gun barrels wiped clean all thought of yesterday, as if it had never happened.

For a brief moment, it touched the yellow sunflowers around the fresh graves that we had left alongside the trail.

***

In the meantime, Mariupol had fallen to other battalions of our division and there was nothing left for us to do but move through it in their wake, amazed. Our route led us through the enormous tank factory which, a few days after the fall of the city, was already working again, but for us. Our objective: Taganrog.

Up to that time, the Red Air Force had been little more than a joke with us. In almost all cases their bombs fell to the right or the left of their targets and their *Ratas*[22] had been repeatedly brought down with small arms. The Red Air Force, both in men and machines, seemed to be far below the standard of their armor and infantry. Our men had a joke: "You can be killed by a Russian bomb falling on your head, but it's your own stupid fault if you are."

---

22 Translator's Note: The generic German term for Russian fighters—in particular, the stubby *Polikarpov I-16* with its radial engine. This aircraft was the most commonly encountered Soviet fighter until 1942. It was markedly inferior to the *Bf 109E/F* that was the standard *Luftwaffe* fighter at that time.

We had never seen a Soviet aircraft fly along a road. They always flew across it, a fruitless business either for fighters or fighter-bombers; they were over and gone before the target could be identified. How were they supposed to do anything that way?

But it was another story on the road from Mariupol to Taganrog, where the Red Air Force gave us a most unpleasant reminder of its existence. From dawn to dusk, without intermission, our lead columns were under continuous attack by hundreds of aircraft. Hour by hour throughout the day, the crash and roar of bombs hammered against our ears. Every few minutes during the night, bombs were scattered as if from a giant shovel on our resting columns. Surprisingly, that hurriedly improvised massed use of Soviet aircraft actually did very little damage. However, the effect of those lame fireworks in course of time was very heavy on our nerves.

It was evening, and I had a roof over my head, an abandoned farmhouse. The broken panes of its window rattled from the shock of distant explosions. Two comrades were sleeping deeply and peacefully beside me; I alone was awake and listening in the moonlight night.

We had been moving for hours. Always eastward, always towards the enemy, whose combat power our companies had shattered. My vehicle had fallen behind the rest of the battalion with engine trouble, and we were steadily overtaking the endless columns of the German advance in an attempt to catch up. The driver, Wilhelm, gazed contentedly ahead into the sunny afternoon. We overtook a light *Flak*; there was another one just ahead. They always made me think of forts on wheels. Then I blinked. The gun in front had stopped with a jerk, its barrel elevating.

"Over to the right," I yelled. At the same moment, the first bombs fell beside the road. Ambushed by *Ratas*! The approach of the enemy aircraft had been drowned by the noise and rattle of the moving column. We vaulted to the ground. There was a small, old house beside the road and, in one leap, we were over the low fence and flat on our faces behind the mud wall. We were no longer just two; a third man from another unit had joined us. I was on the verge of speaking when a fountain of earth shot up beside us, followed, a second later, by rafters and pieces of wall. The house had been hit. Without thinking, I straightened up and yelled through the rattle and crash of gunfire: "Round the corner!" and pushed Wilhelm on in front of me. The other soldier followed close behind.

Lying there, huddled tight together under the mud wall, I thought: "He ought to come in closer," but forgot that thought in the explosion of the next few bombs. There must have been at least a dozen of the Soviet aircraft, scraped together in a desperate attempt to cover their retreat. Another near one, near enough to lift us bodily from the ground. A voice cried out. Wilhelm? I could see nothing in the dense smoke and dust that enveloped us. Then I heard a groan close beside me. It was the other comrade. "Medic!" I shouted. Wilhelm stood up and shouted into the smoke, but one was already on their way. From the eyes of the medic who dressed the wound, I could see there was no hope; the shrapnel had gone straight through his back and chest. Bombs were still falling, but they were a good 100 meters away at that point and spending their force impotently in the open field. Then I saw. The bomb had fallen on the very spot where we had been lying before, barely a meter from the corner of the house. That corner had saved us. But what of the comrade who was now dying?

"You're bleeding," Wilhelm said. I passed my hand over my face. There was a thin line on my neck, a mere scratch, it was nothing. Another centimeter and the story would have been different. I turned to the dying man and found him looking straight at me. That serious, tanned young face—I felt as though I had always known it. I bent over him and smoothed the hair back from his sweat-covered forehead. He smiled. Some men from his own unit had arrived by then and were doing what they could for him. Why hadn't I pulled him in closer? I left him with some trepidation and walked over to our vehicle. Once again, we moved rapidly forward.

It was quiet in the deserted village. A few stray horses, frantic with terror, galloped across the broad meadows. The night sky was red with a flickering glare. A cow lumbered slowly out of the darkness and stood snorting in front of me; it was probably several days since she had been milked. The tanks were rumbling on the road, their tracks clanking heavily through the night. Our advance was continuing. Gradually, the dull pressure which had been weighing on my spirit all day began to lift. I was beginning to understand the meaning of the old house by the roadside: We were in this together.

We were all lying close together. What good would it have done, even if he had moved in closer? Death had come from the left, and a comrade had died so that the others could go on and build the future. Had Cousin Hein[23] come from the right, then *he* would have gone forward into enemy territory. The soldier's hour does not wait for the tolling bell and the peaceful grave. It comes when it comes, and he must heed it.

The air still throbbed with the distant rumble of war. A shiver went down my spine, and I went back into the house. Sleep came to the sound of our tanks grinding on through the night, and the defeated Russian hordes in front of them were running.

The windowpanes rattled softly...

***

Next morning, while the main body continued its advance along the main route of advance, individual vehicles with dispatch riders were sent off to the right and left to reconnoiter the side roads. They remained in visual contact.

We moved along the coastal plain, the road barely wide enough for our vehicles. But we got through. On our left, dark blue waves broke against the narrow sand banks and came riding up in white foam almost to our wheels. On our right, drenched in the autumn sun, were the miserable hovels of fishermen and dockworkers. Delicate threads stretched silver across the road. We arrived in a village and were at once surrounded by people, men and women. We were the first Germans they had seen. Wilhelm, our comrade from Hanover, showed them a few snapshots of his wife and children, and they stared at them, wide-eyed with curiosity. Suddenly, a young woman started to talk excitedly and turned to me, pointing again and again

---

23 Translator's Note: "Cousin Hein" was soldier slang for death.

first to the photographs and then to her own ragged skirt. Then she began to cry, while the rest of them stared silently at their feet. The picture of a well-dressed German worker's wife was too much, the contrast with their own lives too great.

We smoked a couple of cigarettes and then moved on at a leisurely pace. *"Auf Wiedersehen,"* a boy called after us proudly, his only German words. The call to partisan warfare had met as little response from the civilian population there as anywhere else. There were only the two of us German soldiers. The Soviet Empire was creaking at the joints. The people no longer believed. They were finally seeing the truth with their own eyes.

Up on the slope of the hill was a large building with a garish facade, the Air Force Academy. Music came from within, faint at first, then louder, and finally fortissimo—Tchaikovsky—as I entered the gloomy combination lecture hall and dining facility. Outside, our *Flak* were banging away at a few *Ratas*, which vanished like evil spirits across the sea. The pianist, a thin, middle-aged woman, did not pay attention to any of that. She sat, bent over the keyboard, wrapped up in her music. When she saw me, she jumped up in alarm.

"Nitschewo," I soothed her. "Don't let me disturb you."

"Merci, Monsieur," she said in awkward, half-forgotten school French. "It's so long since I sat at a piano. It's a miracle, an absolute miracle."

I stayed for a while, listening. Then I turned and tiptoed out of the room. In the corridor outside, I saw three Russian youths standing round the false god of Soviet Russia, who looked as though he were about to pass into eternity with his fist clenched. They whispered together a moment, then made a grab and, with a crash, the plaster Lenin went hurtling down the stairs. As if shocked by their own temerity, they stood for a moment in silence. But nothing moved. From the movie hall, the music went on, new melodies from Tchaikovsky, full and bracing.

Farther to the rear, at a place where flames and smoke were still pouring from oil tanks that the Russians had fired, our forces were regrouping for a fresh drive into enemy territory, to carry the flag forward in our victorious march. All vehicles were streaming in that direction

Next to us were the azure waters of the Sea of Azov. Then we turned northwest and advanced further into the open country. We were again engulfed by vast fields of sunflowers, endless waving cornfields...on and on, until the enemy turned once more and gave battle.

***

Night lay heavy upon us. The thatched roofs of the Ukrainian village in front loomed dark and spectral against the night sky. It had taken us all day—from first light until late in the evening—to work our way up through the sunflowers, which were tall enough to close in over our helmets and submerge us in a world of fantasy. Again and again, your comrades to the right and left vanished in the tangle of foliage, leaving you alone with the enemy, who was everywhere and nowhere. The Siberians were tough fighters, who disdained death. Many men, ours and theirs, lay in the broad field, wreathed in a final splendor by the yellow heads of the sunflowers.

It was evening before resistance died down. For a while single, individual rounds whipped across the field. Then all was deathly still; even the moans of the wounded had ceased. We were 30 meters or so from the nearest house, of which no more than the merest outline could still be distinguished in the darkness. An open door was creaking in the evening breeze, and we jumped each time we heard it, even though we had long realized that the house had been abandoned and the person who had left the door open in his haste was gone with the four winds.

From over in the west came the clank and clatter of tanks, probably the armor that had been directed to support us coming up under cover of night. Then, suddenly, we jumped again: Over to the right a white cluster of light was setting the night sky aflame. Soon the flares formed a circle in front of us like ghostly Christmas lights, and we heard the monotonous drone of the Martini bombers[24]. However, in a few minutes they faded away in the distance and were lost. But it had given us a look at the small village in front of us, which really did appear to be empty. Gunner One nudged me and whispered: "Let's go."

We crawled out of the sheltering defile slowly. I heard the section leader in front curse softly at a telltale clatter from the light machine gun. We crept on forward, rifles with the safety's off. We had reached the low, wooden fence. Suddenly, all nine of us hit the deck. But nothing happened. Only that damned door had creaked again. A man in front stood up, ran to the door and wrenched it wide open. A flashlight gleamed. Drawers and cupboards stood open and empty, and the simple bed frames were bare. On the floor a jumble of old letters, yellow with age, faded photographs, rubbish of all kinds. A picture of flight.

Outside, we heard the muffled steps of the neighboring forces advancing. All at once, the platoon leader appeared in the doorway. We were to stay in the village for a night's rest, since we had been in action all day. Others pushed straight on through the abandoned village and moved out across the marshy meadowland to establish an outpost line.

We gave the room a perfunctory sweep with an old broom and then lay down, dead to the world, on the well-trodden mud floor. As I sank into sleep I heard what I thought was a soft moan in the distance. But I was too tired to bother with it.

Some time later I awoke, puzzled by my surroundings. A full moon was drenching the room with its pale light. I tried to collect my thoughts. There was Franz beside me and over there Karl. And this was the village we had been unable to take and which Ivan then, in the end, voluntarily evacuated in the evening.

---

24   Translator's Note: Martini refers to American-built "Martin" twin-engine bombers supposedly in Soviet service. "Martin", like "Rata", is a generic term for Soviet twin-engine bombers, including the *SB* and *DB-3*. In fact, there were no US-supplied aircraft in Soviet service at that time. The excellent Douglas A-20 "Havoc" did not see service with the Soviets until 1942.

I heard a thin wail from close by and was immediately awake. Beside me was a tiny white kitten, hardly bigger than my fist, crying quietly to itself. I tried to entice it, but it skipped away and then slowly backed out towards the open door, meowing again. I stood up stiffly and followed. But it slunk away again out into the yard, enticing me on towards the fence, where it stopped in front of a sunflower, emitting sharp little cries. This time it remained still when I approached. Under the sunflower was a big, scrawny cat stretched out gaunt on the ground, with half its head taken off by a piece of shrapnel. The kitten tried repeatedly to get its mother up and circled round her crying. Then it gave up, and stood still staring at me.

I knelt down and stroked it, but it took no notice. I felt how terribly thin it was. The people of the village had probably left several days ago and since then the mother cat must have been keeping herself and her kitten alive on what she could scavenge. I had a sudden idea and felt in my bread bag for my emergency rations, a small tin of sausage, which I opened with a bayonet and then put under the kitten's nose. After a preliminary distrustful sniff, the tiny animal fell to it ravenously, while I looked on contentedly. Suddenly, I heard footsteps in front of me, and I looked up to see the platoon leader standing on the other side of the wooden fence and staring in silence at the scene before him. He had approached silently across the short grass. I jumped up in confusion.

"You ought to be court martialed," he said quietly. "Now get back to sleep." I returned to the house, tired, defeated and incapable of thought. As I fell asleep I heard the rattle of an empty can being chased across the yard, playing cat and mouse the way content cats do.

Next morning, when the platoon leader came in, my heart sank. But he said nothing. Shortly afterwards, the orders came taking us out again into the world of death. As we moved through the village, section by section, along each side of the shell-torn street, a small, white figure stalked up the middle of it, tail in the air, and remained with us until the steppe received us once more.

***

The hour before the attack was always quiet, almost peaceful, though lacking the inward contentment by which alone peace allows happiness. That was because behind each minute death was lurking somewhere out in the endless grain fields or sunflowers.

The 18th Company of the 4th Battalion had received orders to attack.

In a few minutes, the silence would be shattered and the rousing cheer of our men wrest yet another victory from the puppets of the Red Star.

At the last moment, with the intuition of the doomed, a Bolshevist battery dropped a withering barrage on the very sector that the 18th Company was holding. One machine-gun crew was rubbed out. Swearing hard, the company commander, an *Obersturmführer*, pulled a piece of shrapnel out of his leg with his bare hands. Then he stood up and began to hobble forward. The 18th Company's attack had started.

It was met by an inferno of fire. From the shelter of their deep trenches, as tall as a man, the Soviets showered the attacking company with everything they had. Here and there, a brave man staggered.

But soon they were scorning all cover and standing erect above the waving grain, which provided the enemy with such excellent camouflage. Wherever a Bolshevik helmet appeared above the yellow sea, German rifles cracked. It was more like a rat hunt than a battle, except that the quarry also held rifles. Our men literally stood face to face with death in the cornfield. In the middle of it all, one of the Soviets stood up and waved a German helmet. "They're giving up...they're cracking," the men shouted and began to advance with their rifles dropped.

But the *Obersturmführer* was on his toes. "Keep down!" he called and hobbled forward towards the would-be deserter. At that moment, two Russian machine guns opened up on the men diving for cover. Roused to fury by this trick, our men drove the attack relentlessly forward, ever closer to the cunning enemy. A bitter struggle developed, man against man, between the Germans standing upright among the grain and the Soviets crouching at bay in their holes and firing until they ran out of ammunition.

At the right moment, two assault guns arrived in the 18th's sector, and carried the attack, which was being conducted with unheard of fury, farther forward.

One man was severely wounded in the chest. His *Untersturmführer* saw it and immediately dropped beside him, tore open his field dressing and started to bind up the wound. He had barely begun when he was spotted by a lurking Red Army bandit and shot through the head in the middle of his act of mercy.

Our enraged men gave way neither to the enemy's murderous fire nor to his treacherous cunning. Before long, the hill was in our hands.

One of our men waved to a Russian, whom he saw cautiously getting to his feet in the grain, to come over and surrender. The Red Army man smiled in a friendly manner, came a few steps closer and then, with a quick movement, pulled out a hand grenade he had been concealing and threw it at the surprised German who, fortunately, had the presence of mind to throw himself flat on the ground in the grain. A comrade saw it happen, and fired at the cowardly Russian but only wounded him. Then the first man beckoned to him again to come over and give himself up, but he smiled nervously, pulled out another grenade and put it under his chin, whereupon he blew himself up.

Later, we were told by some prisoners that this man was the last surviving commissar of the regiment, which we had defeated so decisively in the fighting of the past two days.

But not all political commissars were so pig-headed nor yet served their masters so abjectly as that fanatic. On several occasions, our men had come across suitcases containing complete civilian outfits, down to shirts, shoes, ties and even cloth caps. They puzzled us for a long time until we were eventually let into the secret by a soured and embittered prisoner: Every commissars had provided himself—secretly, of course—with one of those suitcases, which they hoped would give them a chance of getting away safely if things did finally go wrong. Those "safety suitcases" of Stalin's political commissars said little for the Bolshevik belief in victory. "Fight to the last drop of blood, comrade. By the way, Ivan, where's my suitcase?"

Brilliant sunshine beat down on Hill 180 and the grain bowed low in the morning breeze. The 18th's attack had continued, and now it was standing guard on the river to prevent the enemy from finding a hole in the deadly noose around him. It seemed hard to believe that only yesterday death had marched through this same grain field.

***

We reached the Mius and were engaged in violent hand-to-hand fighting for a village, which the Russians were defending with unbelievable tenacity. In front of us was the city of Taganrog. The Russian artillery was firing like crazy but, to our surprise, very few of their shells were exploding. It was not until some hours later that we realized what the strange miracle had been. They were firing with delayed fuses. When our supply columns closed up toward us—not aware of the danger and cheered to see us—the shells started exploding to the left and the right of the road, but without causing any serious damage.

In the meantime, we had moved on almost unopposed and reached the center of the city, where I received orders to take a squad and comb through a block of streets. There was hardly a soul to be seen and the tall buildings stood silent and forbidding. I forced an entrance into one of them and then worked through the landscaping and courtyard of each building up to the front, opening or forcing open the main gates from inside. But the street outside remained quiet. After a while, we found ourselves in front of a small park. We climbed cautiously over the low wall and, to our amazement, found ourselves confronted by what looked like a palace.

Covered by the rest of the squad, another man and I walked slowly up the wide stone steps, opened the unbarred door and found ourselves in an entrance hall outfitted with magnificent carpets. We crept round the first corner, and were brought up short by the sight of a couple of Tartar warriors dressed in chain mail complete with sword, shield and helmet. We had found the Taganrog city museum.

We walked slowly on through the museum's many rooms. Nothing had been touched and the glass cases were all intact. Paintings by ancient and modern Russian masters looked down on us from the walls. Buddhas and prayer wheels mounted on pedestals stood side by side with the pain-distorted figure of Christ on the Cross. It was the Department of Superstitions.

In one room, we found toys dating from earliest antiquity up to the present day, from dolls of wood and stone at one end to harlequins at the other. I took down a couple of them, one a puppet and the other a plump doll with red cheeks and flaxen hair, and stuck them in my belt beside the hand grenades. Then we went back through the main gates into the street, where everything was still quiet. On the corner of the street, we could see a multi-story block of workers' flats, similar to those in Vienna, only more primitive. I divided the squad into two and we moved cautiously towards it on either side of the street. Suddenly, we stopped short. In the courtyard of the flats were hundreds of people of all ages crowded together and watching our approach with hostile eyes. The machine gunner planted his gun on the ground, cocked it and got into position. It was a bad moment, and I had no idea what to do. I looked at Rudolf, who understood immediately and fell to the rear, ready to race back to the company at the first shot.

Suddenly I became conscious of the fixed stare of a child fastened upon me and looked up in astonishment to see a tiny girl—she must have been about six—gazing spellbound at my belt. Then I knew what I had to do. With a smile, I pulled the red-cheeked doll out of my belt and handed it to the little girl. Her eyes grew round and as big as wagon wheels, then with a shriek of delight she pressed the doll to her body and ran up to a tired-looking woman: "*Mati, mati.*"

I then pulled out the puppet and gave it to a second child, perhaps four years old, who had also come forward inquisitively to see what was happening. That did it. In a moment I was surrounded by dozens of children, all with hands outstretched and overwhelming me with their entreaties. I tried desperately to hold them off and shouted: *"Nema, nema* — that's all I've got." I all but dropped my rifle.

There was a roar of laughter and, in a moment, we were surrounded by friendly people, all talking at once, touching our uniforms, bringing us water because we looked worn out and thirsty. Several even tried to push bread on us.

Never before had I seen such a sudden transformation. There were no more Bolsheviks; the whole place was clear of the enemy.

We had gone another two or three blocks, but the small girl was still with us, trotting along under the shadow of our rifles, the flaxen doll pressed to her heart. Try as we might, there was no driving her away. Wherever we went, we encountered laughing and waving people.

Sleep came slowly that night: I was moved by this small incident, so trivial and so far removed from war.

***

In its struggle to gain power, Bolshevism forgot nothing. It knew how to harness every human weakness for its own ends, from its exploitation of the intolerable living conditions in the Russia of Rasputin to its incitement of the animal instincts of a mass population. It forgot neither the millions of soldiers at the front dying in a hopeless battle for a still more hopeless future, nor the starving factory hands and peasants at home. It forgot neither the dreams of a better life of those always fated to stand outside, outside the windows of the Czar of all the Russians and his selected few, nor the dark passions latent in the soul of the underdogs which, in one unhappy moment, turned a thousand peace loving, unhappy people into raging beasts. It had only forgotten one thing: The human heart.

For those hungry for life, it provided the myth of the communist state in which all would be sheep and none wolves; for the crusading spirits, it provided the myth of world revolution and the Comintern, in the service of which "believers" could live or die according to their needs. And for those of little faith, it provided the secret police, the forced labor camps and the shot in the back of the head. But for real life, for the heart, it provided nothing. Not perhaps, because it did not wish to, but because it did not know how.

Conscious of this deficiency, it then tried to replace the warm instincts of the human heart by cold logic. In the systematic dissection of all things, past, present and future, it found the power of its absolute philosophy. To the pseudoscientific result of this vivisection of all previous human thought and feeling, it gave the grandiose title of the Materialist Concept of History. Dogma and experiment were the pillars on which this philosophy rested. But for the human heart, the only link with life and its deepest secrets, there was no place in this world of materialism. For a while, it beat wildly against the barricades of power, then cried a little in the forced labor camps and, finally, died in the basements of the secret police. Had it tried later to re-enter the world of Bolshevism, its language would not have been understood. The heart had been forgotten, omitted not only in the theory of communism, but above all in its daily life.

How else was it possible for the Soviet dead, fallen for the dream of world domination, to be left unburied for days, often for weeks, in the middle of their towns and villages. How else was it possible for the Soviet medics simply to shoot their wounded, as they often did, as opposed to dressing their wounds? *Nitschewo!* He can't fight like that, so why bother?"

In the middle of Mariupol, a woman camp follower, who had been wounded by shrapnel, had run sobbing through the crowds that had gathered for our entry, desperately begging her fellow citizens for help. Not a single one stirred to help her; most of them had laughed at the way the wretched creature's hair had straggled over her face. Without German help, this female comrade would have bled to death in the middle of her comrades. In Taganrog, a Ukrainian peasant who had been brought from the Dnjepr to dig defenses lay in the middle of the main road leading to the harbor, a bullet through both his legs. Moaning with pain, he had begged the thousands of passersby to bring him a bandage from the looted pharmacy across the way, but nobody had taken the slightest notice, except some youths, who had torn the boots off his feet and taken off. When we found him, the poor devil had been lying in that busy street for 18 hours. No, Bolshevism had forgotten nothing, nothing, that is, but the human heart.

***

In Taganrog, my squad was billeted with an old Ukrainian woman, whom we promptly christened *Babushka*—Granny. She and her two granddaughters—Nada, a young pilot in training, and Maruschka, a medical student—were fervently anticommunist. The *Babushka's* husband, son and daughter-in-law had been deported to Siberia for 10 years' forced labor for alleged conspiracy.

The two girls were friendly and fun, although at the same time they kept us very much at arm's length, so much so that my driver remarked: "I only hope ours are as well behaved."

Babushka, who had worked for a German businessman in her younger days, spoke an atrocious but at least intelligible German. She was on her feet from morning to night, washed our socks and underwear and cooked special tidbits for us. It goes without saying that we shared our military rations, of which there were plenty, with the entire family. Altogether it was a warm and friendly atmosphere, almost a family life.

One day, when I was the commander of the guard for the platoon, I made the acquaintance of a good-looking black-haired Muscovite, who had fled from Moscow with her five-year-old daughter in order to be with her mother in Taganrog. She had been a member of the Moscow State Opera. Having heard that a cabaret was to be formed for the German troops, she was trying to get a job as a singer or pianist, and I promised to make inquiries for her and to meet her again the following day. Next morning, I actually managed to have a word with a fat and bloated looking sergeant, who told me that singers and performers of all kinds were urgently needed. I passed on this information to her when we met next day. I then invited her to go with me to one of the first pubs that had just opened, but we found it so dreary, that I had little difficulty in persuading her to come to my quarters. There we sat for hours, Iniza—that was the name of my great achievement—and Babushka's granddaughters, drinking tea and listening to gramophone music. When I took her home, her mother invited me to tea the following day. On my way back to the billet, I could not help being amused by how conventional, how like life in any small town it all was.

Iniza's little girl, who was a pretty child, as dark-haired as her mother, never left me for a moment and would stand by me for hours when I was on guard duty

One evening, Iniza told me her story. While still a young trainee at the opera, she had met a Jewish editor from the Moscow Party Press office, who eventually married her. When Stalin made his non-aggression pact with Hitler, her husband was among those who had felt this to be a deviation from the party's general policy line and said as much on one occasion to a few of his closest friends. Twelve hours later he was on his way to Siberia. His wife, of course, was no longer acceptable at the opera, and so Iniza was forced to eke out a bare living by giving music lessons. Then, with the rapid German advance on Moscow, she had fled with her little girl to her mother. Despite the new reversal of policy, her husband was not released; he had become an unreliable element.

I have a lot to be grateful to Iniza for. She always pointed out our mistakes to me and showed me the things that should have been avoided in the interests of Russo-German co-operation. At that time, these were still comparatively minor and harmless liberties taken by petty officials, which were easily dealt with, as the front-line troops still had the decisive say in the civil administration of the area.

There was a strict curfew for civilians, which forbade them to be on the streets after dark. Although there was no sabotage nor even partisans at that time, the Soviets were making frequent attempts to cross the frozen Sea of Azov in motor- or wind-driven sleds in order to attack isolated sentry posts and spread alarm in the city by bursts of wild firing.

Late one night, just before twelve, a loud knocking came on our window. We reached for our weapons and pushed it open to find Iniza, shivering with cold and excitement, a large parcel in her hand.

"What the hell are you doing here?" I asked and pulled her into the house.

"The Bolsheviks are going to surround Taganrog early in the morning and kill you all," she said breathlessly. "I've brought you and your friends some of my dead brother's clothes. Hurry up and get into them, and I'll take you across the sea to Mariupol."

We were speechless. "How on earth did you get past the sentries?" I asked. There were, of course, sentries in front of all the larger quarters, headquarters and ammunition stores.

She smiled. "They fired at me, but they missed."

I hardly knew what to say. "How can I thank you, Iniza?" I said. "But things really aren't as bad as all that. I know they've been pushing hard at Sambek since yesterday, but don't worry, our line will hold. And anyway, even if it doesn't, I can't just go off and leave my comrades. Either we all get through or none of us. All of us can't get into your brother's clothes and make a bolt for it across the sea."

She cried a little, but soon quieted down.

Enemy pressure did in fact grow stronger in the morning, but our line held.

With the scarcity of all forms of manufactured goods in the Soviet Union and their high black-market value, it is difficult to say which was the greater sacrifice: Running the gauntlet through our sentries or the offer of material treasures on which the whole family could have lived for months.

That evening, Grigori showed up. He had arrived across the frozen-over Sea of Azov, a deserter from the Red Army.

Up to that point, we had not had a *Hiwi* in our squad, but Grigori not only spoke passable German, he also knew a thing or two about engines. As a result of the biting cold, our maintenance facilities were tremendously overworked. I succeeded in getting both the platoon leader and the company commander to turn a blind eye about keeping him.

Grigori was older than w were—in his mid 40's. He was a quiet type and did his work, almost without anyone directing him to. From that point forward, our vehicles were in good shape.

One evening, I brought him to our quarters. The usual tea and vodka loosened his tongue for the first time. The Ukrainians," he said hesitantly, "have always sought their freedom...

The history of our people is a history of blood and tears. Our huge land has always attracted strangers, just as the honeycomb attracts the bear. Sometimes, it was the Poles, other times, the Turks. Usually, it was the Russians. Under Czarina Katherine II the systematic Russification process started not only for Livonia and a portion of Finland, but also for the Ukraine.

Slowly but surely, they took everything from us; any shred of ethnic individuality, including our language and literature. Then the Great War came. Many thought that General Pawlo Skoropadskyj would be able to pull it off. He formed a central committee, but the dreams disappeared and Bolshevism, which had set up its headquarters in Moscow, reached out for the Ukraine after the collapse of Germany and Austria. Symon Petljura attempted to free the Ukraine one last time. But the Great Russian "White" General Denikin placed Russification over the struggle for freedom in the fight against Bolshevism. His divisions fought both the Red Army and the Ukrainians at the same time.

Even though Lenin had proclaimed the rights of ethnic minorities, there were none for us Ukrainians. When the Ukrainian element within the Communist Party and the Red Army became too strong after the Red victory over the Poles, the Ukrainians were "cleansed". In the effort to divest itself of them, 10,000 leading Communists, officers and specialists were liquidated, only because they were Ukrainian.

He then turned to me: "Months have already gone by but you Germans still don't have any Ukrainian regiments. Don't you want them?"

I was embarrassed. I did not know how to answer him. "It will come," I said, trying the calm down the excited man. "Grigori, you will see, it will come."

"A people," he replied, "do not live solely from bread and meat. A people have to have a flag. If you give us Ukrainians a flag, you will never regret it."

He then stood up and said his good-byes. "I talk too much," he said apologetically. "You're not responsible. If only your leaders really understood the situation."

He said in conclusion: "Unfortunately, it doesn't look that way."

The rest of us stayed behind, lost in thought.

Chapter Five:
Squandered Political Chances

A few days later we launched our large-scale winter offensive against Rostov. Once again we were fighting our way east, this time in the biting cold of a Russian winter. We were a part of *Panzer-Armee Kleist*, which consisted of our *Leibstandarte*, the *60. Infanterie-Division (mot.)* and what was left of the *13. Panzer-Division* and the *14. Panzer-Division*. The nights were indescribable. We had neither greatcoats nor proper winter garments and most of us did not even have gloves. We lay in the Russian trenches, our heads scantily covered with shelter halves stiff with ice, while outside a howling blizzard drove great waves of powdered snow before it. There were numerous cases of frostbite. To urinate caused unspeakable agony and any sheltered corner or hut we could find was used as a latrine rather than as living quarters.

During the night, my teeth chattered so much while I was sleeping that the comrade with whom I was sharing the foxhole woke up, cursing.

On the third day of our attack, a dense blanket of fog covered the ice-bound terrain. All around us, we could hear the heavy grinding of tank tracks. Slowly and cautiously, we groped our way forward into the thick brew, with the company commander halting every few minutes to listen. You could barely see 3 meters in front of you. Finally, after we had once again managed to lose contact on both flanks, we were halted altogether. The fog lifted a little, but it was still impossible to see more than 20 meters. Then we heard movement ahead. Ten minutes later the unmistakable sound of marching feet came to us through the fog and, as a precaution, we took up firing positions in the snow. The company commander still had no idea what was going on, and it might easily have been one of our own units, which, like ourselves, had pushed too far forward. Then the fog lifted for a moment, and we distinctly saw a whole regiment of men with submachine guns about 500 meters in front of us. That meant NKVD.

The old man immediately gave orders to open fire and radioed frantically for help. Within a few minutes, a battery of 88's actually came racing up and unlimbered immediately behind our lines.

The Soviet battle cry—Urrahhh—sounded curiously high-pitched and shrill; they could not have been much more than boys, probably *Komsomols*. Despite the fury of our fire, their attack, which was made with unusual aggressiveness, came rapidly forward. The four 88's firing so close over our heads practically lifted us bodily off the snow with each salvo They tore bloody lanes in the enemy attack.

Then their attack began to waver; our company commander saw this, assembled two platoons and led us in an immediate counterattack, whereupon the remainder of the Russian regiment turned and fled. As our assault swept over the first of their dead, my feet faltered. They were women, budding young women and girls, all around 20. And what a terrible sight they were. The high explosive charge of the 88's had literally torn the clothes from their bodies, and they lay bundled up like discarded dolls from a puppet show. Legs torn off at the hip lay scattered about as if in a butcher's shop, and great patches of blood colored the blinding white of the snow. It was horrific. But our attack went on through the wiped-out regiment of women. It moved quickly and smoothly, until it reached the initial outskirts of Rostov.

***

That night, we were detailed for guard duty at a forward dressing station. Initially we were deliriously happy to be getting warm and having the light duty. But after it was over, we all said: "Never again." With shells dropping so close outside that the windows were blown in with a crash and had to be replaced by cardboard, we inside had to stand and watch the souls of our fellow comrades laid bare.

The medic had just given an injection to a *Rottenführer* who had been shot in the lung. "You're not supposed to talk," I said. "That's

99

the way it is." His glazed eyes followed my every move and he tried to say something once, but I signaled him to be quiet. He breathed heavily. More wounded came, and we had no time to worry about the earlier ones who, in any case, were due to be taken back to the rear at any moment. Suddenly, he called across to me: "There's something I have to say. I want you to hold on to my submachine gun and not hand it over. Some men from my platoon are bound to come and ask for me. Give it to them, they'll need it for street fighting." The physician turned angrily and was about to let fly at the wounded man but stopped himself and merely muttered something unintelligible. "I'll do it, comrade!" I replied. "I'll look after it." As he was being lifted into the ambulance he tried to say something else, but I got in first: "Don't worry, they'll get it." A smile came over his pale face, and then the medic shut the doors.

More and more wounded came from the front; more and more often we had to go out into the twilight-lit field, submachine guns at the ready, to pick them up. For most of them, almost all, help came in time. But a few already had death in their eyes. One, a Bavarian from 17th Company, had been caught in an ambush by a political commissar and shot twice through the head. Now, lying in a small room, he was beyond all care and worries, only his tough body refused to give in. More wounded arrived, among them two more men from the 17th, one with his left arm broken by an enemy round, and the other with a stomach wound. "Who's that making that damned noise in there?" one of them asked and looked stunned when he heard the name. "God! Not Sepp?" The medic, who was tired to the point of exhaustion after nearly 24 hours of continuous work, thought he would not last long. He was already in his death agony. Neither of the two men wanted to be moved to the stove. "Leave us here," they said.

Shells screamed over our forward clearing station in almost continuous succession. On one occasion a Russian rocket launcher—we referred to it as the *Schüttfrost*[25]—fired over our heads, 42 shells in one salvo. A few fell just behind the house and, with a crash, the windows flew out of their frames. Shortly afterwards the field ambulance

25   Translator's Note: Literally: "The Shivers".

arrived again to pick up its next load, in which the two newcomers were due to be included. "Don't send me yet," the one with the arm wound said. "There's plenty of time for me and I can't leave Sepp alone here." The other had to go, though he too tried to hang on. He knew he was in a bad way and that the sooner he got to the main dressing station the more chance he had, yet he begged hard to be left to the next trip.

The work went on. More came, more went. The slightly wounded waited while their comrade fought his last battle. There was nothing they could do to help him. All the physician could do was to make things easier. But they stayed all the same, as if their strong hearts and wills would support their comrade during his final steps.

**

Next day, after a short and very sharp fight, we reached the airfield at Rostov—the Queen of the Don. Just about everywhere in the city there were people cheering us.

Unfortunately, I had to return to Taganrog on duty and, a few days later, our line cracked where it was held by a Saxon division to the north. Rostov was lost again. It was all we could do to halt the Russian counteroffensive in our old positions at Ssambek.

All of the German divisions that had been employed in that sector—the *60. Infanterie-Division (mot.)*, which was where the Red Army had initially broken through, the *Leibstandarte*, the *13. Panzer-Division* and the *14. Panzer-Division*—sustained very heavy losses. This time the number of missing was above average, since the Russian breakthrough had come so suddenly during the night that many *Landser*[26] were surprised in their beds. Many friends and comrades were missing. I was particularly taken aback by the fact that someone from Austria, an *Unterscharführer*, was also missing without a trace. Walter had to be dead; there was no other explanation for it. He would not have allowed himself to be captured alive. With a heavy heart, I wrote his mother a long letter and comforted her with

---

26   Translator's Note: *Landser* is the German term for a foot soldier, not unlike "Tommy" for the British or GI for the US Army.

the though that he might have been captured. Although it was not easy to tell that lie, I was unable to bring myself to tell the woman, whose husband had been killed in the First World War, what I really thought.

While this was going on, the mood was panicky in Taganrog. Rear-area headquarters and civil administration staffs, who were usually only too eager to get as far forward as they could, suddenly found themselves in a great hurry to leave. The logistics officer even forgot to blow up whole tons of ammunition, which actually came in very handy for our division, giving us enough ammunition for every gun to fire at will. That stopped Ivan, despite all his bravado and his willingness to sacrifice human life.

Everything in Taganrog that had made life difficult for us had disappeared. We saw only our own officers and could walk down the street again without getting cramp in the arm. In spite of the bad turn of events things had taken, we remained cheerful and our morale was high. We never had the slightest doubt that we would come out on top. The town militia, a force formed from local anti-communists, made urgent requests to be provided with more ammunition. As a security measure, they had originally been given only five rounds apiece.

This attitude on the part of the town militia strengthened me in my views about our treatment of the Ukrainian people. What a difference between the behavior of these men and that of our own rear-area people! Our sadly depleted division, which we were beginning to call the "Fire Brigade" because it was always called to any spot where things were hot, was in desperate need of reinforcements. But instead of picking up rifles and giving us a hand, these people simply scuttled away as fast as their staff cars would carry them and as far as their gas lasted. Yet there were these simple men of the militia, their lives forfeit and with every reason to escape to the rear, and all they asked for was more ammunition.

It should be mentioned that they did not get it.

But what we got, once the worst danger had passed, was the pleasure of welcoming a functionary from Erich Koch's outfit. The gorgeous brown political leader's uniform, resplendent with gold braid, looked ridiculous to us here in Taganrog. But not to the Russians. They took him—I have forgotten his name—for a very big shot. By that time it had become quite clear that we had no intention of keeping the promise we had given earlier to dissolve the collective farms—a promise which the rural people had greeted with tremendous enthusiasm. Instead, we were trying with our agricultural officers to utilize the large unit cultivation of the collective farms for German needs. This was all very well for the immediate welfare of the German people, but it did immense harm to our cause in the Ukraine. The Germans had made a promise and not kept it—just like the Bolsheviks. The steady flow of Ukrainian volunteers for the German forces were ignored. True, a division here and there accepted volunteers on their own discretion, but then only as auxiliaries for fatigue duties on supply or as kitchen help. And even then they served with no legal rights or status of any kind or description and on conditions entirely dependent on the mood or understanding of the individual unit commanders.

I became sick and tired of thinking about it all.

***

Until one day the truth dawned, and I realized that Germany was not going to seize the great opportunity it had been given in the east. The theory of the *Untermenschen* was too strong and was triumphing over all the dictates of reason and destiny. We were not prepared to grant the enslaved and tormented peoples the freedom and equality they deserved. We were refusing to recognize them as partners and barely agreeing to accept them as auxiliaries. The millions of Ukrainians, who by themselves could have turned the scales in the east, were not only being left unused, but were actually being turned away and disillusioned.

Police methods were replacing the great and splendid idea of the liberation of the east. In place of national independence and freedom, the bit was being drawn tighter. We had taken unto ourselves the antiquated mentality of the Baltic barons, whose feudal world had been drowned in the blood bath of the October Revolution.

This crystal-clear realization preyed on my mind. We had driven like a plough into the endless expanses of Russia and been met with a wave of popular enthusiasm, which we could have channeled into a broad and mighty river. But instead we were doing all we could to curb it and dam it up, and, with a tragic lack of vision, to subordinate it to our own short-term interests. For the sake of immediate gain, we were sacrificing the glittering prize, which we needed only to stretch out our hands to grasp.

Practically all the men with whom I spoke shared my opinion. Those who believed in the tough line and talked, contemptuously about the Burials were usually not among the most intelligent and were rarely to be found where decisions were made with your own blood

I was, to be honest, not primarily concerned with the fate of the Russian peoples, though I had learned to respect and love them in some of the hardest times of my life. As a German, I was concerned first and foremost with the fate of my own nationality. I still had a firm belief in our victory over the Kremlin. But how many rivers of blood would have to flow, and how many mothers' tears would be shed from the North Sea to the Alps before that goal was reached? Still, why should we take the easier and more rational path, if the same result could be achieved with a lot of shouting and cracking of the whip?

Practically all the planning and courses of action that had been based on what we had known of the intellectual, economic and military conditions in the Soviet Union were wrong, because they had been based on completely false assumptions. The frontiers separating East from West are not just accidents of geography, as the naïve would believe—they are total. The greatest experiment in the history of mankind, conceived with a frightful, shattering thoroughness and executed with a ruthless and undeviating logic, had had ample time to bear fruit. That one-time experiment, which had lasted for 40 years and been pursued so unswervingly, had long ceased to be an experiment. It had taken on shape and permanence.

Even a Karl Marx, father of all things collectivist with all his Prussian tautness of thinking, from which even as a Jew he never escaped, never dreamed of this audacious development. It needed a titan such as Lenin, possessed of ice-cold acuity and Kalmuck persistence, to mould the Marxist pseudo-philosophy into reality by a succession of reckless experiments. It is significant of the logic of his thought and deed that before embarking on the economic plan which was to crown his work, he laid the political foundations and, as a result, the intellectual ones.

It was therefore no accident that Bolshevism, true to its slogan that "religion is the opium of the people," inseparably linked its triumph in the east with the complete destruction of all forms of religion. Included among the 20 million dead of the October Revolution were almost all the bishops, priests and members of religious orders of both the Christian churches. The task of destroying all religious thought was entrusted to the state-controlled schools, the trade unions, the party and, above all, the *Komsomol* and the league of atheists. That struggle ended with the complete annihilation in Russia of the Christian concept of thinking.

For 30 years official propaganda had been ramming home at every possible opportunity the idea that there was no God. It had branded every faith as a medieval superstition and a whole generation, since then the parents of a new generation, had grown up in the belief that the cross was no more than a Roman-Jewish scaffold and that God was a man with a white beard, to be classed along with the dwarves of the fairy tales. This deliberate attempt to deprive humanity of the spiritual basis to life, which the idea of God provides, had succeeded all along the line. The experiment in materialism had brought in its train the religious chaos of the steppe. There were, it is true, a few, a very few people—mostly men and women of the older generation and their numerically very small following—who formed secret sects and prayer groups, but it must not be supposed that they wielded the slightest spiritual influence over the people of the Soviet Union as a whole.

As for the Moscow Patriarch, his existence was a patent fraud engineered by the NKVD and is too farcical to warrant any serious consideration. It was a bad mistake to assume that the people behind the fence enclosing what in effect is a new world, are subject to the same emotions and motives as ourselves. The new intellectual approach had brought with it a new emotional approach. Motives and arguments, which to us were of decisive importance, were completely ineffectual in the New Russia, and even sometimes had the exact opposite of the effect intended. The Leninist experiment had in fact led to a complete reshuffling of values and, as a result, to that spiritual isolation of the East, which seemed at first sight so impossible to understand.

On top of all that, there is the fact that the only information that we had previously had on the life of the Russian Sphinx had come from White Russian refugees. It is an established fact that in such questions refugees are usually something of a Greek gift to the country that receives them, for their knowledge of their home country is not only conditioned by their personal feelings, but what is more serious, out of date. Not only was the White Russian ignorant of the Russia of today, but he even tended to paint a wholly imaginary picture of it, born of his own wishful thinking.

The destruction of Czarism and the liquidation of Russian feudalism, bourgeoisie and peasantry brought about a social, economic and spiritual leveling of the proletarian and peasant masses who survived the holocaust. Alongside the economic new order, a new social pattern had to be created for these masses, and it was created. Collectivism outgrew its economic framework and developed into an intellectual concept. Its first victim was the remnant of individualism that had survived the October Revolution and its next victim was the family as a moral force. Eventually, the masses became the "divine" upholder of all life.

These masses, created by a new era, fired with new ideals and provided with new aims, became completely alienated from the rest of the world. Indeed, it no longer understood the outside world, speaking not only a different tongue, but a different language of the mind and heart. There is no doubt that this was a development that was greatly favored by an accident of fate, because this economic experiment could not have succeeded anywhere else in Europe but in the vastness of the Russian space. Its immensity gave room for a constant compensation for failures and, at the same time, made possible the isolation of Russia from Western influences. It was the same with the spiritual experiment, because there were no other people with whom it could have succeeded to the extent that it had. For embedded deep in this people, there was a centuries-old distrust of its neighbors, and a belief that it was ordained to redeem the world. To the Russian, everything was religion, even atheism. Yet a further factor, and not the least important, was that this unhappy development strengthened the great herd instinct of the Slav races. These accidents of race and geography, allied to the Muscovite consistency of purpose, which has never shrunk from shedding oceans of blood in the realization of any of its cherished ambitions, were the most valuable allies of the Bolshevist experiment.

With the German invasion, the experiment found itself in mortal danger. The lid was lifted off Stalin's political preserves and, notwithstanding all the mistakes we made, the peoples of the Soviet Union were given a chance to make comparisons. These, especially where they concerned living standards or the way of life of the individual, were an immediate menace to Bolshevism. The fetters of collectivism burst asunder, and a new world appeared on the horizon. Uncertain and problematical though that world may have been by virtue of the exigencies of war and the manifold German mistakes, it still looked infinitely desirable compared with that of Bolshevism.

At this most decisive moment for mankind, Bolshevism, though politically bankrupt, was saved by the pre-conceived notions ideas we Germans had of Russia and by our resulting treatment of the Russian people. But this was not all. By rousing the Russian people to a Napoleonic fervor, we enabled the Bolsheviks to achieve a political consolidation beyond their wildest dreams and provided their cause with the halo of a "patriotic" war.

As the result of a senseless and rigid administration, terribly reminiscent of the Boyars and Czars, and by a complete misunderstanding of Soviet history and a total neglect of the national and psychological needs of this tortured people, we forced on the Russian masses, just as they were beginning to wake from their stupor, an inexorable choice between a German police state and Bolshevism.

And, in face of the terrible human and political blunders of the Germans, they decided for Bolshevism, which, however little they liked it, at least had the merit of being Russian.

Stalin was quick to see the lifeline thrown unwittingly out to him by the German leaders and, adjusting himself with amazing agility to the new situation, succeeded in producing a lightning revival of the moribund Bolshevism, this time without Marx and Lenin. He brought out the old flags and epaulettes which the Bolsheviks had themselves thrown on the garbage heap and, under the shadow of his devastating defeats, hastily cleansed them of the blood stains of the October Revolution and handed them with full pomp and ceremony to the shattered divisions of the Red Army.

In order to provide for every need of this new found people's soul, even the establishment of an NKVD church was not thought too grotesque, and a special Kremlin patriarch was installed as the licensed minister of the collectivized need for religion, so far as that still existed among the older generation.

Thus, as a result of the blunders of the *Ostpolitik* on the one side and of the greatest piece of political juggling of all times on the other, the communist war became a national war, the war of the Russian nation, and what Stalin had always been striving after, the marriage of Marxism with the Muscovite heritage, now became an accomplished fact. Freed of all theoretical and political principles, a new Machiavellianism with a Soviet flavor was born—a liquidation of bookish communism in favor of Russian imperialism, with its outer forms preserved intact and its basic philosophy unchanged.

This intermarriage between Russian imperialism and Bolshevism constituted the most serious danger to Germany and indeed the whole of Western culture and civilization since the days of Ghengis Khan. Not until he had achieved this union was Stalin able to wring the last ounce of strength out of the Russian soul for use in his armored divisions, his collective farms, his factories, his nuclear and bacteriological research establishments. Not until then was all hope destroyed that the bruised and ravished heart of Russia might itself find the strength to overthrow its masters.

It no longer mattered whether the NKVD or the communist party was hated. Russia herself was at stake. And for the sake of Mother Russia, her children were willing to undergo every affliction and every hardship demanded of them. As a result, it was all beautifully worked out, and the political, military, economic and, most importantly, the psychological factors excellently balanced against each other to secure the "Stalinist Millennium".

Left to itself, Bolshevism could scarcely have survived its defeats. But Russian nationalism alone, faced with a social ferment painstakingly organized since the beginning of the century, would have been just as unequal to the task of carrying the main burden of the war as it had been in 1905 and 1917. The defeat of 1917 was in fact only a after effect of the failure of the Russian ruling classes in 1905.

It was the unification by Stalin of these two spiritual and physical forces, Russian nationalism and Bolshevism, which brought into being the deadliest of all dangers for the whole of the non-communist world.

All this was plain and tangible enough for us to see. But the most terrible thing about it was that we ourselves had given up thinking. We had become mechanized in our actions and even in our desires, and it was with a shock that I compared our state of mind with that of the Bolsheviks. We had preserved our inner freedom in minor and secondary matters only, in the side issues. On all the really important questions, however, we no longer thought; others did the thinking for us. That was certainly true in military matters. Of course, in that profession, it was the same throughout the world. No general can ask his officers or men how he should conduct the battle whether to attack or to retreat. Ultimately, an army is a type of mechanism, although it can be saved or brought to destruction by an individual act of courage or cowardice. Even there, in the military field, a man as an individual may sometimes decide the issue.

But really fundamental issues of politics cannot be treated mechanically, that is, if one is not confusing experiments with politics and culture. Especially when it is plain for all to see that the experiment is a failure.

It was about this time that we began to hear a new name: Grigory Zhukov.

Whenever things were going badly for us, whenever we felt the presence of a powerful and flexible opponent, our commanders gave a knowing smile: Zhukov.

In Grigory Zhukov, the Red Army had discovered a military leader of real stature, a Napoleon of Bolshevism. His tactical and strategic skill put all the musty civil war heroes in the shade as though they had never existed. The "Heroes of Red October"—Budyonny, Timoshenko, and Stalin's old friend and brother-in-arms, Voroshilov—paled into insignificance beside the great general. It was he who, after the shameful defeats of the Kremlin party generals, offered the first real resistance to the German armies and then went over to the offensive after a debilitating defense.[27]

But on our side, the man of the Eastern campaign, the spirit behind the victorious *Panzerwaffe*—Guderian—had been condemned to a galling inactivity, having fallen in disgrace for not having reached his designated objective.

As everyone knew, however, the only reason why he had not been able to reach Moscow was because Hitler had rejected his plan of attack on the advice of the older generation of generals.

***

I felt an overwhelming urge to go back home. I *felt* that there must be a way of getting these facts to the men in power, of giving a true picture of the situation to those who themselves had had no di-

---

27 Translator's Note: Zhukov became known as the general who never lost a battle. In reality, he did suffer a major defeat during Operation Mars in 1942. However, the Soviets consigned that disastrous defeat, with its more than 300,000 casualties, to almost complete obscurity.

rect experience of the Eastern Front. It was simply inconceivable that this greatest of all opportunities was going to be thrown away.

In fact, it soon happened that I received orders to proceed on several months of a work leave in the *Westmark*[28].

As I sat in the icy carriage of the train, rattling homewards, my thoughts were not on the relief I felt at escaping from the horrors of the Eastern Front for a few months, but on ways and means of penetrating to the highest offices in the land.

When I arrived home, I made an open and frank report to *Gauleiter* Josef Bürckel, who had previously always been most receptive to anything I had to say or suggest. On this occasion, however, he brusquely refused to hear a lecture by me on the Eastern question.

I also received a serious warning from a very good friend of mine, the well-known Viennese journalist, Ernst Handschmann, when I met him. "You're going to hurt yourself if you go round everywhere banging your head against a wall," he said. "The Old Man has had some very curious things to say about you...that the Eastern Front doesn't suit you very well. And you want to watch out for the *SD*[29], they've got their eyes on you."

"Did you ever watch out," I answered quickly, "in the years when the Party was struggling for power, when there were big things at stake and you thought you had the right answer?"

"But look! You're only an *Unterscharführer*. Do you think you can see things as clearly as the men at the top?"

"I've been there. I can't be mistaken. Our whole Eastern policy is one big failure, and not just in the small things either. It's the major issues I'm worried about, the things that are going to decide our future one way or the other."

---

28   Translator's Note: Just as the area of Austria that was incorporated into the *Reich* as the *Ostmark*, the Saarpfalz area in the west was referred to as the *Westmark* after its incorporation into the *Reich*.

29   Translator's Note: = *Sicherheitsdienst* or security service (the security branch of the *SS*).

We parted coolly.

***

When I arrived in the editorial office, I found myself swamped with routine work that was awaiting me. Nevertheless, I found time to draw up a brief but unambiguous report on the mistakes Germany was making in the East and to send it to the Anti-Comintern, to the *Reichsführer SS*, to Goebbels and to the Ministry for Eastern Affairs. I also sent a copy to Josef Bürckel. For a while, I heard nothing, but noticed that a number of my friends began to distance themselves from me. Eventually, I was asked to go to Berlin, first to the Anti-Comintern, where I had a short but very enlightening conversation in the *Cafe Kaiserhof*. Finally, I was ordered to *Hauptmann* Hadamowsky, who was Goebbels' right-hand man. He received me with icy coldness, and I saw that my memorandum was in front of him. I began to talk about it, but he cut me short by saying: "Presumably you've thought the whole matter over by this time? "

"Thought it over...why?"

"You're aware, I hope, of the full implications of the statements you've made, and of which, incidentally, you are unable to offer any kind of proof."

"I can prove everything," I retorted heatedly. "But I'm not worrying just about the Russkies, it's Germany and Europe I'm interested in."

He gave an icy smile. "So you're determined to molest the minister with this affair?"

"There's no question of molesting him; I am a German journalist and have been directed to report observations of consequence."

Hadamowsky stood up. "All right, then. I suppose you know best what you can answer for."

"I'm not worried."

A few minutes later I was received by Goebbels. I had never met him before, but he went out of his way to be cordial and attentive. I talked for about 20 minutes, after which he smiled. "I'm glad you're telling me what's on your mind," he said, his voice courteous and amiable, "but I can only say that during the historic events on a continental scale that we are witnessing today an occasional creak in the machine can appear occasionally. Let us suppose that your observations actually are objective and not just a one-sided picture you have formed under the impact of your personal experience; even then there is nothing to worry about. At the most, they are a credit to you for having had the courage to stand by them. But you must understand that for the grand design, the really grand design of things, you must trust the *Führer*, who is kept informed of everything in the greatest detail and pursues his course without wavering."

With that, he stood up, thanked me cordially for my information and shook me by the hand.

Outside again, I realized that statements of the kind I had made were not welcome. Moreover, from his smooth and unruffled manner I also concluded that they were not even anything new.

So, tired and disappointed, I returned to the *Westmark*. There was still no word from the *Reichsführer SS* or from the Eastern Affairs Ministry.

Shortly after that, I was married, and a few weeks later my "work leave" was up. I sent a telegram to Bürckel putting a stop to an attempt he was making to get it extended. When I went to say good-bye to him, he seemed curiously animated. "Stop worrying," he said cordially. "You think more than is good for you, unlike most Austrians, but it'll all work out all right...of that I'm quite sure. I've read your memorandum, and thought a lot about it. I've also ceased believing that Erich Koch is the right man in his job. He's in a key position, right at the hub of things, where a man can make bad things worse or good things better. But as for the general line of policy, there's nothing he can do about that. Anyway, come home in one piece and look after yourself. Somehow, I don't much like your going away again;

there are fewer and fewer left who are prepared to do the job for its own sake."

***

We detrained at Stalino and moved towards Rostov. The offensive in the Caucasus was now well under way. As we passed through Taganrog, I managed to get twelve hours of leave and rushed around in a staff car to visit the old places that held so many painful and joyful memories for me.

I headed straight for my old billets, where I was aware of something strange in the air as soon as I entered the courtyard. I climbed out of the vehicle and ran up the steps to my former quarters, but old Babushka shrank back in fear when I suddenly appeared in the room. "Babushka," I cried, disappointed, "don't you recognize me?" She came closer to peer at me, and then with a shriek threw her arms round my neck. "Pan Erich, Pan Erich...oh, Erich, why did you ever leave Taganrog?"

I tried to calm her.

"Where's Nada?"

Her face darkened. "In the brothel."

I stared at her. Beautiful, little Nada. "How did that happen?" I stammered.

"Don't ask," she replied.

"And what about Marushka?"

"She's somewhere in Germany. They came in the middle of the night and took her away. She's working in a saw mill. I've had two letters so far. She's having a pretty rough time, not much to eat."

We sat and talked for about an hour. I asked questions, and she answered them. I heard nothing I wanted to hear. "Not all Germans are good," she said finally, with a set face. "I know what you're going to say, great God, I know" she crossed herself quickly. "The Russians aren't good either. But we had such high hopes of you, and you prom-ised so much."

I stood up with feet like lead and brought bread and cans of food from the vehicle. The old woman kissed my hand, her eyes stream-ing with tears. "May God protect you." Then in a whisper she added: "Come back, please, you and your comrades, and chase away the po-lice and the wicked commandants."

As if in a dream, I walked through the streets, which were quite elegant compared to the previous year and had large businesses.

My feet faltered as I reached the large block of apartments where Iniza lived. I forced myself on up the stairs. She was at home and recognized me immediately, but approached me with funny mincing little steps. "So you're around again. And how's the world treating you?" she asked in her hard German pronunciation, in which I ob-served a decided improvement.

"That's what I wanted to ask you," I said, more seriously than I had intended.

Tears began to roll down her cheeks, which were heavy with make-up. "Oh, Erich! Life is so difficult. You know—my mother and my little girl—and always the fear of being denounced to the *Gesta-po* because my husband was a Jew. It's all so different from what we dreamed, so very different from what you and your friends told us it would be like. Did you know that the people in the building still talk about you and your friends? The first, they say, were the liberators, the second the enslavers, and the third the hangmen."

"It's not really going to be like that, you know," I said evasively. "The war's not over yet..."

"The war never will be over," she whispered. "These town com-mandants of yours, your Gestapo and your labor offices...they're sim-ply driving more and more people over to the partisans, the very same people who risked death to welcome you when you came. But now what they say is 'if we've got to be enslaved and deported then let's have our own executioners, at least we can talk to them.' Anyway, papa Stalin has promised that everything is going to be quite, quite different."

"Do you believe it?"

She smiled bitterly. "No, I don't, but there's plenty who do. You've only got to put across a good story to a Russian for him to believe it. He's very susceptible to propaganda, and he forgets easily, like a child. You Germans could have had it all your own way. If it turns out otherwise, it'll be all over for me. I play and sing in a soldiers' cabaret. I'll be shot if they come back; and they will come back," she concluded in a flat voice.

"Don't be absurd," I broke in, "the Caucasus is about to fall."

"Perhaps...perhaps not. But here we are talking about politics and you must be hungry."

"No, stay here. I want to hear more."

"Oh, leave it for God's sake. I'm sick and tired of it all. Come over here." She tried to pull me across to her, but I did not move.

"Oh, you needn't be afraid, you're safe enough with me."

She smiled through her tears. "Your Iniza has to go and see the doctor every other day, otherwise she wouldn't be allowed to sing in the cabaret..." Suddenly, she put her hands over her face. "Oh, God! What have we done to deserve it all? First the NKVD and death always round the corner, and now this..."

I stood up and tiptoed out. There was nothing I could say.

Down in the yard Iniza's little girl recognized me and came running up in great excitement.

"*Pan* Erich, *Pan* Erich!" I gave her the whole of my day's rations and stuffed her pockets full of rubles and marks. "Remember me to *Mamushka*."

Chapter Six:
Tank Warfare
in the Caucasus

The vehicle was roaring. Rostov had fallen. Laid to ruins by an unusual massed attack by the *Luftwaffe*. Across its main street, a streamer was prominently displayed: "Soldier Beware! Deadly Asiatic Venereal Diseases!"

Before our vehicle turned off to the big bridge across the Don, we stopped for a short while. We wanted to take a look at the places where we had taken quarters and were in position the previous December.

The people were fearful. Rostov had been virtually destroyed by the *Stukas*. An *Unterscharführer* came out of a building, whose roof had been burned away. I closed my eyes for a moment, but he had recognized me and approached me, laughing.

"Walter," I said, confused, "how is that possible?"

He took a deep breath and looked at his wristwatch. "My leave train is heading home in three hours. I'll be using those 14 days, you can believe me on that!" He joined us in the vehicle and rolled a cigarette with a jerky hand. He began to tell us his story...

In the middle of the night, the *Spieß* shook us awake. His face was a white as a sheet. "We're all goners," he stammered. "Ivan's already in the city."

We were up in a flash. The *Spieß* did not know much more than we did. We had never put on our uniforms as fast as we did then. Of course, the vehicle would not start. While the driver cursed and worked like a madman to get it started, a dispatch rider arrived. He had already been wounded.

"You won't be able to get out through there any more," he yelled. And, in fact, we actually heard small-arms fire coming from the road in the direction of Taganrog to our rear. A cold chill went down my spine.

An *Untersturmführer*, who apparently had also been asleep, linked up with us. "Just keep your nerves, men!" he said in an effort to calm us down. A round from an antitank gun howled on its way shortly above our heads, heading along the road and into the wall of a building.

"How impolite!" The *Untersturmführer* laughed. "That could backfire!" In the middle of his sentence, he stopped and fell quite slowly to the ground.

"Medic!" The *Spieß* yelled for no apparent reason, since a medic was already tending to the *Untersturmführer*. His entire chest had been opened up. "Leave me alone!" he sputtered out with some effort. "Just get away!"

Naturally, we lifted the *Untersturmführer* onto the first vehicle that finally started. Our own vehicle continued to hold out for a while, but it also sprang to life eventually. There was heavy firing already raging on the next street over. In addition, there was a cold that took your breath away. Just as we were about to mount our vehicle, a burst of machine-gun fire from a very short range landed right in our midst. Since I had not yet been standing on the vehicle, I didn't get scratched. All of the other comrades who were mounting up—about 8 in all—got hit. The *Spieß* collapsed with a cackle in front of my feet. He had been the father of four children.

Get out of there! I thought to myself. Get out of there! I ran back into the courtyard and collided with someone. It was the blonde, Katjuscha. In the place we were staying, you need to know, was also this blonde. I though she was probably over 30, but I later discovered she was only 25. She had been very cold toward us, and I had barely spoken to her.

Without a word, she took me by the hand and jerked me into the house. We didn't go up the stairs to the 2nd floor, however, where she

118

lived. Instead down into the basement. She led me all the way to the back of it, opened a small storage area and told me to lay down in it. She then covered me up with a couple of old canvas sacks and disappeared. So, I was lying there with my pistol in my hand, ready to fire. I don't know whether it was the cold or the excitement, but I will not deny that I was shaking. Outside, they were firing like crazy. Suddenly, I heard a young, high-pitched and raised voice: "Don't take a lot of time, you bastards!" A few shots were fired, then it turned quiet. A few coarse boot steps stamped down the stairs. I slowly raised my pistol. Although there was only a dim light in the basement, I immediately recognized the padded uniforms and the fur caps.

All of a sudden, the blonde stood next to them and laughed. She said something and then approached me. So that's what's going to happen! The thought shot through my head in a flash. But then she turned around and left the basement with the Red Army men. Despite the cold, I was bathed in sweat as it became quiet in the basement again.

A few hours later, the woman returned and brought me an entire loaf of bread. Then she indicated with a hand movement that I should remain quiet where I was. It was not until the next evening that she came again, bringing me some hot soup and some bread. This game was repeated for an entire week. I then turned feverish; I had caught a cold. Katjuscha took my temperature with her hand and shook her head in a worried manner. That evening, she brought me two blankets and a bottle with hot tea and vodka. Despite all that, I believe a spent more than a week in the basement half unconscious and dozing in and out. By the time I finally felt better, or forces had already pulled back some 80 kilometers. I was far in the Red's rear area. One night, the Ukrainian woman brought me a wadded jacket and a fur cap. She hid my uniform cap, overcoat and tunic completely behind the sacks and took me up to her apartment. I was given a hiding place behind the beds in which Katjuschka and her old mother slept. I spent the entire day there. It was only at night, when the apartment was locked up and the windows carefully covered, that I was allowed to crawl out of my hiding place.

I was there, month after month, while she went to work at an armaments factory as a book keeper. I was literally buried alive. Only the old mother of Katjuschka knew of my existence. Then, suddenly, the front started to get closer again, and all of Rostov was swarming with Red Army men. All agitated, Katjuschka took me back down to the basement one night. She feared soldiers would be quartered in her building.

Toward morning, I awoke, startled. An ear-deafening thunder filled the room. *Stukas* were bombing Rostov. The entire building was shaking and trembled like a ship in a storm. The two women! I though to myself, agitated. I wanted to head upstairs when a direct hit put an end to all my thoughts. When I awoke, it was broad daylight. Light was falling into the basement through a gaping hole. Infantry small-arms fires and the creaking of tanks tracks could be distinctly heard.

"More to the right!" A voice shouted outside. I shuddered as if I bolt of lightning had hit me. The words had been in German.

I bellowed loudly for help.

And they actually heard me. "Move back." One of them yelled in. "We'll open up your cage." I felt my way back, and when the charge went off I thought the air had been sucked out of me. But the crack was wide enough, and I was able to force my way through with some difficulty.

Outside, I found myself looking into the rifle barrels of mechanized infantrymen from "Viking"[30], who were here going about their business.

Stumbling, I made my report to the *Untersturmführer* with some difficulty. Then I wanted to take a look after the woman, but the house was a pile of rubble. There were no survivors.

---

30   Translator's Note: The narrator, Walter, is referring to men of *SS-Panzer-Grenadier-Division "Wiking"*. The division was famous for having contingents from many different European countries, especially from Belgium, the Netherlands and Scandinavia. By the end of the war, its official designation would be the *5. SS-Panzer-Division "Wiking"*.

"Then they interrogated me, and I made a statement...and now," he concluded, its time for leave!"

"Walter," I said, as I slapped him on the shoulder, "you're one lucky guy!"

He looked at me and nodded. Then we shook hands in silence. He went to the local military administration headquarters and we moved on.

We finally reached the "Viking" Division, which was in the process of preparing to cross the Kuban. I was assigned to the tank-destroyer battalion.

We moved again through shoulder-high tobacco fields in full bloom, through sunflower fields and past waving grain. To me it was a release when I found myself in the thick of heavy fighting a few hours later.

The antitank battalion was composed almost entirely of self-propelled guns armed with the former Russian 7.62cm gun, a very respectable caliber. Unfortunately, they suffered from the disadvantage that they were as big as a barn door, being more than 3 meters high and just as long. Yet with all that, their armor was so pitifully thin that any antitank round went straight through like a knife through butter. We were in fact only protected against infantry weapons and not even that completely, as Number One, the gunner, and Number Two, the loader, were exposed in the back. We suffered many casualties as a result.[31]

We had reached the Maikop area, and the village ahead of us was held by the enemy, who hung on tenaciously and would not give way. We made a snap decision and set the thatched roofs alight to burn the enemy out. Within a few moments of opening fire with incendiary rounds, the first houses were on fire. The infantry then began to make good progress. In accordance with my orders, I moved my gun forward to the center of the village square to cover the infantry attack

31 Translator's Note: These vehicles were the *Sd.Kfz 139, Marder III*, introduced in April/May 1942. The chassis was that of the *Panzer 38(t)*, a tank of Czech origin

against possible surprises from the south. But there was not a single enemy tank to be seen. I dismounted for a moment as the infantry came up. As I did so, an old woman ran out into the street from inside one of the burning houses, her hair straggling over her face.

"Germanski!" she called breathlessly. "Tell me, German, is there a God?-*Bog jest?"*

I stared at her and then nodded. *"Da, Da. Bog jest.*

The old woman turned triumphantly towards a group of younger women and youths and shouted with a very loud voice: "Here you are, here's the first German. You must believe him, you've never believed what I told you. He says there is a God. God exists, and He'll make everything right again."

I climbed back into my gun-commander's position, and we moved on beside the advancing infantry as far as the end of the village.

That was Russia. Their houses on fire, the world collapsing about their ears, and the old woman thinks nothing of saving herself or her belongings, because God is more important. God and the bearing of witness for Him.

How was one to rule this people with rational laws and programs? Unless of course, by the methods of the Bolsheviks, of the system we were out to destroy.

***

Our division then pressed on past Maikop high up into the mountainous country above Tuapse, where it was to act as a covering force. In fact, we seemed as if we were on rest and relaxation.

A blissful calm existed up there in the Northern Caucasian forests. The Soviets, who had been forced back against the high mountain slopes, where they were leading a wretched existence, were barely able to have any influence on our movements, let alone interfere with them.

The people in this part of the world were poor, desperately poor. Far worse nourished and clad than any we had seen elsewhere. They were mainly Russians from White Russia who had settled there as lumberjacks. Most of them lived in lumberjack colonies, pathetic clusters of small wooden cabins and tiny plots of land. Somehow, I could never quite make these people out, for, with all their wretchedness, they had a streak of slyness and cunning. Altogether, they presented a startling difference from the cheerful Ukrainians, who, in spite of Bolshevism, were almost well off in comparison.

With the exception of outpost skirmishes and combat patrols, there was not a lot happening. Despite the peace and quiet of life in the high forest, we were not sorry when we were suddenly pulled out and put on the road to the east again. Our positions were taken over by Alpine troops, part of those gallant and doomed formations, which were later almost completely bled white—in vain, unfortunately—in the fighting round Tuapse.

On again to the east, past Armavir and Prochladny. Looking at a map was bad for the nerves; it showed that we were 3,000 kilometers from the frontiers of Germany. And still we were heading east.

Rumor had it that we were to push right through to the Caspian Sea in order to turn the left flank of the Caucasus. But suddenly we found ourselves approaching the Terek, which we crossed in the dead of night over a wooden bridge. After a lull of several weeks, the Red Air Force was becoming active again and accompanying us day and night. So heavily camouflaged were our guns with small trees and branches, that they looked like nothing other than travelling bushes.

Once across the Terek, we came across a large village which struck us both for its neatness and cleanliness and for its complete lack of life. One of the houses, we noticed, had a shop sign written in German in elaborate Gothic print: *Brotladen*[32]. Every house had a small rose garden in front and rose-covered arbors and hedges around it. The church gleamed a blinding white. We were in the last German settlement: Gnadenburg.

---

32   Translator's Note: "Bread Shop" (bakery).

At some time during the course of the nineteenth century, a religious sect had been founded in Wuerttemberg by people who believed they could find the road to Paradise. In order to safeguard their road, this sect asked permission of the Czar to found a number of villages in and about this area, and he, being only too glad to get a few hard-working and industrious Germans in his country, readily assented. Seven large villages then rose in rapid succession along the Black Sea and the Sea of Azov, across the Kuban and out here into the Caucasus. They were to act as rest stations for the German pilgrims on their journey to Paradise.

Then the flow of the faithful ceased, and like a handful of wind-strewn grain, these seven villages remained in the middle of the Russian Empire, symbols at once, of German sectarianism, German piety and German industry. The people of Gnadenburg soon got on friendly terms with the Cossacks, and even with their neighbors, the Karachevs and Karbardines, to one of whose tribes they paid a yearly tribute, thus insuring themselves against fire-raising raids of the fierce hill tribes. If anybody from outside ever had designs on Gnadenburg, Moslem Caucasians and German Christians fought side by side against the invaders.

But the village had been swept clean by the NKVD, and there was not a single German woman or child to be seen. In the first few days of the war, 98 men of the village, along with the village schoolmaster, had been deported to the Ukraine, where they had been forced to dig tank trenches and construct defenses. Led by their gallant schoolmaster, they had taken the opportunity provided by a surprise German attack to make their way across to the German lines and had since served as interpreters and guides in many different German regiments. All 99 of them had come back home, standing hopelessly in front of their damaged, plundered and now empty houses.

They walked as if in a dream through stables and houses. They touched boards they had nailed tight a few years back; they stroked damaged crucifixes which their wives had brought with them into the marriage. Then they stood helplessly around in bewildered groups in the neat little village street.

"My mother is 62," the schoolmaster said to me with an expressionless face. "Where did she die? Where is she starving and freezing at this moment? It is a heavy cross that God has given us to bear. I don't know what we've done to deserve it. Our whole lives have been spent in ceaseless labor and rectitude, like the story of Gnadenburg itself. But God must know what He wants. In all this madness of the last few decades there must be Someone who knows where we're heading."

***

Shortly after leaving Gnadenburg, our mission became clear: To clear the old Georgian military road, the *Grusinkaja daroga,* and then push on towards Wladikawkas, or Ordshonikidse, as it had been renamed by the Bolsheviks, in order to open the road to Tiflis.

Our hearts sank slightly at the sight of the high Caucasian mountains on the horizon, but we nevertheless approached the coming battle full of confidence. The next morning, we were showered with leaflets among the bombs for the Red Air Force. These read: "Everyone of you is marching to his death. The Caucasus will be the meat grinder of Hitler's armies."

The men laughed and threw them away or else put them to a more useful purpose as we were very short of paper.

I was in a better humor than I had been for a long time, because it looked as though the German Command was trying to avoid making the same mistakes in the Caucasus as it had done in the Ukraine.

Relations were particularly good with the Muslim tribes. Volunteer cavalry units were being raised all over the Caucasus, which later rendered valuable service as reconnaissance and even as small combat forces, and we were constantly seeing the green flag of the prophet fluttering side-by-side with our own. A strict order was issued stating that the Caucasian tribes were our friends and that they were to be treated as such in all circumstances, even down to the most trivial things. Energetic propaganda was being directed at an attempt to foster mutual understanding with considerable success, except for a few minor cases.

The men principally responsible for this intelligent and proper treatment of the Caucasian peoples were two political advisers attached to *Generaloberst* Kleist's Staff, *General der Kavallerie* Koestrin and *General der Kavallerie* von Herwart. Koestrin, who was the son of a German bookseller in Moscow, had spent his youth in the Russian capital. At the beginning of the Russian campaign, he had fallen into disfavor for having drawn attention to the true strength of the Red Army, and had then sat in the Grunewald, a forgotten man, until Kleist remembered him and asked for him to be detailed as his political adviser, an arrangement which turned out to be as much in the German interest as in that of the many Caucasian tribes: The Karachevs, Karbardines, Ossetians, Ingushts, Azerbaijanis, and Kalmucks.

This historic country, in whose mountain villages the Promethean legend is as alive today as it was a 1,000 years ago, has always been a problem child for the Russians. It was there that Schamyl, the 19th century leader of the Moslem hill tribes, engaged in his epic life-long struggle. It was also there that Russian divisions had to use tanks, artillery and aircraft to break the last resistance of the mountain hill tribes in 1934. This fertile and strangely beautiful country, which some say is the cradle of mankind, could not be made to submit to the men of the Kremlin.

German tanks were rolling into this land of magic. Golden eagles described their eternal circles high in the deep blue sky; the black kite, most beautiful of all Caucasian birds of prey, swooped down inquisitively on our lumbering columns. Falcons planed swiftly past, and wolves and bears drew back shyly into the endless forests at our approach. In the shadows of the Caucasian high forest, the black panthers peered down suspiciously on our Alpine troops as they hoisted the German flag on the steep mountain crests.

***

We received our first classes concerning the civil population. One of the most important things to remember was never to express admiration. It is a risky thing to say to a Caucasian: "What are a nice-looking pair of trousers!" or "What a lovely horse!". The owner will instantly present it to you, however precious or valuable it may be, expecting, of course, an equally valuable gift in return. To fail in this is regarded was a breach of etiquette and resulted in a serious loss of face.

Much as we were amused at these instructions when we first received them, we were grateful enough for them later. For example, I was invited to a banquet by the Ossetian in whose house I was quartered. Fortunately, I was careful to seek advice as to the correct behavior before I went.

When the dish arrived on the table—it was a whole roasted lamb—my host ceremonially cut off the head and handed it, as a mark of respect, to me as his guest of honor. I then, equally ceremonially, passed the brain back to my host and his wife. Obviously surprised by such excellent manners, my Ossetian host bowed. But when I then proceeded to cut off the left ear and pass it to the eldest son, I was really accepted and, from that moment on, the whole village regarded me as a man of the world, as somebody who knew how things were.

But, unfortunately, not everybody took the same precautions. At the end of the month-long fast of Ramadan, the Karachevs of Kislewotsk gave an immense and magnificent Bairam feast for the German armed forces. A representative of the Ministry for Eastern Affairs came over from Berlin specially for the occasion.

One can imagine our horror when he began to hold forth in a booming voice after the feast:

Men and women of the Karachevs. We, the German people, have liberated you from the shackles of Bolshevism. You are now free. But that does not mean you can do as you like. You must show yourselves worthy of your new freedom and get to work. You must rub your hands together and get at the enemy. This is not the time to hang it up...

And so it went on. Though not word for word, this is a fair, if somewhat toned down rendering of the homilies of this gentleman who, with his gorgeous brown uniform, liberally plastered with braid, was gazed at spellbound by his Karachev hosts.

127

To our great good fortune they had not understood a word, though the thundering voice and sweeping gestures had obviously made a deep impression. Then *Rittmeister Baron* Hahn, who had been detailed to act as interpreter, rose to his feet and, accompanied by the knowing smiles of the other interpreters present, gave a brilliant translation of the speech in a form completely acceptable to the Caucasian mentality. It ran more or less like this:

Karachevs! Word came to us long ago that here, in the high Caucasus, was a worthy and noble people, the Karachevs. So we thought long and hard how best we could help you. And now our *Führer* has sent his armed forces and liberated you...

And so on in the same style. When he sat down, the Karachevs burst into frenzied applause and their elders assured us that they would do all they could to help us.

We sighed with relief. Had the speech of the gentleman from Berlin been translated literally, it would have been considered a gross insult and might well have led to political disaster in the Caucasus.

The political expert from Berlin was immensely surprised at the laughter that greeted him when he later said conceitedly, pumping out his chest: "You see, gentlemen. That's the way to talk to these people; that's the language they understand. It hits home."

No one said anything. It would have been too dangerous. Moreover, the mentality of these Caucasian tribes offered us tremendous opportunities, though it needed an ability to empathize and a certain amount of sensitivity. This was strikingly demonstrated by the case of the "Special Adviser to the Kalmucks," whose name I shall not mention as he is now living in the Eastern Zone of Germany[33]. This brilliant and enterprising ethnic German from the Sudetenland devoted himself unsparingly to the cause of the Kalmuck tribes and induced in them such confidence that they were soon prepared to submit

---

33 Translator's Note: The reader is reminded that this book was first written right after the war, when there was a divided Germany, and statements about wartime activities or accomplishments could carry serious repercussions in the Soviet-occupied zone.

their problems unconditionally to his judgment. Among his friends and acquaintances he became known as the "King of the Kalmucks."

None of us took our friend's work very seriously, looking on it rather as a personal avocation. One can imagine our surprise, therefore, when a delegation of Kalmuck elders appeared at von Kleist's headquarters one day to inform him that all the elders had sent orders through underground channels to their tribesmen in the Red Army to return at once to the Caucasus in order to fight on our side against Bolshevism. They also said that the Buddhist Kalmucks had even sent messengers to Tibet to inform the Dalai Lama of events in the Caucasus and to advance Germany's interests there.

This was far more fruitful work than the interminable discussions that took place over what was to be done about the mountain Jews of Daghestan, once we had taken its capital, the Caspian port of Makhach-Kala. In about the year 1000 a number of larger mountain tribes living in the Daghestan, which are the highlands of Eastern Caucasia, became converted to the Jewish faith although by race and ancestry they were purely Aryan. Though remaining faithful to their newly adopted religion, they avoided all racial intermixture and so were, beyond all doubt, genuine Aryan Jews. Ethnologists even went so far as to say that they were directly descended from the Goths.

So what were they? Aryans or Jews? Were we to class them as friends or enemies?

Military developments relieved our theorists of any such moral quandary; we never got to Daghestan.

***

In general, our handling of the population in the Caucasus was a hundred times better than it had been in the fertile plains of the Ukraine, where the first partisan groups of any size were just then beginning to make their appearance.

In fact, I did not know that Koch and Sauckel were just starting their wholesale conscription of labor throughout the Eastern territories and that the Caucasus was in fact the sole praiseworthy exception along all of the Eastern Front.

We knew none of that. All we knew was that we were moving our gun into position at Kishnyi-Kub. My gun was well camouflaged, being half-dug into a deep gully, and we had spent the night free from the attentions of enemy aircraft. When the runner came to wake us in the morning, all five of us were already up and about. Our Hein, a young soldier from Schleswig Holstein, pulled me aside for a moment. I was surprised, because for all his youth, Hein was already an old warrior, and it is usually only raw troops who hand over letters for home before a battle.

Hein held out two photographs, each of a girl; one very pretty, and the other rather plain. "Which one do you think I ought to marry? " he asked.

"That's a hell of a question to answer on an empty belly," I said, trying to dodge the issue, because I knew that as far as Hein was concerned my judgment was infallible.

"What about this one, what do you think of her?" He held out the plain one.

"Looks reliable," I answered, for want of anything better to say.

The 19-year-old boy's face brightened. "That's exactly what I think. She's had a child by me, and she's always writing and sending me parcels, she's so worried about me. I've decided to write to my old man today. I want the boy to go on the farm if I should ever pack it in."

We laughed. Then came the order: "Start up the engines!"

In a few minutes, we began to move and immediately there was activity in every defile. I had not realized the night before just how big our force was. There must have been at least a 100 armored vehicles, vehicles of all sizes. All of Mühlenkamp's battalion[34] was there.

---

34 Translator's Note: *SS-Sturmbannführer* Johannes-Rudolph Mühlenkamp was the long-time commander of the tank battalion of *SS-Panzer-Grenadier-Divi-*

Our company, the 3rd Antitank Company, was located somewhere about the center of the force. Safe enough. But we had not gone far from Nishnyj-Kub when we received the order: The company was to close up to the lead tanks. Up front after all, our usual luck. Everything was still quiet, and we rolled on forward over hills and through deep defiles. Suddenly, a thunderous crash from far ahead shattered the peace of the morning air. Very heavy calibers. The shells were already impacting. A wide and deep tank trench gaped across our path just ahead.

Armored engineers dismounted from their vehicles and calmly worked their way forward with their demolition charges. There came a smart rap against the side of my crew compartment. So, there were infantry there. That was something we had not expected. They were dug deep shafts in the gullies, which were overgrown by tall mountain grass, and were holding out there. No muzzle flashes could be seen, but there was no mistake about the sound of bullets. Fascinated, I watched through my sights, as a tall *Oberscharführer* walked forward through the hail of fire, completely without cover, and attached charges against the wall of the tank trench. There was a sudden crash. The bastards had shot up my scope. By the time I raised my head above the gun shield, the *Oberscharführer* was gone, torn literally to bits by a shell. The next man crawled forward and lit the fuse. Then I saw him give a jerk, roll over and lie still. Meanwhile, bullets were whistling close overhead, and I had to get my head down. An enemy section was obviously giving us special attention, probably because, being on the extreme left flank, we offered the best target.

Heavy shells were now dropping around us continuously, and I looked enviously at the tanks closing their hatches, while we remained exposed above and to the rear.

Then the first charge went up, and a moment later the second. And then another. How the sappers had done it in the face of such fire was a mystery to me. The first tanks were already making their

sion *"Wiking"*. He was awarded the Knight's Cross on 3 September 1942. He later served as the acting commander of the division, where he received the Oakleaves to the Knight's Cross, and ended the war as the Inspector General of the *SS Panzer* forces.

way across the ditch, which had not been able to hold up our attack. Following close on their heels, my gun lurched down and then up again. On the way up, I saw to my horror that two of our tanks were already on fire, either from direct hits or mines. But I had no time to lose, shells were falling all around us. I continually shifted position and varied speed during the advance, using every possible maneuver to decrease the danger. Suddenly, I felt something wet on the back of my neck. It was blood. I felt again, but I wasn't wounded. Then I saw blood, deep red blood, dripping through the crevices round the gunner's position.

I shouted through the intercom to the gunner: "Are you wounded, Karl?"

"No, not me," he answered, and then a second later his voice came again: "It's Hein. Pass me a field dressing...quick!"

I handed him up the first-aid kit, but a little later he said in a low voice: "I think he's had it. I've already used five dressings. Hein's unconscious."

"Watch out," I shouted, "keep your head down." I had barely finished speaking when I heard him cry out. I promptly pulled myself up by the gun shield and, with a wild somersault, landed on top by Karl's side. He'd been hit fairly harmlessly in the jaw. But Hein was in a bad way. An explosive bullet had torn open his lower belly. After dressing Karl's wound, I shoved the first round of HE into the barrel, had the gun roughly swung round and then fired at the nearest defile. And then again. The enemy fire actually did slacken a little, although I had had to fire in the blind. Suddenly, the radio operator, who also manned the hull machine gun, shouted: "Something moving over there!" He swung his machine gun and fired several bursts. Then, cursing, he stopped. One of the invisible snipers had put a bullet through his right arm. I jumped down back to the gun-commander's position and gave him a field dressing. Then we stopped by the commander's vehicle. *Hauptsturmführer* Oeck was furious. "Get back as fast as you can and wait at the combat trains...you'll find them near Nishnyj-Kub."

We swung round and moved out at top speed. I was surprised to discover that we had advanced a good nine kilometers and that the infantry was still way back at Nishnyj-Kub. As we moved back by ourselves, the whole countryside seemed to spring to life suddenly, and we were met by a hail of fire. Red Army soldiers appeared from every nook and cranny. Despite his wound, the radio operator opened up with the machine gun and fired into the thick of them, leaving a trail of bodies behind us. I sat at the rear of the gun with Karl, taking turns with the submachine gun and throwing hand grenades, which we simply threw behind us. One of them went straight down a hole, and a Red Army man was hurled out of it a moment later. There was one man who trotted along quite carefree behind us carrying an anti-tank mine, which he was apparently determined to throw at our gun. I actually had a liking for him, he kept it up so cheerfully and indefatigably, completely undeterred by the sting in our tail. But he meant no good, and had to be dealt with.

At last, we saw the first buildings of Nishnyj-Kub, and I asked for directions to the main dressing station. Hein was still alive when we lifted him out, but he was gone by the time the doctor bent over him. Shaken, I received his effects, among them the two snapshots. His letter had remained unwritten.

The two wounded members of my crew remained at the dressing station. It was not easy to leave them. "Just my damned luck!" Karl kept repeating angrily. The radio operator several times asked me "not to be angry" with him, saying that he would much rather have stayed with the gun.

Tired and depressed, the driver and I moved out and found the combat trains not far away in a defile. Just as we decided to get some sleep, the first bombs came screaming down.

***

Towards evening, three replacements reported for duty as the new gun crew. Shortly afterwards, the *Spieß* came over and instructed us to accompany the ration trucks up to the front after it got dark.

133

After some minor skirmishing on the way, we eventually arrived back at the front with the two heavy trucks to find that our battalion had formed a "hedgehog"[35] in a huge field of maize in the meantime. We had hardly arrived when the first salvoes of "Stalin Organs" came down—miraculously, without causing the slightest damage. I slept soundly and without dreaming.

We were under way again at dawn. The wide valley lay shrouded in mist, and the peaks of the hills glowed fiery red. Off to our left front, the oil town of Malgobek began to take shape against the slopes of the *Dreihügelberg*[36]. A large white house stood out from the darkness, caught by the first rays of the rising sun. The squat fuel tanks were still hidden in shadow.

Below in the valley, to the right of Malgobek, was Sakoptschin, standing like a sentinel in front of the narrow defile that formed the gateway to the Georgian military road. For how many hundreds, or even thousands of years had soldiers marched, driven or ridden down this road? How much blood had seeped into this fuel-sodden soil?

The sun hung large and red in front of us and the mechanized infantry riding into battle on their vehicles hummed the age-old soldiers' song of a red dawn lighting the way to an early grave.

A T34 swung into view about a mile in front, then another. Our leading tanks halted and a round screamed through the morning air. It was a direct hit, and the first Soviet tank burst into flames. We moved on at top speed, the first wave of tanks in front, with our 3rd Company close behind them. Once again, we were the outside gun on the left flank.

In front of us fifty Russian tanks swung into view, then there were a hundred. There was general relief. The hour of decision had struck and we were in for a major fight.

---

35   Translator's Note: A "hedgehog" defense was the popular expression referring to an all-round defense established on a temporary basis during operations.

36   Translator's Note: Literally, "Three Hill Mountain".

The Russian armor was steadily reinforced as more and more tanks appeared out of the hiding places in which they had waited for us—from small defiles, from behind houses and haystacks. As they advanced towards us and opened fire, the hills around suddenly sprang into life. Artillery, antitank guns and antiaircraft guns rained a fiendish hail of shells and rounds of all calibers into our midst.

Great fountains of earth splayed up in the midst of our force. But there was no work for my gun yet; it was still quiet on the left flank. I critically observed the full length of my sector, including the town on the *Dreihügelberg*, which was by this time slightly to the rear of our left flank. Suddenly, I saw a flash immediately to the right of the white house. A muzzle flash! Out of habit, I counted: One, two, three...at five, the round landed three meters to our left, making the gun rock. I promptly changed position over to the left. Another flash from above, and I counted again. The round impacted at "five," this time about ten meters away to our right.

A moment later the company commander raced past in his command vehicle, and I reported: "Enemy fire from Malgobek."

He laughed loudly. "You're crazy. Malgobek's been in our hands since early this morning." Then he moved off, shaking his head at such ignorance on the part of a gun commander.

Another flash from above, and I changed position again, this time moving backwards. The round landed on the exact spot we had been. Before long I was able to pick out at least three batteries firing on us from above.

A little later the commander moved up again. "You were right, damn it. The infantry regiment that attacked the town this morning was badly cut up in its assault. You'd better open fire on the Malgobek batteries for the time being. There's nothing going on here anyway."

We pivoted in place. By then, our driver down below was beside himself. "What the hell's going on up there? Are we turning tail?" There is nobody worse off in a tank engagement than the driver. With only his narrow vision port to look through, he can never see what is going on and, what is worse, can never get a real feel for the battlefield. At this point, of course, we were having to turn our unprotected rear towards the enemy attack. We then fired off round after round in rapid succession against the high ground. Our rounds were soon striking the white house and then, at last, on the forward battery. We saw debris hurled into the air. All the time I was having to shift position at ever more frequent intervals, because the remaining enemy guns were obviously concentrating all their efforts on finishing us off.

During a short pause in the firing, I took the opportunity to have a quick look round. Things were not looking too good and there must have been some 30 of our guns and tanks on fire. There was also a healthy looking bonfire over in the enemy's side, but to make up for that at least 300 T-34's were massing against us.

Then the loader reported: "Three more AT rounds left."

I stiffened up. In my firing fever, I had completely forgotten the need for economy and had fired off all our ammunition. Now we were in a nice mess. I maneuvered immediately over to the commander to report. The CO said nothing. I offered to move back and reload to the gunwales, but he shook his head. "The ammo carriers will be along any moment," he said. "Try to keep going as best you can until then. And don't stay too long in anyone spot, or you'll be pinpointed."

We raced around the battlefield for a while. Not a pleasant feeling having to hang around like a fifth wheel and act like a target in a shooting gallery for the enemy. A few minutes later the driver reported laconically: "Fuel for another 10 kilometers at most."

I looked around desperately for the ammo carrier, but it was still nowhere to be seen. In fact, it had been knocked out long before without our knowing it. The news about the fuel was the last straw. Could a piece of shrapnel have found our fuel tank? But whatever it was, it made no difference—we were finished. A little way to our left, I could see a shallow dip in the ground, and I had the gun moved to its deepest point—less than three quarters of a meter deep—and halted there.

"Well now, gentlemen," said the gunner with gallows' humor, "make yourselves comfortable."

I squatted down at my station and feverishly tried to think of a way out. No matter how hard I tried, I could think of nothing. A shadow fell across me, and I looked up and saw the Number Two, a young recruit fighting his first battle, looking enviously at my station, which was better protected against shrapnel than his own.

"Would you mind changing places?" I asked him quietly. " I want to come up top for a bit."

He nodded quickly and clambered down while I went and hung out next to the gunner. He said nothing, and I also had nothing to say. We were both in our second year in the east, and we knew only too well what our situation meant.

Next to the seat the recruit had left was a crumpled dime novel. I picked it up and opened it. "The red light in the bar alternated with blue and green in a majestic play of color. Soft music brought an atmosphere of delicate refinement..." I smiled and read on. Shells were bursting all round us and shrapnel screamed past in a frenzy of destruction; but I was sunk in my dime-novel world. All of a sudden, I felt a terrific blow in the pit of my stomach and found myself hurtling upwards. For a split second, I saw the gunner flying beside me and a fiery hell below. By the time I hit the ground, I had realized that it was a direct hit. Lying dazed on the fuel-sodden earth, I caught sight of the young recruit trying frantically to extricate himself from the burning gun, but he fell back into the sea of flame as I jumped up. Exploding ammunition and grenades arcing upward forced me back to the ground. Close beside me I heard a low groan. I looked around and saw the company commander dragging himself along the ground, bleeding and dripping with sweat. "What's going on?" he asked faintly. I pointed to the burning gun.

"How many rounds do you have in your pistol?"

I did not understand. "The usual, 16."

He pointed to the Soviet tanks, which had approached to within 200 meters and were swarming with mounted infantry. Our own tanks were rolling back.

Just in front of us there was a narrow puddle filled with fuel about half a meter wide and around 30 centimeters deep. We crawled through it. The commander was having a rough go of it—we later discovered that he had 14 small pieces of shrapnel in his shoulder—and our progress was painfully slow. Meanwhile, our tanks launched an immediate counterattack and managed to throw Ivan back almost a kilometer in spite of his superior numbers. In response, the Russian batteries redoubled their fire, which rose to a pitch of absolute frenzy and, with shells dropping in unbroken succession and shrapnel whistling and sizzling just above us, we did not even dare to raise our heads to look around.

Eventually, we arrived at a depression, where we found the mechanized infantry had assembled. With a sigh of relief, we joined them. Saved! Shortly afterwards, a large formation of about 80 aircraft appeared on the horizon and approached us. Ours at last; it was about time! Another sigh of relief through the ranks. But then a brittle voice said: "They're Reds." It was true enough. We had not recognized them. They were American, part of the first deliveries of American aid to Russia. A second later, the first aircraft started its strafing run and machine-gun rounds began to strike in our ranks. Bombs screamed down and tore great gaps in the huddle of humanity below.

During these few minutes, or hours—that awful eternity—we lay rigid on our backs, with hands clenched, waiting for death. Wounded men cried out 20 meters yards in front of us and again 20 behind. Many cried no more; they were the lucky ones.

Then at last the skies were empty. Two German fighters raced in.

Two German fighters!

You didn't know whether to laugh or cry. We has long since used up all of our field dressings. We then squirmed over the heaps of dead and wounded—the enemy fire had not abated for a second—and reached a gun from a neighboring company which was damaged and on its way back. A few tank rounds followed us, but they fell short. I wiped the blood off my face, some of it my own from a few shrapnel scratches I had received and some of it from my comrades. When I looked in a mirror, I recoiled in horror. My face was blackened all over from the explosion and slightly scorched by hot oil or fuel. I had noticed nothing.

When the gun halted at Nishnyj-Kub, I fell off exhausted and remained where I had fallen. I was completely exhausted. But not so the company commander, Oeck, who, in spite of his 14 pieces of shrapnel, picked up a couple of repaired guns from the maintenance company, found crews for them and headed out to the aid of our hard-pressed comrades. A little later I heard the news that a close friend of mine, Fritsch, had been killed just beyond the tank ditch, the 30th man of my parent unit to go. Our, division lost some 1,500 men in the fighting around Malgobek and Sakoptschin, and the graves beside the tank ditch grew to a small city of the dead.

A few days later, we again found ourselves in heavy fighting round Malgobek, which we at last managed to take. This town was the key to the whole position, and without it our attack had had little chance of success. I could not understand why the Russians had not simply taken a dozen tanks and a handful of infantry and closed the fourth side of the wide valley, of which they already held the other three. Not a single man of us would have got out.

***

Shortly afterwards, a special assignment took me to Kislewotsk, yet another Russia. There were lovely, well-cared-for little towns from Czarist times, with the addition of course of the usual monumental palaces of Soviet bureaucracy. Such were Jesentuki, Piatigorsk and Kislewotsk.

In Piatigorsk, the town where Lermentov had written <u>A Hero of Our Time</u> and was shot in 1841, and where Pushkin wrote his <u>Caucasian Prisoners</u>, I met friends from home. We talked and drank until dawn. From there, I moved on into nearby Kislewotsk, where relations with the civilian population were obviously on a happy and normal footing, especially with the Muslims, who were well disposed towards us and intensely anti-communist. As I drove into the town, I encountered a Karachev cavalry battalion on its way to the mountains, singing and playing roughhouse. They were splendid slender and bronzed men, who sat in the saddle as if molded there.

In Kislewotsk, I struck up a chance acquaintanceship with a number of professors from the university in Leningrad, mainly from the Medical Faculty. They had been evacuated from Leningrad to the Caucasus, probably in order to prevent any members of the Russian intelligentsia from falling into our hands. They were all working in German military hospitals.

These men were serious older medical professionals, many of whom had studied in Germany and Vienna, yet the stories they had to tell of Leningrad might well have come from the lurid imagination of a Dostoyevsky.

The city had been so badly supplied that a complete state of famine had set in only a few weeks after the beginning of the German siege. Dogs, cats and rats soon came to be regarded as delicacies beyond the reach of ordinary mortals. Scenes of cannibalism, reminiscent of the great famine of 1921, were daily occurrences and a man was barely safe from his neighbor. Deaths were kept secret for weeks on end so that the next-of-kin or other people in the building could go on drawing the dead person's rations; the bodies lay rotting under the beds. Anybody sick or feeble who ventured on the streets was immediately surrounded by gangs of starving children or youths, as if by a pack of wolves. Anybody who had the misfortune of collapsing out of doors was immediately stripped of his clothes and shoes. There was a strict law that the caretaker of any house in front of which a person was found dead was responsible for burial. The result was that most caretakers maintained a constant watch and the moment anybody died, promptly stripped the body of all its belongings and dragged it along to the next house, so as to burden the man next door with the work, which all had grown too weak to do.

When the first evacuation trains finally left the dying town, the bodies of the people who died on the journey were simply heaved out of the window at every station; one could not travel with them and the other passengers needed the space. The railway track was lined with naked corpses.

"It was sheer hell," an old professor said, shuddering and covering his eyes with his trembling hands. "I don't know where we found the strength to survive it all. And it wouldn't really have been so difficult to supply the city with foodstuffs. But it was easier like this. Only the privileged and the army were needed alive; we were condemned to death, to a horrible, ghastly death."

Most of the professors had lost many relatives in the charnel house of Leningrad. I left the Russian scholars' colony numb with horror.

Measured against such an experience, even the bloodiest of battles lost half its terror. I wandered aimlessly through the streets. The strains of the balalaika filtered out from cafes and bars. Wounded soldiers paraded down the promenade arm-in-arm with Caucasian girls or Norwegian or Flemish nurses. In the dusk, the candles in the small Orthodox church flickered mildly inside the wide-open door. I hesitated a moment, and then went in. There were a few worshippers, old men and women, down on their knees on the stone floor.

God had given us a great mission—of that I was certain—a difficult but noble mission. If only we would realize it and prove ourselves worthy. May the giving German heart grapple with it and pour out all its strength in its discharge. May the blood of the millions of our dead be the seed from which eternal friendship with the liberated peoples of the steppes and the eastern mountains may spring—to the benefit of all mankind.

***

I went into a small bar where Caucasian and Mohammedan music was being played. The monotony of it had driven all German troops away, and the place was left almost exclusively to the locals. A

Luftwaffe Hauptmann asked me if there was room at my table. Gradually, we got talking.

"You know, that's just how I feel about it," he said in a tone of relief. "I've just come back from leave in western Germany where my father-in-law runs a big ammunition factory. The Russian women workers there, most of them Ukrainians, are all housed in barracks surrounded by barbed-wire. These wretched women, a lot of whom are even volunteers who were brought to Germany with grandiose promises, are kept cooped up like convicts, only being allowed out in pairs under escort, just like in an orphanage. It's complete lunacy. I did what I could to make people understand. But it's like drop of water on a hot stove."

***

I was then posted to the Salt Steppe, which links the Kalmuck Steppe with the Caspian Sea, the country north of Mostok, Edissja, Stepnoj and Atschikulak. We were quartered in carpet-weaving villages, which had been founded by refugee Armenian settlers. During our stay there, we encountered a regiment of Cossacks, which was doing magnificent work against the enemy in that area.

The few hours I spent with the old colonel of this regiment were an absolute tonic. This East Prussian officer, a man of some 60 years of age, was the idol of his Cossacks, whom he treated as equals. He could get anything from them. He treated them as human beings and was, in turn, respected as a human being by them. A long time later I heard that this regiment, like the Kirghizian division, had been wiped out to the very last man after the death of its colonel. Not a single Cossack had surrendered, even though their position covering to the German retreat was hopeless.

But at that time there was still no thought of retreat. Nalchik fell, the capital of the "autonomous" Soviet Republic of the Karachevs and Karbardines.

***

Shortly after that, I was summoned home for the second time to spend another few months getting everything in the office back in order. This time, I kept very quiet. The story I had been told by the *Luftwaffe Hauptmann* was fully confirmed by what I saw. In fact, conditions in some places were worse.

After I had been back a week, Josef Bürckel sent for me. "How's things in the East?"

"Just as reported in the German Armed Forces Daily Reports," I replied laconically.

He said nothing.

"I see the Ukrainians are being treated like convicts. They came here to help us defeat Bolshevism and are now sitting behind barbed wire. They're worse fed than the German people, but are expected to do the hardest work. If that happens here, what do you think's going on in the East?"

Bürckel quickly changed the subject, asking me about the morale of the troops and the fighting in which I had taken part. I gave him the straight truth.

A few days later, I noticed that he had begun to make surprise inspections of the Ukrainian workers' housing and feeding arrangements. Some weeks later, I happened to see a confidential directive to factory managers to treat their workers from the East with humanity and justice.

He became increasingly friendly to me every time we met, and we had frequent long conversations, almost invariably about the East. Hoping, as I was, for a new turn in the situation there, I soon found out that he was toying with a plan for replacing the nefarious Erich Koch in the Ukraine, a project which would have been wholly to Germany's good, but which never came to anything, being wrecked on the rocks of party intrigue. However, I was relieved that I had managed to win over at least one man, who, even if he was not in the top rank, undoubtedly wielded great influence.

In general, I noticed for the first time that old and trusted National Socialists were at last beginning to think independently and to apply their thought in a sharply critical manner to the course of events.

On one occasion, shortly before I returned to the front, Bürckel summoned me and, in a fury of indignation, laid on the table a handout which had been issued by Dr. Robert Ley's office[37]. It was a report of a wildly abusive speech attacking the Catholic clergy, which Ley had delivered to a class of disabled soldiers under training for service with the party.

"To think that that man has to go and pour out this sort of filth at a time like this," Bürckel began furiously. "The Allies have only got to print it in leaflets and drop them over our Catholic districts, and they'll have a bigger effect than any bombs. Sometimes it's difficult to know whether you're dealing with fools or criminals."

I opened my mouth to speak, but shut it again. I would not as yet have been understood.

It was not only on tactical grounds that this policy towards the Church was to be condemned, but also on moral grounds. Was it not Frederick the Great who said: "Let every man in my kingdom find Paradise after his own fashion."

Although we never let slip an opportunity for quoting old Fritz, this was one of his sayings we had completely forgotten.

And that was not all: For this struggle we were waging, covertly of course, against Christianity was somehow dilettantish, even childish. For many centuries the entire German people, from the peasants of Styria and the Tyrol to the fishermen of the North Sea, had lived

---

37   Translator's Note: Ley was the head of the German Labor Front—*Deutsche Arbeiterfront*—and was fairly notorious within the Nazi party for his personal, often irresponsible, behavior. He was implicated at Nuremberg after the war for the mistreatment of foreign workers and sentenced to death. He escaped the hangman, however, by committing suicide in his cell at Spandau, an incident that caused the Allie to review their security procedures to prevent similar occurrences among the other condemned men.

within the orbit of Christian culture and under the spiritual leadership of the Christian churches. All of a sudden, this whole race was to change its creed, in double time, with the help of such spiritual aids as Alfred Rosenberg's <u>Myth of the Twentieth Century</u>[38], which most of the higher party officials frankly admitted they had never understood, even though they had read it two or three times.

It was an attempt to take something away from the people, without having anything to offer of even approximately the same value in return. Small wonder that the effort was a shipwreck with the great mass of the people.

There was yet another factor which should have been considered. The horror of battle was not easy for any man to endure, except perhaps the fanatic nationalist who set his country above all else, even above life, and was happy to die for it. But there were not many of those. The German Army was a mass army and most of its men needed something to which they could cling in their hour of dread and which would help them at the moment when a man's heart weighs in the balance. But that was something Rosenberg could not supply and, at such a time, the great majority of men turned back to the faith of their fathers and mothers. Time after time, I saw Alpine troops cross themselves at the moment of attack. And not only Alpine troops...

But instead of these self-evident facts being realized and taken into account, the campaign against religion continued to be waged as obdurately and bigotedly as ever, in the middle of the most dangerous situation which Germany had ever faced.

***

To add to all this, the air raids in the West were gradually becoming painful. In our district in particular, which contributed no small

---

38   Translator's Note: Alfred Rosenberg was consider to be one of the chief ideologues of the Nazi Party and the cited book as well as other writings were influential in shaping policy. He was also the Minister of the Occupied Eastern Territories. Although he was one of the proponents of the theories of the *Untermenschen*, he held a relatively benign view of the Eastern Peoples and hoped to enlist their help in fighting for the *Reich* and against the Soviets. He was convicted at Nuremberg and hanged for war crimes.

part to the overall production program, target dates were seldom being met. First it was Saarbrücken's turn, then Mannheim's, then Ludwigshafen's. It was patently obvious that the *Luftwaffe* was no longer capable of protecting the *Reich*.

I was talking about this one day to a friend of mine, who as an *Untersturmführer* in Himmler's entourage, was responsible for reports on air warfare. During our last meeting together, he said: "Udet[39] knew what he was doing all right when he shot himself."

"Shot himself? What on earth are you talking about? He crashed, didn't he?"

"Who said he crashed?" Arthur replied quickly. "The official statement said he had been killed testing a new weapon. And it was perfectly true, he had. As Inspector General of the Air Force and an old hand at the game, Udet was only too well aware that with the start of the Eastern campaign our air production program was not going to be sufficient to meet the pressure from the West as well as its other commitments. As Inspector General he bore the whole responsibility—to his conscience, to history and to his people. But when he voiced his fears he was laughed out of court. So, one fine morning, he picked up a brand new RAF revolver and shot himself. The official report was perfectly true: He was killed trying out a new weapon."

What could I have said to that?

---

39   Translator's Note: Ernst Udet was a famous aviator, who had distinguished himself in the First World War as part of the "Flying Circus." He helped in the build-up of the pre-war *Luftwaffe*, becoming a major proponent of dive bombing. Ideologically, he grew ever more estranged from Göring, however, leading ultimately to his suicide, which was disguised from the German public. Udet was Germany's highest scoring "ace" still alive at the end of World War 1. His final total was 62 aerial victories, second only to Manfred von Richthofen.

A friendly face, a little Ukrainian girl is greeting us.

Inspecting the abandoned Russian armored car, type BA-10, the crew was still in the vehicle.

The *Wehrmacht* made extensive use of the bicycle enabling the Infantry to advance up to 20 km (12 miles) per hour, depending on road conditions and the terrain.

A Sturmgeschütz III with an Infantry squad during the early stage of operation   *"Barbarossa"*, June 1941.

The famous 8,8 cm Flak in action against Soviet armor. The weapon could fire up to 15 rds per minute, when operated by a well trained crew.

The 8 t *Zugmaschine* (8 ton prime mover) is rushing 200 ltr. gasoline drums to the Panzers on the front line. The soldier next to the driver is armed with a captured Russian 7,62 mm tank machine gun.

A wounded prisoner is given first aid
by Panzer crew members.

This Sturmgeschütz III (assault gun) is
returning from the front with provisions
and Russian wounded.

The light scout car Sd.Kfz. 222 after a raid behind the enemy line. The Red Army
prisoners appear to be rather relieved to be out of the fight. August 1941.

Unteroffizier (sergeant) is giving this badly injured comrad first aid treatment.

Infantry armed with Karabiner 98K and Gew. 41 are engaged in house to house fighting in an Ukrainian village, July 1941.

Soviet prisoners - giving up.

An ever growing number of Red infantry is surrendering to German Panzer II and Panzer III's. In the foreground, note some of the POW's are still armed.

The masses of POW's captured in the early weeks of the campaign on the Eastern Front surprised the German soldiers at the front.

A number of Soviets played dead and had to be dealt with harshly.

Female Red Army - soldiers proudly display their newly issued *Tukarev* M 1940 semi-automatic rifle.

A battery of abandoned Soviet *"Stalin Orgel"* rocket launchers mounted land and lease Studebaker trucks.

A group of Red Army prisoners, escorted by the author and one grenadier

The execution of captured partisans.

Ukrainian villagers are welcoming the German liberator.

Taganrog, *Babuska* (Granny) in the door of her humble dwelling.

Female Red Army soldiers having a good time repairing the shoulder boards of their embarrassed guard.

The green hell of the Ukrainian cornfields.

The *Sturmgeschütz* III was a 24 ton killing machine armed by a 7,5 cm gun able to knock out a T-34 at a range up to 1,500 meters.

Russian T-34/76 tanks, abandoned on railcars behind the German lines.

After combat, medals are rewarded in the field. Here the company commander is issuing the Iron Cross 1st Class.

The three man crew of a 8cm Granatwerfer 34 is readying the weapon to assist the advancing infantry. Six rounds of HE (high explosive) shells per minute could be fired at a range up to 2,4000 m.

Hand grenades at ready, these troops are awaiting the attackers advancing through the ripening wheat fields, summer 1941.

After the battle, if possible, the fallen comrades are getting a Christian burial.

Many Soviet soldiers defected to the German units.

Captured Red Army female soldiers.

Many ethnic soldiers from the many countries under the Soviet domain were encountered on the western border of the Soviet Empire in the first weeks of the war.

A never ending stream of prisoners filled the German camps, August 1941.

A Sturmgeschütz III is advancing towards an abandoned hamlet.

After the town is taken, abandoned Russian T-26A light tanks are searched for injured or dead crews to be removed via the waiting ambulance vehicle parked in the background.

The Uzbek prisoner is interrogated by a fellow countryman in German uniform. The German *Sonderführer* is standing by in the back.

We lit our cigarettes - a dangerous encounter turned into a great party.

The old Ukrainian.

A cigarette and a piece of bread.

The faces of the enemy. A German officer face to face with his former fierce enemy, relieved that the suffering is over.

Ukrainian villagers are greeting a PK (propaganda) motorcycle rider. Tobacco or cigars are exchanged for bread, milk or soap.

Villagers are greeting the Wehrmacht entering the Ukraine as liberators. The crew of a *Züundapp Ks 750 Beiwagenmaschine* (combination) of the 16. Pz. Division.

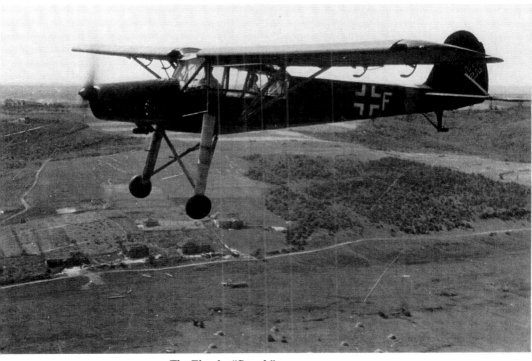

The Fieseler *"Storch"*.

SS-Troopers in a Volkswagen *"Kübelwagen"*. The soldier is holding a MG34 machine gun.

A Soviet officer's barrack room.

The self-propelled gun, *Panzerjäger* 7,62 cm Pak (Russ.) auf Sf. 38 (Sd.Kfz. 139), a combination of a Czech tank and Russian anti-tank gun.

Karachaev elders in their traditional clothing are sitting in front of their simple dwellings.

Stahl and his *Kameraden* enthusiastically participated as guests of the local population in their traditional festivals.

Volunteer cavalry from the Caucasus tribes are joining the German Army, acting as scouts, reconnaissance and even combat units.

This Panzer III was hit by a T-34 and burned.

T-34/76 left abandoned in front of the German line.

The first round hit this T-34. Ammunition and diesel fuel turned the enemy into a burning hell.

This Marder 38 is returning with its crew bandaged up - but alive.

A Ukrainian farmer and his wife. The woman is cutting slices of the typical Russian heavy black bread.

A peasant family with their worldly goods and their children on their way back to the village after the front moved further east.

Only the Orthodox church survived.

The great trek to the West.

The German Cavalry General Helmut von Pannwitz. Von Pannwitz started to organize the Cossacks in the summer of 1942. He was to be the commander of Cossack Units. *Kommandierender General des Kosakenkavallerie Korps.* Captured by the British on *12. May 1945, handed over to the Bolsheviks, and executed in the UdssR on 16. January 1947,*

This Cossack from the Kaukasus poses with his wife. He is wearing the traditional costume *(Tscherkeska).* On his chest are the German eagle and the Edelweiss of the *Gebirgsjäger* (Mountain Troops) is affixed to his right arm.

Oberstleutnant Burg Graf zu Dohna, commander of the 1.Don Cossack Rgt., 1943.

A Soviet officer after his capture.

Gebirgsjäger (Mountain Troops) on the march in the Caucasus, 3000 km from the German frontier.

Three comrades of the *"Leibstandarte"*.

This young *Rottenführer* (corporal) of the *"Totenkopf"* Division is armed with an MP 40 machine pistol. The magazine pouches each hold three 32 round magazines.

The SS man is firing his carbine 98k at the approaching Soviets. The ammunition pouches each hold 2 clips of 7.92 mm rifle ammo (5 rds per clip).

The 3 men machine gun team in action with their 7.92 mm MG 34. The trooper left is carrying a *Laufschützer* 34 (spare barrel carrier) on his back.

With mud running into their boots, the soldiers are carrying the MP 40 machine pistol. The second trooper mans the MG 42 machine gun which has a rate of fire of 1,200 rds per minute (25 rds per second).

Soviet Infantry armed with sub-machine guns during an attack. The Russian PPS 41 had a rate of fire, cyclic 700 rpm (rounds per minute)

With MP40 submachine gun at ready, the *Landser* is urging the wounded Red Army soldier to come out of his dugout, August 1941.

A hand grenade did the job to this Soviet Maxim-machine gun crew.

Sturmbannführer Otto Skorzeny and his Chief of Staff SS *Untersturm*führer Adrian von
Foelkersam in Budapest, 16. October 1944.

Oberst Hans-Ulrich Rudel.

Truck loaded with military and civilian
personnel waiting for the final end of
the War, May 1945.

Chapter Seven: Stalingrad

A few weeks later, I received the news in Germany of the cruelest blow in the whole of its history—Stalingrad. Although I did not realize at the time that this spelt the doom of the Eastern Front. What I also did not know was that this was the beginning of the end. What I did know was that Hitler had said that Stalingrad would be our beacon in the east. Beacon it was, a beacon that shed its cruel light over our destruction. For nights on end I could find no rest. I was haunted by the image of hundreds of thousands of men: Exhausted, starving and betrayed, yet ready to fight to the last in a hopeless cause.

This was not the first time that Stalingrad, the former Zarizyn, had played a decisive part in Russian history. In 1918-1919, this "City of the Empress," which first became an established community in the 17th Century and, as Zarizyn, had led an inconspicuous existence as an ordinary little Volga town—far outshone by the splendors of Nishny-Nowgorod or Kazan—found itself almost overnight a key center in the history of Bolshevism.

The counter revolution of the White Guards, spreading rapidly from the south and east, had succeeded in kindling a flame that was on the point of achieving the complete destruction of Bolshevism. The operational objective of the White command was to unite its divisions fighting in southern Russia with those of the Far East. The success of this move was bound to result in the suffocation of the Leninist revolt.

And so their divisions marched singing and victorious from the east to the southwest and from the south to the northeast. At the intersection of these great strategic moves was the Volga.

The divisions of old Russia, Cossacks at their head, marched along the river of rivers, the mighty Volga. The Cossacks were the first to have their horses drink from the waters of the Volga. The White Army stood before Zarizyn.

The battle for this small town, which at that time boasted barely 60,000 souls, was of decisive importance, even though the soldiers did not realize it.

But the Bolshevik leaders knew what was at stake. They had sized up the situation and realized that the future of their revolution would be decided one way or the other at this small town on the Middle Volga. If the White Armies were to succeed in uniting, then the fate of Bolshevism would be sealed, its power broken, and the grief and fury of the Russian people would sweep over its followers like a hurricane.

So Lenin vested two Special Commissioners with extraordinary powers and sent them to Zarizyn with personal instructions from himself: Joseph Stalin as his special envoy and Voroshilov as his military commissar.

Fate decided against the Czarist generals and their divisions, perhaps because they had not grasped the significance of the battle, perhaps merely because the fickle gods of war were more kindly disposed that day towards the Red troops. Whatever it was, Bolshevism was saved and the counter-revolution lost. What followed was no more than a succession of fighting pursuits and retreats.

As a result, the town of Zarizyn was renamed Stalingrad in honor of Lenin's special envoy and later developed into a center of industry on the Volga. Then, at the decisive moment of the Second World War, this same town, with its vast tractor works and other industries, and its population swollen to many hundred thousands, stood once again at the crossroads of history.

The two fated generals of this genocidal struggle, *Generaloberst* Paulus[40] and Marshal Rokossovsky, met for the decisive round. Once again, fate decided for the Kremlin outside the gates of Stalingrad.

---

40   Translator's Note: Paulus was only promoted to *Generalfeldmarschall* after his forces had been surrounded and the battle seemed lost. Hitler promoted the general with the admonition that no German field marshal had ever been captured

On 23 November 1942, 22 German divisions were encircled in the city, 3,000 kilometers from the German frontier, and 300 kilometers from the German front. On 2 February 1943, the last battle group surrendered.

***

A few weeks later, I was in a small wine bar in Saarbrücken when a young lieutenant friend of mine, a man I had known since his Hitler Youth Leader days, came up and spoke to me. I had not seen him for some time and was shocked to see how much he had aged. When I told him of this, he smiled wearily and said: "I was one of the last wounded to be flown out of Stalingrad."

Then in this little tavern in the Saarland there grew up before my eyes the awful picture of that greatest of all battles on the Eastern Front: Stalingrad[41].

When the Rumanian divisions holding the line north and south of the city had been smashed and broken by the weight of Russian artillery, Soviet tanks and infantry moved into the vacuum and the *6. Armee* was encircled.

Things at first did not look too bad. Ammunition and rations were plentiful, and the Russian attacks were hurled back with terrible losses. Deterioration set in, almost imperceptibly at first, but then with dramatic suddenness. The *Luftwaffe* was no longer capable of supplying the encircled army; Göring having once again promised more than he could perform. From the end of November onwards, Paulus issued no more overarching orders and the Commanding Generals of the corps acted on their own initiative.[42]

---

alive. Apparently, Paulus did not take those words to heart, since he surrendered with what remained of his forces and later collaborated with the Soviets.

41 Translator's Note: The author advances the common viewpoint of the early post-war years that defined Stalingrad as a major turning point in the war in the East. Most historians now consider the fighting around Kursk in July 1943 to be the actual strategic turning point of that conflict.

42 Translator's Note: Von Paulus was probably one of the worst choices that could have been made as the commander of *6. Armee*. He had a quite undistin-

In the middle of December, *Panzergruppe Hube* worked its way up to within 48 kilometers of the Stalingrad pocket, and the beleaguered troops jubilantly watched the light of their flares and artillery bursts in the night sky. Feverish preparations were made for a breakout.

Then came the *Führer* order that there was to be no breakout, and that Stalingrad was to be held as a key position on the Volga.

Rations steadily worsened. Soon, only six to eight supply aircraft were arriving each day. Six to eight aircraft a day to supply the entire *6. Armee*! Daily casualty reports grew to between 1,000 and 2,000 men, most of them deaths from hunger, cold or starvation.

Nevertheless the forces, both officers and men, acquitted themselves well, so well, in fact, that at the end of the battle the Russians were forced to admit in their official report that of the 600,000 men who had taken part, 360,000 had been killed or wounded. Some 60,000 guns, 1,000 "Stalin Organs" and about 5,000 armored vehicles had to be used to break the resistance of the German Army in Stalingrad.

When the end came, the German defenders had 80 armored vehicles—80 armored vehicles without fuel or ammunition against 5,000. That was the picture of Stalingrad.

Paulus gave his last order to his men on the 25 January: "All ranks are authorized to attempt to break out of the Stalingrad pocket without asking permission."

On 24 January, *General* Daniels took independent action to surrender his infantry division in the southern sector. This permitted the Russians to thrust into the gap and thousands of Stalingrad fighters paid with their lives for Daniel's action.

---

guished command record, having led nothing larger than a battalion (briefly) and having no combat command experience at all. He was by all accounts a very good staff officer, but he an ineffectual field-army commander. He also lacked the moral courage to oppose Hitler's "hold fast" command and order a breakout when this was still possible.

The beginning of the end came on the 29 January. The Russians succeeded in driving a wedge through the pocket, which at that time was 5 kilometers long by 2 kilometers wide, cutting it into two separate parts: One in the north with the few remaining tanks and heavy weapons, and the other in the south containing only infantry without ammunition.

The over-all command post was in the southern half of the pocket, housed in the cellars of the GPU prison. Paulus himself was incapable of addressing a single word to his officers. He was a broken man.

The last German forces laid down their arms in the northern pocket on 2 February 1943, and the curtain fell on the most decisive battle of the Eastern Front.

The young *Leutnant* finished his story and we sat silent, looking absently into the air. The air-raid sirens howled. We slowly stood up and drained our glasses. Bombs were dropping close at hand in the area around the railway station, but we were past caring.

***

At that time, I still had no conception of the full extent of the political and military consequences of Stalingrad. But it was not long before I realized that Stalin had given the war an entirely new turn. The war of Communist world revolution was over. The nationalist war of Russian Bolshevism had taken its place, and we had cleared the way for it by our own folly.

We were now facing our third winter of war in Russia. It had very quickly been brought home to us when we first began to move east that there was something lacking in our armory, something we had to buy dearly and which in fact we never fully acquired: Accurate information about the Soviet Union as an arms forge and a political and psychological understanding of the extent to which Bolshevism had taken the mechanization and conditioning of the soul of the Russian people.

On the material side, the courage and military experience of our troops were capable, albeit with the most tremendous efforts, of destroying the Russian arsenals and pulverizing their products of many years, but on the political and psychological side, there was no one to inform us of the terrible extent of the mechanization of people's minds. We were faced with a new problem, the Soviet man. Knowledge of Dostoyevsky's novels, however thorough, could not help us, or the poems of Pushkin. We found neither Tolstoy's Anna Karenina, nor a blessed resurrection of Gogol's dead souls. That world had been buried forever along with the Cossack officers, the priests and the Kulaks in the mass graves of the Cheka, and only lived on as a ghostly spark in the cabarets of the "old" world. It had died in the bloodiest of all Lenin's experiments, which his Georgian apostle had inherited and then molded to his own way of thinking. We had to find our way in this "new" world in the east, just as that world had itself had to find its own way in the beginning.

Bolshevism had used the human masses that had been delivered up to it in its hermetically sealed laboratory to demonstrate to the world the thesis of materialism; it had subordinated all life regardless of the cost to the claims of a doctrinaire revolution. The road has since become only too familiar.

This world of appearances, the greatest contradiction between theory and practice ever known, had been shattered in the fatal year of 1941, when the skill of our generals and the courage of our troops broke through the iron curtain separating the peoples of the Soviet Union from real life. It was not only the direct effect of our victories that proved so damaging to the Bolshevist era, but also the indirect effect. Millions of faithful or perhaps ignorant Russians had realized from the German soldier's behavior, uniform and actions that they had been systematically deceived and betrayed.

Stalin then faced political bankruptcy. His laboratory had been pried open and smashed and his propaganda became ineffectual and patently absurd. Yet this picture had changed, through our fault, and our fault alone. Without as yet realizing it we were in the middle of a political and, resulting from that, a military collapse.

THE GREAT RETREAT

Chapter Eight:
The Specter Of Tauroggen

Soon afterwards, I left again for the front. The powerful counter-offensive at Kharkov had fizzled out, the enemy having been shrewd enough to allow our spring offensive, for all the dash and courage with which it had been mounted, to run itself to death. The unending waves of British and American bombers were beginning to have their effect as well.[46]

---

46   Since the Convention of Tauroggen may not be familiar to English readers, and a rudimentary knowledge of it is necessary to fully understand the author later in the chapter, the following information is provided from Wikipedia (http://en.wikipedia.org/wiki/Convention_of_Tauroggen):

The Convention of Tauroggen was a truce signed 30 December 1812 at Tauroggen (now Taurage, Lithuania), between *Generalleutnant* Hans David Ludwig Yorck von Wartenburg on behalf of his Prussian troops, and by General Hans Karl von Diebitsch of the Russian Army. Yorck's act is considered a turning point of Prussian history, triggering an insurgency against Napoleon in the Rheinbund.

According to the Treaty of Tilsit, Prussia had to support Napoleon's invasion of Russia. This resulted in some Prussians leaving their army to avoid serving the French, like Carl von Clausewitz, who joined Russian services.

When Yorck's immediate French superior Marshal Macdonald, retreated before the corps of Diebitsch, Yorck found himself isolated. As a soldier his duty was to break through, but as a Prussian patriot, his position was more difficult. He had to judge whether the moment was favorable for starting a war of liberation; and, whatever might be the enthusiasm of his junior staff officers, Yorck had no illusions as to the safety of his own head, and negotiated with Carl von Clausewitz.

On top of all that, we were beginning to hear whispers about the lunacy of our production policy, about the continual stream of modifications and improvements that were being proposed for our tanks and aircraft. No doubt these new tanks were far and away superior to those of the enemy, who was still turning out a steady stream of his old T-34's, but these frequent changes of design meant equally frequent retooling and reconstruction of factory plant and machine tools. Those in the know told us that to retool a factory for a new type of tank often took months—months during which all production was at a standstill. And all that time the Russians were turning out T-34 after T-34 after T-34...

The result was that when these new tanks of ours finally went into action, they were faced with such an overwhelming mass of enemy armor that their superior qualities hardly counted. And from all we heard, it was exactly the same with the Air Force. The whole thing was beyond the comprehension of the fighting man on the Eastern Front, at any rate that of the junior officers and noncommissioned officers. We could see only one ray of light and that was that the *Führer*, who, after all, had the last word in everything, was bound to know what was going on and would see to it that everything would be set straight. But in the meantime, we were losing more and more ground and our cemeteries were growing seemingly without end on a daily basis.

Gritting our teeth, we often fell back before an enemy who was inferior to us in all but numbers and looked to the west for new tanks and new artillery pieces. But in the west they were busy designing, planning, modifying...seemingly as an end unto itself.

What was needed, and needed desperately, was a huge input of guns, tanks and aircraft. What we got was no more than a trickle.

The Convention of Tauroggen armistice, signed by Diebitsch and Yorck, "neutralized" the Prussian corps without consent of their king. The news was received with the wildest enthusiasm in Prussia, but the Prussian Court dared not yet throw off the mask, and an order was dispatched suspending Yorck from his command pending a court-martial. Diebitsch refused to let the bearer pass through his lines, and the general was finally absolved when the Treaty of Kalisch definitely ranged Prussia on the side of the Allies.

The race against time was on—and with a vengeance.

The answer that the command in the East gave to this situation was to take onto itself the Soviet "scorched earth" tactics and attempt to make up for its lack of material numbers by creating an empty space in front of the Dnieper in which the great mass of the Red Army would run itself to exhaustion.

***

Awestruck and dumb, I stood watching the unending torrent roll past: Horse-drawn carts, hundreds upon hundreds of vehicles, endless columns of civilians—men, women and children—all staggering beneath the weight of their last worldly possessions. Regiment after regiment: Artillery, tanks, infantry, Cossacks and German cavalry. Everything was moving west towards the setting sun.

Gradually, the exodus began to assume the proportions of a catastrophe. Behind it in the east, towns and villages were already burning and the twilight creeping up towards the broad river, which seemed chosen to become our fate, grew aflame with a fiery glow. From the shot-up wall of a building, where I was positioned with my squad, I could look down onto the riverbank and see thousands upon thousands of milling, bawling cattle being pressed forward. A shout from their Cossack herders, and the exhausted animals, their heads hanging, waded slowly into the rushing water, and the river came alive with a great host of heads all striving for the western bank.

On the western bank—that's where we were to find our extended defensive lines—over there on the western bank. What a change from only two years before, when we had stormed across that same Dnieper with the tatters of the Red Army flying before us. And now?

Ever since the summer, the steppe had been pressing in on Europe with an unbelievable weight of men and materiel. The people of the Soviet Union were storming west in battles dwarfing anything the world had yet seen.

Burnt-out tanks, shattered aircraft, cannon, machine guns, countless mortars and hundreds of thousands of dead bodies littered the battlefield.

It was once again the hour of great decision; this time, more than ever before, a choice of bend or break. The German command had weighed all the possibilities open to it and chosen the one that seemed to promise the greatest chance of success with the least cost in lives, and the result was an exodus without parallel from the area east of the Dnieper. The country itself was to slip away from Bolshevism: People, towns, factories, cattle and grain. Nothing was to be left but a vast empty void that the Red Army would require months to overcome—months of delay, during which the German defense line would be made impregnable.

The harvest that was pouring out of the east was heading for a railway station just short of the river, from which it was being sent off across the Dnieper bridge to the west. Trains were pulling out of the station at 10-minute intervals, each carrying its precious load: Machines of every conceivable kind, whole industrial plants, grain, grain and yet more grain. There was human freight too: Men, women and children, swarming over the roofs, even hanging on the side like bunches of ripe grapes—all with one aim, to escape the return of Bolshevism.

Slowly, the day faded. More and more cattle trotted down to the river, surrounded by Cossacks and Caucasians from the mountains, all mounted on agile steeds. The animals cautiously dipped their hooves into the cool water and then slowly, patiently, lowing sullenly to themselves, slid into the stream, beast after beast. More and more herds came and swam away, like vast rafts on the wide river. From farther downstream came the grunt and squeal of thousands of pigs crossing on the big ferry. And so it continued, hour by hour, day by day, night by night. Trains whistled in the distance, their wagons full of the precious grain around which this great greatest hunger offensive of history was being waged.

Absorbed by this awful spectacle, we completely forgot all time and place. A Martin bomber made a forlorn attempt to approach the one bridge but our *Flak* ringed it with fire and drove it off. Our relief arrived, and we made our way back to our billets through the deserted streets. The glare of burning villages was now brightening a great arc of the evening sky.

The thunderous boom of a heavy explosion came from somewhere far away, and the sky deepened to a blood red. That night our forces disengaged in accordance with their orders, leaving the enemy to follow up in the morning. To follow up into a void, without villages, without towns, without man or beast and, most serious of all, without the grain they so desperately needed. To follow up into a desolate void, which was to swallow and halt their offensive.

***

The success of our withdrawal to the Dnjepr was complete, and only a very few of our men fell into enemy hands. The days of our real losses were yet to come.

But on the western bank there was a surprise awaiting us, a terrible surprise: There was no defensive line—the much-vaunted Dnjepr line simply did not exist. We dug ourselves in as best we could under the fire of the enemy, anger and disillusionment tearing at us all, officers and men alike. It was only the iron discipline of all ranks that prevented mutiny and revolt against the people responsible.

At several points, the Russians crossed the river at almost the same moment as us. The river that was to determine our fate did so indeed, but in a manner we had not hoped for.

It soon became crystal clear to us: There was no East Wall. Indeed, the Dnjepr defense line did not exist. A river alone, mere water, has never in the history of war formed a decisive defensive line. Our leaders had built their hopes on sand in the truest sense of the word, and blood, our blood, would have to stem the flood alone. Yet it was in those very days of retreat, far more than in the forward march of victory, that the German soldier on the Eastern Front showed his true stature.

***

157

Retreat! How often had we sensed the hot breath of panic spreading through the enemy's ranks before that fatal cry was raised. We had always been the ones to go forward, on every front, north and west, southeast and south and, above all, in the east, hunting the routed enemy into bloody defeat. Then, when we had had to go back for the first time during those grim winter days of 1941, we too had felt the horror of retreat. Even our later offensives, which had carried our banners further into the vastness of the east, could not wipe away that dread from our memories, the dread which retreat brings to every man, whether general or private.

Later on we realized that we had become soldiers during those days of fear and hardship, soldiers who had seen and overcome the ultimate horror of war. We came to realize that much of what we had hitherto taken to be proof of victory, such as taking several hundred kilometers of terrain to the east or the west, was not really conclusive. We saw that this war, which had long since outgrown its boundaries, embraced possibilities of every conceivable kind, both in our favor and against us—possibilities that went unnoticed during our years of conquest. We put away our ideas of a "cake-walk" victory, our illusions of a war already won. We no longer counted up the tokens of success, but began, quietly and humbly, to watch the rules under which the deadly game between the enemy and ourselves was being played; we learned at last to take the long look at things and to react accordingly. This new knowledge was something more than just an incident in a soldier's memory. It was the prerequisite for our future action as a nation; and it came not a moment too soon. The political setback we had experienced in the south, following our military crisis there, demanded from us that ultimate courage that can face the truth, however hard. Undaunted by the harlequin theater going on about us, this spirit of absolute devotion to duty carried us through on all fronts, through all the skirmishing, the partisan warfare, the battles of attrition. An event that a year before would have thrown the victorious German armed forces into a turmoil of excitement, was now registered by the German soldier with displeasure, but with no surprise. News of a successful response on our part was treated as a matter of course.

During this period we had to undergo the severest test of all: To pull back without having been defeated. A thousand times the question was asked—Why are we going back?—never to be answered satisfactorily. Commanders were continually being asked by their men to explain this move, which was inexplicably and irrevocably threatening to destroy what had been the mainspring of every soldier's life: The success of our arms and his confidence in victory. In addition, there was the fact that this gigantic withdrawal, with its deliberate creation of a dead and empty space by yielding territory, often without contact with the enemy, contained within it the gravest dangers to discipline and morale. There were endless herds of cattle streaming back past our men, poultry and livestock being carried west in countless thousands. Whole mountains of valuable goods lying unguarded by the roadside waiting for transport. Then there were the civilians, trekking slowly along the railway tracks carrying the trains laden with the unending flow of grain. Kilometer after kilometer of people—young girls in their teens, women with children at their breasts, and men—all with one thought, to escape the death advancing from the east in the form of Bolshevism.

What army could have withstood a withdrawal of such dimensions in its fifth year of war without suffering serious damage or even the considerable disintegration of its psychological and organic integrity? Dangerous as this withdrawal was for the rear services, it provided a test of purgatorial dimensions for the fighting forces. Stalin, of course, concentrated for the pursuit every man who had survived the heavy fighting of his Ukrainian offensive and was trying, at whatever cost, to turn this unprecedented migration of millions of souls over hundreds of kilometers to his own decisive advantage. Occasionally, the enemy would not follow up at all, and our movements took place without enemy interference. Then he would throw in everything he had to break through our defensive screen, penetrate into our bridgeheads and make a cheap haul out of our retreating elements. But he never succeeded. Despite the difficult strategic and tactical situations into which this plan, by its very nature, was bound to bring us, the enemy was at no place and at no time able to disturb our intentions for any length of time, let alone thwart them.

This deliberate withdrawal from the Donez to the Dnjepr was one of the greatest operations undertaken in the history of war. Never before had a command placed itself so completely in the hands of the troops. There was little it could do to mitigate their hardships or ease their psychological anxieties. For tactical reasons, it could rarely let the men know even the operational objectives or the direction of march. There was only one thing for it to do: Place a blind confidence in the German soldier. And he never betrayed that confidence, carrying on even when he neither understood nor could understand the orders given him or the command that issued them. In the course of this withdrawal, it became clear that the German soldier had outgrown the mere obedience of the parade ground and had attained a state of absolute devotion to duty.

***

We soon saw what our withdrawal meant for this unhappy country in terms of individual lives.

He had joined our company many months before, attached himself to us sort of like a stray dog in one of the many villages we had captured. At first he was everyone's favorite, but the *Spieß* soon had him put on kitchen duty. There he stayed, the young Schura Matchujin from Poltava, a 13-year-old boy whom a *Komsomol* unit had dragged to the front. One of our units had taken him prisoner, but it had released him on account of his age.

It was not long before he was speaking amazingly good German and settling down to the daily routine as if he had always belonged to the company. When the division advanced east and took up positions beyond Poltava, Schura took to slipping away at frequent intervals to his native village, which at that time was just behind the lines, to return shortly afterwards with a sack full of eggs, so that we were never sorry to see him go off on one of his trips. It never entered our heads that he might not come back or might even desert to the enemy. Schura was the most dependable person you could imagine, both in his work and even, if men were short, in battle.

For that reason, the mood of the entire company was even gloomier when it was suddenly discovered in the middle of the major withdrawal that Schura had vanished without a trace. "Man, oh man, can you believe it?" the mess sergeant said angrily. "Schura of all people." Even the company commander was upset. The *Spieß* growled: "Just because we're going back this time. Who would have thought..." He turned down the many volunteers who came in: "No...Schura was enough."

Day followed night and night followed day and train after train rattled westwards laden with the grain. The countryside reverberated under the hooves of tens of thousands of cattle, all moving west. Night was turned to day by the light of blazing towns and villages which, deserted by the people and laid flat by fire, would no longer offer shelter to the oncoming Soviets. As the endless file of peasant carts drew past, a man would every now and then point to one of the many boys riding on them: "Looks like our young Schura!"

We came to a riverbank. Farther upstream there was a continual procession of farm produce, machinery, refugees and, of course, troops pouring across a bridge. A large ferryboat was shuttling backwards and forwards at our crossing point. During the previous few days we had been withdrawing steadily, covering the allotted distance each day, almost without enemy interference. But now that the Russians seemed suddenly to have realized that we really meant it, they were making desperate efforts to catch up with us and take possession of the riverbank themselves.

Everything was ready for the crossing. The combat trains were already, and the first platoons on their way over. Then the ferry returned once more to carry the last platoon across under covering fire from the opposite bank. The first Russian assault groups had already reached the river on either side of our debarkation point.

The whole platoon was quickly aboard. Russian artillery was firing too high and dropping its shells far behind us into the water. Our infantry guns were replying in kind, all very much like gunnery. Fortunately, the river was wide.

Suddenly, there was a shout from the men watching the bank we had just given up to the Russians. A boy had appeared among the Red Army men, then another and a third. "If that isn't Schura, I don't know who is." "If we get a direct hit, it won't matter anyway," said another. "One shell will be enough." He reached for his sniper's rifle. "But at least we'll give him something to remember us by." He took aim, and then lowered his rifle. Over on the bank the three boys had suddenly run to the water's edge, dived in before the Russians had realized what was happening, and were swimming with long strokes after the German ferry.

The men crowded to the stern of the ferry, which then threatened to capsize. Two of them untied a boat, and rowed to meet the swimmers halfway. The barrage was forgotten. Nothing mattered but the three foolhardy young swimmers. Just as our ferry touched the bank, having come unscathed through the hail of fire, our two men dragged the first of the boys into the boat. German machine guns kept up a tornado of fire, putting down a complete screen of fire over the boat, which, endless minutes later, also reached the bank unharmed. One of the boys had been wounded through the arm: It was Schura.

Before the medical orderly had finished bandaging his arm, he was already greedily swallowing his first bite of bread. "Please don't be angry with me, *Nastchalnik*," he begged our company commander, "but when we started pulling back, I couldn't stand it any longer. I simply had to go home and see my mother. But the Bolsheviks had already occupied our village and either taken away or killed all the men and women. Only my two brothers were left, hidden away in one of our hideouts. I found them at night and we set off straight away to catch up with you. We tried all the time to find a gap in the Red Army we could slip through, but it was impossible. We didn't give up though, but slept during the day and went on trying to find a way through at night, until we found you, just before the river. And now," he finished his story exhausted, "now I've found you at last and everything's going to be all right."

He tried to say something else but sank limply back and was asleep. The men stood in a circle round him and said nothing. Our *Spieß* picked up a shelter half and put it gently over the sleeping boy.

And this is the story of old *Babushka*—just one portrait among many—the portrait of an unknown, simple Ukrainian woman. But for me it is a memory, a memory of the great river.

"A thousand thanks," said the ancient *Babushka*, bowing low over and over again, so low that I feared she would bump her head on the ground. We watched amused as she hastily picked up the big pot with the remains of the chicken soup we had been unable to eat and disappeared with it through the low doorway. At midday she was back. And so it happened that the old woman took to coming every day to fetch the leftovers for herself and her four grandchildren. Two of her sons were in Siberia, a third had been killed in the Red Army. Her two daughters-in-law had been taken off by the Bolsheviks to dig defenses, and she was left alone with four perpetually hungry grandchildren. She was soon known to the whole company as *Babushka*, little grandmother.

But we were not the only givers; she too gave in her own way. There might be an enormous hole in somebody's socks, which she could still mend far more quickly than any of us, in spite of her old fingers, or perhaps a shirt or a pair of trousers to be washed. There was no need to tell her. She came unasked day after day, and mothered us all in her own fashion. But it was the serious, taciturn Rudolf whom she took most to her heart. Probably because, as she said, Rudolf had the same blue eyes as her son Jacob, who had gone to Siberia five years earlier.

At that time, we had been holding a narrow wedge that we had driven into enemy territory and were going to give up again shortly afterwards under the overwhelming pressure. It went without saying that all of us knew the situation and had reckoned with this withdrawal. In the end, it turned out as it always did, everything in a mad rush. We just thought ourselves lucky to be getting our personal items out at all. Just as our personnel carrier was rattling out of the village, Rudolf muttered angrily to himself: "You idiot, I've left my old shirt with *Babushka*."

Things were very hot for the next few days and many a good man fell on that sandy soil, so that those at home could continue to live and work. The broad Russian heavens stretched their gentle fields of glittering stars in cloudless nighttime skies over the graves in the East and held watch over their quietude. Our taciturn, brave Rudolf also waited somewhere in the vast expanse of the East for the bells that will ring in peace throughout the world.

Shortly after Rudolf's quiet death, we counterattacked over the bare stubble of the freshly harvested sunflower field where he had died and threw the enemy line back by retaking our old village. The women and children lined the roadside the same as the first time, but the glow in their eyes was gone, their smiles frozen. We walked through the familiar streets asking about this and that person. Suddenly, we found ourselves in front of *Babushka's* small house.

There was no sign of life. Old Waska from the hut next door slowly dragged himself up to the low wooden fence. "*Babushka kaputt*," he said in a flat voice. "Many *kaputt*." He pointed with trembling fingers to a tattered brown rag that fluttered like a storm signal from the low gable on the roof.

"God damn! "Wilhelm cried. "It's Rudolf's shirt!"

My story is short, just as life is mostly short in Russia, and there is no happy ending, as there is none to Bolshevism. The Red Army commissar who had taken over the village saw the brown shirt on the gable where Babushka had always dried our laundry. Perhaps a small-minded person had begrudged the old woman the food she had had taken from us and denounced her. But perhaps it really was the shirt that betrayed her. "You've helped those Hitler swine," the commissar roared at the frightened old woman. "You've betrayed the world revolution."

It did not help her that she cried and said that the children would surely have starved if the Germans had not given her food. And whoever eats must work. Didn't the great comrade Karl Marx say: "He who does not work, neither shall he eat."

So *Babushka* was shot, together with all the other "traitors" and "fascists," those shirt-washers and sock-menders and even the old man who had gone so far as to cut wood for the mess. And because they had cried and clung to her skirt, the four children had had to accompany their grandmother on her last long journey.

Silently, we trooped into Babushka's house, where we took a yellowed old photograph showing her in her younger days from the wall. We sent it as a memento to Rudolf's mother far away in the west.

When, a few weeks later, we were forced to evacuate the village again in order to shorten the front, we pulled the burning embers out of the stove and into the dry straw. No one who came here under the blood red flag of the east was going to find a roof over his head in this house.

At the edge of the village, we stood silent a moment and looked back at the burning house. Rudolf's tattered old shirt fluttered from the gables, engulfed by a cascade of flying sparks. Then we moved off to await the enemy in our new line.

Later that day, I happened to overhear a *Sturmbannführer* say casually: "No need to waste any pity on that scum."

He must have gathered from my expression what I felt: "Maybe you don't agree?"

My throat felt parched, but I managed to say quietly: "*Sturmbannführer*, I don't."

He looked at me in astonishment and then turned and muttered something to his adjutant about German sentimentality. The rest of the men crowded round me and shook my hand in silence.

At about that time I began to notice from the whole attitude of the company that a profound change was taking place amongst our men. Both officers and men of the fighting units were beginning to examine things and to arrive at conclusions very close to my own. It was only in the places where the decisive orders came from that all appeared to remain completely deaf and blind.

However, the severity of the fighting and the stupendous enemy superiority did not leave much time for discussion, let alone thinking. Over and over again we attacked, and again and again we threw back the enemy hordes. But it was always the same story: The enemy yielded under our pressure, but thrust forward again on either flank, forcing us to give ground to avoid being encircled. Our losses were heavy, because our blood could not make up the missing East Wall, with its concrete pillboxes, deeply echeloned trench lines and strongpoints. What tremendous stories, both official and unofficial, had been concocted about that wall. And though it would not have surprised us to find that things were not exactly what they had been made out to be...to find nothing, nothing whatsoever, nothing but this fantastic make-believe story—that was too much.

For the first time, I was overcome by fear. I felt like a man deserted, fighting in a hopeless cause; and with me the entire German Army in the East. In front of us a pitiless, treacherous enemy, quick to exploit his every chance, and behind us a command that lacked all understanding of the enemy's real nature and sacrificed every opportunity it had to paper programs and obsolete ideas.

I was faced with the greatest decision of my life. We had received the appeal of Seydlitz and Company, showered down on us in millions of leaflets. The specter of Tauroggen was on the prowl for more souls. The sudden appearance of this "National Committee of Free Germany" and "League of German Officers" came to us in the east, prisoners and fighting troops alike, like thunder from a clear sky. Erich Weinert, German communist leader and writer, and Walther von Seydlitz, the bearer of a great Prussian general's name, had given their names to the organization of an intellectual German revolt behind the barbed-wire fences of the Russian and Siberian steppes. Then, later, a new name began to be heard, faintly at first, but then with increasing force, a name which to the German people personified the fate of hundreds of thousands of our Stalingrad soldiers—the name of *Generalfeldmarschall* Friedrich von Paulus.

There is no denying that this revolt was brilliantly planned and executed. Conceived in the Politburo with all the craft and experience of the old professional agitator and watched over by the revolvers of the Kremlin commissars, its foundations were the two tenets of Bismarck's political testament: Never to expose Germany to the danger of war on two fronts, and support for the traditional idea of a Prusso-Russian alliance, the whole being given luster by the historic Prussian breach of faith at Tauroggen.

Among the millions of German prisoners, the reaction was surprisingly weak, especially among the noncommissioned officers and men. Apart from the thin layer of political opportunists and turncoats, it won very few adherents and those were mostly incorrigible German romantics who derived their inspiration less from the tragic figure of the forsaken Stalingrad Marshal than from the legendary rebellion of *Generalleutnant* Yorck and his officers.

Among the German soldiers fighting on the Eastern Front, the reaction was outright rejection and deep contempt.

Nevertheless the galaxy of brilliant names of the officer rebels burst like a thunderbolt on the astounded ears of the German soldiers and prisoners in the east. There was Seydlitz, of course, and *Generalleutnant* Edler von Daniels, *Oberst* van Hooven, *Oberst* Steidle, *Generalmajor* Kortes, *General* Lattmann, *Major* von Frankenburg und Proschitz, *Major* von Knobelsdorf-Brenkenhoff, *Oberleutnant* Gerlach. And since the Soviet strategists naively believed that the Germany of that time had to have an unknown corporal, there was plain *Gefreiter* Emmendorfer bravely lined-up alongside all that eminence.

But the name that really shook the Eastern Front soldier was that of Friedrich Paulus.

This relatively young general, who had once been Reichenau's Chief-of-Staff and had been appointed personally by Hitler—over the heads of a number of senior generals—to succeed him, had at one time been the most hated of all German generals by the Russians.

It had not been so long since Ilya Ehrenburg, Stalin's personal journalist-in-waiting, had named Paulus the "Butcher of Kharkov" because he had used force to crush an incipient revolt in that city. His *volte-face* was a mystery. Yet not even his example could do anything to lessen the morale of the German Eastern Front soldier.

Behind it all were the grinning masks of Stalin and Kaganovitch, their aim the bolshevization of Europe. It was all too obvious. Even though our way may have been wrong, were we to expose our country, countless women and children, to that threat? Though we were marching to our doom, could we fail to hear the call to duty and loyalty given us by the graves of our comrades, ploughed up and destroyed by the Bolsheviks though they were?

I decided to continue the path, to continue it to the end, however bitter, though with seeing eyes and doing all that was in my power to do. Perhaps a higher power would spare me the results of the defeat and place me with my silenced comrades.

I decided in the knowledge not only that our road was wrong but also our guide. But were we not trapped, were we not caught in a net far more terrible and embracing than anything the Soviet divisions could contrive for us, the net of our own awakening realization?

How was it indeed possible for a person to know everything, to see everything, to feel everything and do everything? This deification works only as long as nothing stronger appears on the scene. But when it does, the lack of a real bond uniting the community has its effect. Because everything waits for the one man, who is expected to work miracles, even though he is only human, with human virtues and human weaknesses; simply a man.

One man may certainly take bold decisions and sweep the whole people along with him. But the same one man may also blunder and err and drag the whole people down with him.

The way of the community, halting and bumpy though it may be, is slower whichever way it leads, uphill or down. The eyes of many see more than the eyes of one; the ears of many hear more than the ears of one. No, never again totalitarianism, that I swore. If only we could once avert this mortal danger, if only we could throw back Bolshevism, then we would unite with all our strength for the revolution of reason. The sacrifices we were having to make at the altar of the *Führerprinzip* were too great.

And back then I still had no idea whatsoever of how great those sacrifices had been.

***

It was just at this period, during the agony of doubt and indecision, that the affair of the dying deserter took place.

We had seen the Russian regiments mown down in front of our machine guns hundreds of times. Hundreds of times, we had been faced by the riddle of this war in the East. How could a people, tortured and oppressed as no others in the world, be so ready to die for their torturers? Of course, we did not find in the Red Army man the same conscious devotion to duty or the same understanding of the ultimate truth that our own men displayed. But that utter disregard of their own lives, that ruthlessness towards their enemy and themselves alike, was a riddle we had never answered.

If the Bolshevist experiment had succeeded in anything it was in the mechanization of living. From the Stakhanovite-influenced worker whose very sleeping and waking, whose laughing and crying, whose meals and digestion must be reduced to a norm if he is to attain his target, to the Red Army soldier and his way of fighting, all things show the triumph of materialism and mechanization. The heart is dead. And the soul of the Russian peoples dies before the muzzles of the execution squad, and yet everything goes on its appointed way in its appointed mechanical order. Though enthusiasm is dead in the men of the Red Army, the men who must pay the reckoning for those whose account is unsettled and likely to remain unsettled for all eternity, these same Red Army men fight and die like wound-up puppets, like robots, for problems that are not theirs and phrases that they have never understood. They die as they have lived—like machines.

We sometimes found that enemy defenders would cover us with a hail of fire from their automatic weapons right up to the last moment and then jump out of their holes, throw away their rifles and ask us with a cheerful grin for *Papirossi* — cigarettes. Sometimes, companies yelling the *Urräh* battle cry would carry their attack to a point just short of our lines and then, what was left of them, would crawl across to us through our fire to offer us their rifles and ammunition. With my own eyes, I have seen Russian prisoners snatch up the rifles lying around to fire on a Soviet bomber that had chosen us for its target, the very same prisoners who, a short time before, had been fiercely and stubbornly defending their line against us.

Dusk was upon us. We were positioned on the slight rise from which we were to carry our attack forward next morning into the frost-covered terrain ahead of us. There was a howling bitter wind that constantly stirred up a dusting of frost. Suddenly, our outposts saw a man fighting his way through the storm. "Don't shoot," the *Unterscharführer* shouted. "Let him come in!" At that moment, shots were heard from the other side, and the man dropped, either wounded or dead. "A deserter," we complained. "Shit!" Shortly afterwards, a patrol of three men crawled out in front of our lines to find him, but they were soon back. Although badly wounded, he had gone on dragging himself towards our lines. The medic examined him and shook his head. Stomach wounds, three of them.

Later in our dugout with his wounds roughly dressed, the deserter waved away our sympathy. *"Nitschevo,"* he said, almost to himself. "Better this way than the other." I lit a cigarette and pushed it between his lips. "Ukrainian?" I asked. He shook his head. He had been a worker in the Urals and had once upon a time believed in the fiction of liberty, equality, fraternity. But that was long, long ago. "But why then," I asked, "are you all so willing to die for the system?"

The mortally wounded man breathed heavily: "That's something you'll never understand, never. The Red Army, the *Robotsche-kristianskaja-krasnaya-armija*—the Red Army of Workers and Peasants—it's like a fly struggling in a spider's web, a web with no end."

As dusk grew deeper and billows of fog rose from the bottom land, he drew for us in his dying voice a picture of this workers' army.

The backbone of the Red Army was not the commanding officer, not even the specialist. It was the *Politruk* or, to give him his full title, the *Polititscheski Rukowoditel,* the Political Commissar. In the smallest unit, which was the platoon, his function, according to regulations, was performed by the *Pompolitruk,* who was assisted by what was known officially as the *Informatory,* three or four informers whose identity nobody knew, not even the platoon leader. The *Informatory* was made up of ordinary soldiers selected by the *Pompolitruk* and required by him to report their comrades' every conversation and every move, however harmless. It was practically impossible in the Red Army to say a single word without its getting to the ears of the *Politruk.* The *Politruk* proper worked at the company level; if he had done long service he may have held the rank of a *Starschi Politruk.* In the battalion, the work was in the hands of the *Batalyonnyi Commissar,* in the regiment *(Polk)* of the *Polkowoi Commissar,* who similarly may have held the rank of a *Starschi Polkowoi Commissar.* In the brigade, it was the *Brigadni Commissar,* in division the *Divisionnyi Commissar,* in corps the *Corpusnoi Commissar* and, in a field army, the *Armeiski Commissar pyervogo ranga*—that is, first grade. Over him, he had the *Armeiski Commissar vtorogo ranga*—second grade. On top of this hierarchy of super-informers, all of whom wore an official uniform and were regarded as at least the equal of the officers, sat the Supreme Political Commissar of the RKKA (Red Army), the *Natschalnik polititcheskogo upravlienja RKKA.* All the threads of that endless and deadly web ran together with him. None could escape from it once they were caught in its meshes, and that meant every Red Army soldier, every man, was helpless in the face of this chain of spies and traitors.

"You think you've found a friend and pour out your heart to him," the deserter whispered, "and perhaps he really is your friend. It's just that he is also one of those involuntary bloodhounds, who stir up and hunt the masses of peasants and workers who have been herded together. Suppose he has a heart and doesn't report you. Then the *Politruk* is told by another informer, who perhaps doesn't even know the first, that the two of you have been having a long conversation. Then come the questions. Until finally your friend breaks down and lets out part of what was said between you. That is the end. Next morning you are liquidated."

The sound of a shot came from the distance. "It might be an outpost," the wounded man said hoarsely, "or it might be the *Politruk's* pistol having the final say. You're under the magnifying glass day and night and whatever you do is seen and heard. And then you ask why the Red Army is so ready to die for its hangmen? The net holds us all prisoner, all of us from the greatest to the humblest, from our first steps in the barrack square till our last tumble into the mass grave."

Our shells rumbled overhead and farther down the line an anti-tank gun barked. The dying man turned quiet. But before he left the misery of his wretched life, he opened his eyes once more. "Break it," he whispered, "break open the net, you Germans..." Over by the woods, Red Army men were shouting their last *Urräh* for their Bolshevik masters. But the deserter heard no more. We lay by our rifles and listened to the sound of massed dying.

Chapter Nine: Bridgehead Narva

Right in the middle of the difficult fighting retreat, which was casualty intensive, the news reached me of the death of Franz Roth, one of the most successful combat photographers for the German side in World War 2.

A short while later, orders reached me in the Kirowograd area to move to the capital of Croatia, where a new corps was being formed, the *III. (germanisches) SS-Panzer-Korps.* This formation was to consist mainly of volunteers from the Germanic countries: Holland, Flanders, Denmark and Norway. Its commander was to be *General der Waffen-SS* Felix Steiner[47].

I was both happy and sad to be leaving the Eastern Front after nearly three years. I had often envied my comrades in Italy and France, having the time of their lives in Biarritz and Capri, while we had to spend our days and nights dodging death in the Russian steppe. Yet for all that, I felt a touch of sadness and melancholy. There is a curious haunting quality in the wide Russian landscape. It repels and enthralls at the same moment. It sickens a man and yet leaves him yearning. Even today, after years of unimaginable horror and strain, there is hardly a man who has served on the Eastern Front who does not at some time feel a nostalgic yearning for the unending space of the Russian land and the boundlessness of the Russian character.

---

47   Translator's Note: Steiner was one of the more famous *Waffen-SS* commanders, who had to come to the armed branch of the *SS* via long service in the Army. He had previously commander *SS-Panzer-Grenadier-Division "Wiking"*, which was another formation famous for its complement of Germanic volunteers from all parts of western and northern Europe. Steiner would end the war as a field-army commander and one of the Germany military's most highly decorated soldiers. He went on to defend the reputation of the *Waffen-SS* after the war and became an author in his own write.

But my stay in Croatia was to be short, mercifully short, for it was the same there; the same sorry story of one mistake after the other made by our Command.

***

An order came taking us away from the fertile fields of Croatia away to the far north to "Bridgehead Narva."

We detrained at Jövi and moved by motor march to the narrow bridgehead, which stretched little more than two kilometers wide across the deep blue waters of the Narva.

Columns of black smoke and flame were belching up from the opposite bank just across from Hungerburg, the Estonian seaside resort on the Gulf of Finland, where one of our shells had scored a direct hill on a Russian fuel depot. In front of us, in Narva itself, however, all was quiet. There was a lull all along the front and the silence was oppressive. We felt that all hell might break loose at any moment and shatter this unaccustomed calm.

Soon we began to encounter roadside warnings: "Road under enemy observation." "Warning! Road under artillery fire!" A column of wagons drawn by small, shaggy horses moved unconcernedly down the dangerous stretch of road. Then shells began to drop on either side of us, but we got through unharmed. We made it to an improved road, with the first buildings of Narva on each side. "*Godverdomme!*" a sentry called out, "that was a near one." It was a Dutchman of the Netherlands Brigade,[48] which was standing guard in that area.

Then we entered Narva, that strange and mysterious city of Northern Europe, which has been fought over and stormed so many times in history and has yet survived through the centuries into our own time. Standing between the ambitions of two worlds, Europe and Russia, its walls have forever been ringed by war and destruction.

---

48   Translator's Note: The brigade was officially known as the *6. SS-Freiwilligen-Sturm-Brigade (mot.) "Langemarck"*. It was later redesignated as a division, although it never really possessed more than a brigade's complement of men and equipment.

All that was left of its beauty and splendor was ruin. Barrage fires and bombing had transformed this Pearl of the North into one of Europe's worst rubble heaps. Yet the magic of its past still lived on in some of its winding lanes, in the midst of its shattered houses. The old gate of the city church still vaunted its six skulls and two fiery torches, and the cupids still looked down from the gateway of the Fonne House. The stork standing on one leg on the tower of the City Hall still looked out with distrust towards the east, the origin of the continuous metal greetings of the little Red Father to his "beloved" Estonians.

And towering over all were the twin symbols of this gallant old town: the *Hermannsfestung* and its younger rival Iwangorod, symbols of the struggle which, throughout the centuries, has been inseparable from its life.[49] And now to-day again, Narva was once more the focus of North European history.

The city of Narva was founded in the 13th century by Germanic tribes, principally the Danes, as a bastion against the rising danger from the east. Some time later it was taken over by the Teutonic Knights and enlarged into a major European stronghold against Russia. Its biggest tower, the "Long Hermann", was erected under the Grand Master of the Order, Hermann von Brüggeney-Hasenkampf.

Opposite the fortress rises Iwangorod, massive and defiant, visible proof of Russia's determination never to renounce her claims on Europe. Legend has it that Ivan III, Grand Duke of Russia, engaged for its construction a Greek architect whom he then rewarded for this unique achievement in the Russian north by having him blinded to prevent him from ever again attempting a similar task.

Narva saw the victory of the 17-year-old Swedish king, Karl XII, over a Russian enemy four times his superior; it also saw the crushing

---

49 Translator's Note: "Hermann's Fortress" was erected in Narwa. Ivan the Great had Iwanograd erected as a Russian counterpoint, guaranteeing access to the Baltic for the Russians. The Narva separates the two countries. The author goes on to explain this in greater detail.

defeat inflicted on the Swedes by Peter the Great, who made Narva a Russian town for centuries to come, not unlike Dorpat.[50]

Not until 1918 were German soldiers to march once again into the age-old citadel, only to leave it again in the fatal November of the same year, after which the Bolsheviks occupied the undefended town and installed their terror regime. Then Estonian, German and Finnish volunteers, fighting side-by-side with the regiments of the White Russian General Judenitch, finally beat the Bolsheviks back and pushed on deep into Russian territory.

Estonia's independence, which the Soviets were then forced to recognize, lasted a short 20 years, after which the hordes from the east again streamed across the Narva and, under thin pretexts of security, occupied the old Estonian and German lands. In August 1941, it was once more the German soldiers' turn to throw the enemy back across the Narva, northern Europe's eternal bulwark against the east, and pursue him eastwards towards Leningrad.

After the many German withdrawals and the shortening of the front, Narva had once again become the gateway between Europe and the east, just as it had been 700 years before. In dugouts and trenches, in pillboxes and out in no-man's-land, men in the ranks of the *Waffen-SS* from all the Nordic countries were fighting side-by-side with Estonian volunteers for the survival of Europe. Thus Narva remained, right into our own troubled times, what it had been for centuries past: The key to northern Europe. The future of our continent would be decided there. This was the dividing line of the world.

But we were not the only ones to realize this; the Bolsheviks did too and launched attack after attack in their bid to win this heap of rubble and thence strike the final blow against northern Europe. Savage air attacks swept over the town and our bridgehead. Sudden barrages were dropped on our line in order to undermine the morale of the defense. Soviet tanks tried to force their way through to the strongly defended riverbank. But it was all in vain. The men whose

---

50   Translator's Note: Dorpat is the German name for Tartu, the second-largest city of Estonia, and another city that was heavily influenced by Germanic life and culture.

176

ancestors had once fought under the Teutonic Knights, who before that had conquered under the Danes and the Dutch, threw back the Russian masses and held the tiny Narva bridgehead like a breakwater in the midst of the red flood, forcing the Kremlin to postpone its grandiose plans for the redistribution of the Baltic regions.

The Estonians fighting for their native land in the ranks of the *20. Waffen-Grenadier-Division der SS (estnische Nr. 1)*, coined a battle cry that became the watchword of the whole Narva front: "Out of the rubble grows revenge."

The Kremlin had little to hope for in that sector.

Fighting together for freedom, side-by-side with the Dutch and Norwegians, the Flemish and the Danes, stood these descendents of the old military frontier established by Prince Eugene, descendants of the old pioneers and settlers from all German districts. From the Banat and the fertile Batschka country, from the forests of Transylvania and the Rumanian mountains, they had come here to the far north in the unaccustomed surroundings of North Estonia to defend their families, their homes and their country, their bloodlines and their empire, and had proven themselves magnificently. Between these men from the southeast and the men from the north and west, fighting together at Narva for the future of Europe itself, there grew a comradeship and a bond, the bond of a common experience, a common danger, a common fight.

***

The Russian shells did not always fall on their target, and despite the best efforts of their gunners, the spire of the city hall, so reminiscent of Amsterdam and Haarlem, still stood proudly intact above its shell-pitted roof.

"It's all the same now whether they hit it or not," said the old washerwoman who acted as mother to the company. "Narva is dead."

The German church had been badly damaged, and only its massive corner buttresses, still blinding white, told of its former baroque beauty, created by industrious hands in the 17th Century. Also in ruins was the ancient Bourse, where once the courage and endurance of sailors, peasants and soldiers had been transformed into golden coin. Of the old apothecary, only the bare front wall was still standing, rather like a bad stage set. Here and there among the rubble of vanished houses stood a gracious old gateway, a striking contrast to the ruins around. The dates chiseled into the facades from more than four centuries told of the wealth of this old fortress town on the Narva.

Quick swallows soared past us, straight and swift as arrows, turned and climbed steeply into the arch of the sky. They came to Narva with the late spring, as they had always come. They had seen the King of Sweden reduce the mighty power of Russia to ruin. They had swooped round the stonemasons building Hasenkampf's "Long Hermann" and soared above the blinded Greek as he cursed the Czar in front of his own creation, the mighty fortress of Iwangorod. They had seen the Hammer and Sickle rise and fall, and German battle standards flying alongside the blue, black and white flag of the brave people of Estonia. And still they came, nothing deterred them: Neither fire nor smoke, neither bursting shells nor the battle cry of men throughout the centuries. War, sorrow and joy came and went and came again. But in the late spring, the swallows returned to Narva.

The iron crosses in the cemetery stood out black against the pale glow of the northern night. Stars twinkled through the roof of the big chapel, shattered by a Russian shell. Golden icons lay scattered about the floor. We picked our way carefully across the churchyard with its flowers and blossoming trees. The narrow path was churned up by shell bursts and many of the trees lay broken and dead across our path. Generation on generation of the burghers of Narva lay buried here in the churchyard of the old Hanseatic and Teutonic town: Germans, Swedes, Danes, Dutch, Estonians. Here and there a White Russian officer or a priest.

The song of the Sprossers, Estonian cousins of the European nightingale, sounded insistent and magical through the grey night. Above us the chug and groan of heavy shells. Forward in the sap, a machine gun rattled. Again the moan of shells, close this time. We threw ourselves down among the graves and the hail of shrapnel spent itself harmlessly above us. As I stood up, my eyes fell on a big cross.

Jacob Nikodemus Budde
Merchant And Seafarer Of Narva, Born 21 May...

The year had been effaced by shrapnel. Only the epitaph was legible:

All Thou canst give, oh Lord,
Hast Thou made mine;
Joy and sorrow,
Work and strife.

Give, oh Lord, to those
who follow the greatest in life:
Joy and sorrow,
work and not least strife.[51]

Some hours later, as I was on my way back to my billets, we decided to make another attempt to decipher the date of this curious dead man. We were spared the trouble, because the cross had been shattered to fragments by a Russian shell.

At the other end of the town, towards Krenholm, two wooden houses were blazing, like giant torches in the morning wind. A small group of Dutch engineers marched down the road, singing. In the middle of the clear morning birdsong rumbled the distant sound of our heavy guns.

The old washerwoman was wrong. Narva was not dead. It lived. Its beauty shone out from its ruins, from the rubble inside the baroque gateways, from the elaborately carved dates, from the haunting charm of its landscape.

---

51   Translator's Note: In the original German: *Alles, was Du geben kannst, oh Herr, / hast Du mir gegeben: Die Freud und / das Leid, die Albeit und den Kampf. / Oh gib ouch denim, die nacho uns kommen / des Lebens Größtes: / Die Freud, das Leid, die Albeit und night / zuletzt den Kampf.*

And what gave this old town its life and strength was its age-old unbroken spirit of resistance to the east.

***

We were positioned close to the enemy, in places no more than 35 meters from their lines.

Dead silence reigned in the narrow strip of shell-torn land between us and the Soviet sap. Only occasionally did a heavy shell rumble across our positions. Once in a while, off to the right, we heard the rapid staccato of the "Hitler siren", as the Russians called our machine gun[52]. Then silence, heavy and oppressive, dropped again over the spectral landscape. Rain fell in a steady monotony out of a pale grey sky. Water stood knee high in the trenches and gurgled over the edge of our rubber boots.

Undeterred by the weather, men stood here and there in the trenches gazing motionless towards the Russian line. For hours at a time, sometimes the entire day. Often alone, sometimes in pairs, one with the field glasses, and the other resting to save his strength for the strike.

A youth's eyes gazed hard and cool towards the enemy trench. From the corner of his mouth came the whisper: "Nothing out of the ordinary to report." Two men were walking, bent and stooping, along the trench towards us. They straightened a little as they passed and, in the same moment, a sharp report rent the sodden air like the crack of a whip. We ducked. Who wanted to die in the dreary grey of a wet morning? Again the deathlike silence came down and we went on our way. But the sniper team in the front line at Narva stood motionless, gazing into the coming day.

There were more of them farther along the line, this time two boys from Transylvania, Rudolf, aged 19, and Michael, aged 24. We talked to them about their homes, about the war, about everything.

---

52 Translator's note: Undoubtedly referring to the *MG42*, which was capable of firing up to twenty five rounds a second for a short period of time.

Rudolf's father was a hunter, his brother a hunters; he had it in his blood. Put a gun in his hand and his eye looked for a target. Michael had seen his first hunt while still a boy. Now they were back at hunting stand, but here the quarry fired back. "We only have to fire occasionally, but we have to hit when we do," Rudolf said, his eyes alight. "Otherwise we give ourselves away."

A Bolshevik showed himself in the opposite trench. A quick aim — crack! He fell forward. Had he been hit or had he merely ducked for cover? More hours of waiting and then at last a target. Another shot. The man on the other side stopped and finally tilted over backwards. A pencil mark on the wooden dugout walls. That one counted. I asked what they thought about as they stood there crossing them off one after the other: "That guy won't be shooting at my comrades any more or at me."

Sometimes the opposite numbers across the way spotted one of our snipers. Where was he? Once the target was sighted, a duel developed in which every conceivable trick was used, every scrap of cunning. A whole magazine might be fired off from a feint position, then a quick dash back to the old stand to see if the enemy would reply. Once the position was located it was usually the end of the duel. Sometimes, it was our man who lost. Then another took his place as the eyes of the forward line, behind whose vigilance the others could afford to relax.

***

One evening, in this bitterly contested Narva bridgehead, we had an experience that instantaneously showed us something of the Soviet mentality.

In the falling dusk, Dutch and ethnic German SS grenadiers stood at the parapet, watching tensely out into no-man's-land. The Russian barrage had lifted, and they would be coming at any moment. A pale fog billowed out of the vegetation and the spit of woods. In front of us, Ivan was laying smoke to cover his attack on our company's forward position. Nevertheless, our bullets were soon cutting like a swathe into his ranks from all sides. Artillery laid a barrage beyond them, and the remainder of the force that had penetrated our position was flung back at the point of the bayonet. A few dozen Red Army men had paid with their lives for Stalin's world revolution.

Some time later, one of our patrols went out to reconnoiter towards the woods, where we had seen strange lights flickering. They oriented on them. They stopped in surprise at the sight of the first of the enemy dead, who lay only a short distance in front of our lines. The bodies were charred and burnt. Farther on they could see fires still burning in the grey night. Was one of them moving there? The Dutchman bent over him, but he was dead. Then the *SS* men realized what had happened. When the commissars saw that they could not bring in their dead—and probably even the badly wounded—they covered them with gas or some other flammable and set them alight.

Forward, comrades! World Revolution is waiting!

And when the moment comes, a bottle of gas and...burn faster, comrade! Burn faster. Papa Stalin not only needs your life, he especially needs your death...

***

The next morning I had orders to report to *SS-Brigadeführer* Wagner[53]. A new division that had just been formed—the *14. Waffen-Grenadier-Division der SS (galizische Nr. 1)*[54]— was in urgent need of officers and noncommissioned officers.

I was posted to it; probably because somebody had remembered my feelings towards the peoples of the east. Anyway, I was to take charge of a platoon immediately. The division was to fight in Gali-

---

53   Translator's Note: *SS-Brigadeführer und Generalmajor der Waffen-SS* Wagner was the commander of the *SS-Freiwilligen-Panzer-Grenadier-Brigade "Nederland"*, the soldiers to which the author was assigned at the time. Wagner was a recipient of the Oakleaves to the Knight's Cross as commander of the Dutch. After the war, he was tried and executed in Belgrade (5 April 1947).

54   Translator's Note: The division was primarily formed from ethnic Germans and Ukrainians.

cia.[55] The only pleasant part about it as far as I was concerned was that I would be travelling by way of Vienna and would be able to see my wife.

My farewell from the Dutchmen was affectionate, almost tearful.

---

55   Translator's Note: Generally speaking, Galicia can be considered an ethnic enclave of the southwestern portion of the Ukraine.

Chapter Ten:
Fighting in Galicia

Back in Vienna, I was surprised to find what little idea most people, even my closest relations, had of the true situation in the east. They talked all the time about our wonderful new weapons, the secret weapons. When I ventured to point out that we had never actually seen any, badly needed as they were, I was brushed aside impatiently with gestures of disbelief. It even went so far that I almost came to blows with my father-in-law, who was an old captain in the militia. They all knew the situation so much better than I or my comrades did, although we were unfortunate enough to represent the Eastern Front. The accounts I gave of our acts of injustice and political insanity met with a flat disbelief. Resentful, I held my tongue.

As so often before, I felt a sense of relief to be moving east again. It was in Cracow that I first heard the fantastic rumor that things weren't too good in Lemberg (Lvov). It was then my turn to disbelieve. Wasn't Lemberg supposed to be the great strategic defensive focal point—of immense psychological importance—for Galicia and the Galician *SS* division? I tried to find out more about it but there was no more information to be had. To be on the safe side, I cut my stay in Cracow short and was on the move again a few hours later. One station outside of Przemysl, the old, historic fortress town of the Hapsburg Monarchy, the train suddenly stopped and a *Major* appeared accompanied by a horde of military police, all in steel helmets and shouldered submachine guns. A fine martial sight, almost too martial.

"Combat teams are being formed here to seal off a temporary breakthrough."

The men on the train looked at each other knowingly. So there was something wrong at Lemberg, after all. I made my apologies to the *Major* and showed him my movement order and special pass. He was equally apologetic, but said that no exceptions could be made. I pointed out that I was headed for the front, not for the rear, but I was wasting my time, this *Major* was as keen on getting every last private as the devil is for an available soul. We were crowded together in bare and gloomy quarters and left for hours with nothing to do but hang around and sleep. I was in a furious temper. Then, towards evening, we were entrained again and eventually headed off for Przemysl. At first, I decided to make a break for it, but on second thought realized that I would probably be unable to get through alone—although you could never be sure by then whether there really was an emergency or it was just a flap with people throwing their weight around.

At Przemysl, we were put into a large barracks, which at least gave us room enough to stretch out on the floor. During the night, an air-raid alarm was sounded and orders came round for all ranks to leave barracks and take cover in the trenches outside. Somewhere in the distance tracer shells sprayed up from a lonely battery, and one or two tired Soviet aircraft crawled across the sky. A few small bombs were dropped a long way off. The whole thing reeked of the rear area. The language among the men and officers was colorful, to say the least. We went back to our rooms long before the show was over.

Next morning, there was still no news. Our numbers had grown to at least 3,000 men. If there really was an emergency, why on earth were we not formed into units and sent to the front? In any case, there was no firing to be heard and a breakthrough without artillery was something new to me. Then, at last, companies and platoons began to be formed, and I was detailed as a platoon leader. For the first time I noticed that I was the only member of the *Waffen-SS* in the garrison.

Once again, nothing happened. We lounged around the parade ground between the barracks and the other buildings, bored to tears. Strident military marches blared out of the radio all day. Suddenly, an icy silence fell over the garrison.

The words echoed clearly from the loudspeakers: "...a great crime prevented...the attempt failed...the *Führer* unhurt...the criminal revolt crushed."

General uproar followed, in which only the officers were silent. Wild denunciations and reproaches were leveled against the officers who had contrived the plot. I said nothing. I was too shaken by the news. Gradually, I became aware of an empty space forming around me. I stood alone, and knew that it was my uniform they were drawing back from. It was like a vision, lasting perhaps two or three minutes. Then they all began talking to me hurriedly and eagerly, as if to erase the impression. But I was able never to forget it.

The music went on without a break. Then Goebbels spoke. About an hour later, as I was looking through the barbed-wire around the garrison, beyond which we were not allowed to move, not even for a walk, I suddenly saw a *Hauptsturmführer* whom I knew driving past in a vehicle. In desperation, I shouted out to him. He recognized me, stopped and went straight to the *Major* on my behalf. Ten minutes later, I was released from this curious "combat operation." The *Hauptsturmführer* invited me to lunch and promised to get me transport to Lemberg. He told me that the new Galician division actually was encircled and that there was heavy fighting in the outskirts of the western Ukrainian capital.

***

Lunch brought a great surprise. The only other guests apart from myself were a Russian general, a close associate of Vlasov, and his young wife. She spoke fluent German and with her help, the general and I started an animated conversation. His attitude to our political mistakes was also one of resignation. "You've made these mistakes and are still making them," he said softly, "because, in spite of all your high-sounding phrases, you still don't realize the peril of the situation, both for yourselves and Europe. Bolshevism is something consistent and absolute. But you only talk about it and go on playing around with something between good intentions and indifference. Take the case of Vlasov himself. After he had already been chosen to become an ally of yours in the fight against Bolshevism, he went to the supply room of the camp he was in to ask for a replacement for the ragged trousers he was wearing. The supply sergeant initially bawled him out indignantly, and then gave him the trousers. I always think of that story as illustrative of your eastern policy."

He paused a moment and then went on: "Do you realize that three million Russian prisoners of war starved to death in the winter of 1941? I don't know whether it was some diabolical plot to annihilate us 'sub-humans,' or perhaps an administrative blunder or perhaps only your famous indifference, which strikes me as almost Russian. If it was deliberate, then why didn't you save the anti-communists, and deliberately liquidate the representatives of the Bolsheviks? That's what Bolshevism would have done in your place. Why didn't you just shoot them all systematically, or poison them or get rid of them some other way? As it is, you've got millions of innocent people on your conscience, hundreds of thousands of them probably deserters, and you've lost the sympathy of the Ukraine in the bargain. But the Communist Central Organization goes on working quite happily and almost untouched. But let's suppose it was all a mistake. After all, that's not impossible. But where are the guilty? Where are their gallows? Punishment of these people might have given a new boost to popular feeling. But no, these incompetent fools were allowed to remain and the most valuable political capital in the east was sacrificed to a pack of villains. Do you know what Bolshevism would have done in your place? It would have let these millions starve just the same, perhaps twice as many. But then it would have staged a show trial of its own agents, convicted them of deliberate sabotage on behalf of the enemy and then had them solemnly executed. But you'll never learn. And that's why you're where you are today."

I said nothing for some time. Our host was obviously embarrassed, because he too had no serious counterarguments to offer. Eventually I asked: "If this is the case, *Herr General*, then why have you thrown in your lot with us?"

He looked at me with his large, dark eyes before he spoke in a melancholy fashion. "Because I know Bolshevism, that terrible synthesis of madness and crime that holds my poor, unhappy people in its grip, all because our fathers once made the same mistakes that you're making today. Your eastern policy has forced on every Russian a terrible choice—Red Bolshevism or Brown Bolshevism, Nagan pistols or Mausers—and if there has got to be torture, suffering and death, most Russians, however much they hate the Kremlin, will choose the

Bolsheviks, because they can at least talk to them in their own language. You mustn't delude yourself that those of us who've decided for Germany have done so out of love for you. We haven't; we've done it because we know that there isn't a hope of gaining freedom for Russia from within. We'll be satisfied with the part of Russia you leave us. Or if we aren't, then we'll fight against you for Russia's freedom once the Red plague has been stamped out. But even if you Germans lose your war, we Russian patriots will not give up the struggle. Don't forget: We're not fighting for Germany, but for Russia."

***

That conversation had moved me more that I let on.

Later that afternoon, the *Hauptsturmführer* put me in charge of an ambulance, which I was to take up to my division. With two drivers, neither of whom spoke a word of German, I set off shortly afterwards for Lemberg, which I reached in the middle of the night. When I arrived, shells from medium Russian artillery were dropping in the streets and alleys of the town and small groups of Martin bombers droned high across the night sky. There was not a single soul to be seen, far and wide. Neither civilians nor German soldiers. We drove slowly and cautiously through the streets of the dead city. In the light of our blacked-out headlights I finally saw two unguarded German vehicles parked in front of a big building. I had the ambulance stop and pushed open the gate to the house. I heard the sound of carousing and raucous singing coming from an apartment on the second floor. Inside the flat I received a rowdy welcome; an *Untersturmführer*, whom I knew, a *Hauptscharführer* and three Ukrainians were having a good time. Like me, they had been trying to find the division and, tired of their search, had settled themselves down comfortably in a deserted apartment that had once belonged to a German officer.

My drivers and I sat down and joined the others at the big table. About an hour later, I began to inquire about the situation from the *Untersturmführer*, who was quite drunk by then. But he knew as little as I did, having arrived from the same direction as I had only a few hours earlier. I was gradually beginning to feel thoroughly uneasy about the whole affair. I slowly walked out into the corridor. As I left the apartment, I heard another door closing quietly behind me and, from the floor above, came the unmistakable sound of soft footsteps. Out in the street there was still no sign of movement. A few buildings were on fire in the distance, coloring the sky with a deep glow, and a salvo of rockets from a "Stalin Organ" crashed down a few blocks away. Several bursts of heavy machine-gun fire came from somewhere close at hand.

I went back to the apartment and tried to persuade the *Untersturmführer* to make an attempt at establishing contact with our own fighting elements. But he would not hear of it at that time of night, it was too late. So I left the revelers to it; in any case, they were hopelessly drunk by then. Out in the dark corridor, I heard the same creak of a door. I stopped and pulled out my pistol. "Where are you going?" asked a faint woman's voice, speaking the hard German of a Ukrainian. "There's death waiting outside. None of us can escape it. But tonight...tonight we're still alive..." A hot, almost feverishly hot hand groped its way under my arm. "Come in with me, German." After some hesitation, I followed the pressure of her hand into an apartment, which was as dark as the corridor outside. I struck a match, but she blew it out immediately. "Why do you want to see? " she asked and led my uncertain hands to her firm breasts. "I'm young and yet I've got to die."

"Why don't you get away then?" I whispered back.

"My mother is very ill," she said quietly, "she would die if I left her, so we'll just die together. It's better that way."

"For God's sake, why do you keep talking about dying? " I said irritably, trying to shake off the gloom that lay heavy on me. "You're an Ukrainian, and they're your own countrymen who're coming."

The young woman laughed softly. "I've loved a German. They shot off both his legs and he was taken away, far away to Germany where he has a wife and two children. I shall never see him again. I've loved a German, and the NKVD shoots women and girls for much less. Come, stay with me; it's my last night. You needn't be afraid," she added eagerly. "I'm not ill, I'm not a…I was a medical student when the war started, and he was a doctor at the hospital. Stay with me, just because you are a German. I'll be able to feel him saying goodbye to me through you, and then everything will seem all right…"

As I took her in my arms, I felt a flood of tears streaming uncontrollably down her face. It was nearly morning when I stood up and, without a word, groped my way out into the dark corridor. Over in the other apartment, I gathered up the young officer, who by that time was completely out, and had him carried into the ambulance, which was the only vehicle still outside the door; the other two had gone. Out in the street, I encountered one of our patrols, which told me that our division was in action to the south of Lemberg. The rest of the men with me piled into the ambulance and we moved off, driving in a general southerly direction. As we were leaving the city, we missed our road and got too far over to the east into a working-class district of residences. Street fighting was starting to flair up on the outskirts of the city.

There was no German soldier to be seen far and wide. Only civilians were standing in front of the buildings, dark and aloof. I asked for directions. Nobody answered for a moment, and then one man pointed firmly in a direction, which my compass told me would take us even farther east. I asked him if he was sure it was right and he answered affirmatively. The rest of them confirmed what he said, all except a young girl—she must have been about 14—who looked at me hard and gave an almost imperceptible shake of her head. I cautiously moved out in the opposite direction, and ran into a Flak position a few minutes later, where we were directed on our way. We moved off again, this time in the direction of Przemysl. On the way, I stopped several times to take wounded aboard.

***

In Przemysl, I received the unhappy news that my division really was surrounded. I was given a dispatch to the general and ordered to make my way through at all costs. Using a motorcycle with a sidecar I set off late in the afternoon out into the Galician countryside, once again with a Ukrainian driver who knew no German.

It was a gorgeous evening. The sky arched in a deep blue over the shining gold of the harvest fields, almost as though the whole countryside had hoisted the blue and gold colors of Ukrainian freedom in defiance of the menacing rumble of the guns moving in from the east. The oncoming night was only signaled by the rising misty veils from the steep mountain slopes of the nearby Beskides and the endless forests of the distant Carpathians. The road beside us, ahead of us and all the way back behind us was full of refugees—an endless procession of creaking and groaning carts, crying children and cattle lowing in their longing for rest and their lost stalls. Dust covered and motionless, the people squatted and sprawled among the scanty remains of their worldly goods, gazing all the time ahead of them to the west, always west. An old Galician peasant trudged past clutching his new plough, guarding it like a precious treasure. The Lemken, in their close-fitting white trousers, standing in front of their huts and gazing wide-eyed on this procession of misery and despair, gave the old man a slow farewell nod as he passed. What indeed would Galicia have been without the plough? A young woman from Podolia held on desperately to a yellowed Madonna, which she was carrying under her arm. Both of her children, she told us, had been killed the day before by Russian aircraft. Ukrainian police in black uniforms, the blue and gold cockade on their caps, guarded the column. From away in the distance came the monotonous thunder of battle, and here on the road was the monotonous rumble of the westbound carts. Up and down; up and down. But always onward, onward towards the west.

***

Up and down; up and down; it is the history of Galicia itself, this country between the fertile black earth plains along the Zbrucz and the dark pine forests of the Carpathians and the sunny slopes of the Beskides. Always the sport of others, but ready ever again to maintain itself by its own strength. And ever again thrown back into the cauldron of war, plunder and violent death. Down through the centuries, ever since the day when the legendary Daniel Romaowitch had himself crowned king of the Galician and Lodomeric peoples in the castle at Halicz, the struggle for the independence of this fertile country has been kept alive.

The German victory of 1939 saw the dawn of a new era of re-construction for Galicia, except, of course, for the districts on the Russian side of the San River demarcation line, which became once again the scene of brutal pacification, arrests, deportations and murder. This terror lasted until 1941, when despite the many mistakes we made when in this area, though not on the same scale as farther east, it was almost forgotten in the general wave of rejoicing which swept the country. Galicia became a new gateway into Europe, through which passed the golden flood of its own rich harvests, and it was to find its place in the sun at last. But death was on the march from the east again and trampling like a ravaging beast over Galicia's peaceful farms, villages and cities. Once again, its blue sky was dark with the smoke and stench of burning homes and, once again, the Ukrainians of Galicia were dying for no other reason than that fate had made of them a human frontier between east and west.

And so the people of Galicia were fighting side-by-side with the Germans in a desperate attempt to defend their homeland. The whole country was up in arms. As mothers and children, women and old men drug their carts in endless columns towards the west, the men and boys picked up spade and gun. Galicia's road to peace and happiness had again grown longer, for the dice of history were now rolling in the Beskides and the Carpathians, in the Balkans, up north in Latvia and along the Narva.

**

Just outside of Grossno, we encountered a tall and powerfully built *Oberst*, a Knight's Cross recipient, standing on the crossroads. Around him were a couple of young *Leutnants* and senior noncommissioned officers. All of them with hand grenades tucked in their belts and submachine guns shouldered. Damn, I thought, surely Ivan hasn't got this far?

A *Leutnant* examined my papers: "I'm sorry, I'm afraid you can't pass."

At that moment, the *Oberst* walked across and I gave him a brief account of my mission. "All right," he said, "you'll be able to go on later. But stay here for the moment and attach yourselves to us."

I obeyed his order, still very mystified by what was going on. Shortly afterwards, an artillery battalion came rattling up to the cross-roads: Guns, limbers, ammunition column, everything complete and in apple-pie order. The *Oberst* halted them. "Where are you going? "

A plump *Oberstleutnant* turned his head slightly. "Assembling in Cracow, *Herr Oberst*."

The *Oberst* did not move a muscle. "You will remain here. My liaison officer will show you into position."

"Sorry, *Herr Oberst*, afraid you're mistaken," the battalion commander smiled. "We're going to Cracow."

Sub-machine guns were raised, and the *Oberst* took direct aim at the artillery commander. "You will take up position here. Army group orders. If you attempt to move on, I will arrest you as a deserter."

The *Oberstleutnant* grew as pale as a sheet, but he turned without a word and followed the young *Leutnant*, who was to direct him into position.

We waited at those crossroads for four hours, halting column after column. Most of them were happy enough to find themselves again under a command that knew what it was after and had not lost its head. A few showed signs of resistance, but all obeyed in the end. Months later, I heard in the Armed Forces Daily Report that our line in the Grossno area was still holding and that we were inflicting very heavy losses on the enemy. That was all the work of a single man who was courageous to the marrow of his bones. He was not just a person who wore a uniform; he was a soldier from head to toe.

***

Late at night, we moved on. Gradually, the military columns and the long lines of refugees thinned out until finally we saw no more. We drove on and on. Just before dawn, we overtook a squadron of

193

cavalry moving west, their horses plodding slowly and tiredly down the road. A light battery was firing close by, and I concluded that we had to be at the main line of resistance shortly. Suddenly, my blood ran cold. An officer just ahead of me had shouted *"Stoj!* Had he meant it meant for us? My driver gunned the engine as much as he could. We were surrounded by Russians, even the column of riders had been Russian. With great presence of mind, the driver swung his vehicle around into a side road at the other end of which, not two hundred yards away, we saw to our horror more Russian cavalry cantering past on a road parallel to the one we had just been on.

At that precise moment, our engine stopped. I shouted to the driver: *"Dawai, dawai!"* But he merely shrugged his shoulders and said laconically, *"Maschine kaputt."* My heart stopped. I immediately ripped my overseas cap with its death's head insignia from my head and turn up my collar with its *SS* runes. Meanwhile, the driver had begun to tinker with the engine, apparently oblivious to our peril. With painful slowness he took out the spark plugs one-by-one one and blew on them to clear away the accumulated dirt. I released the safety of my sub-machine gun and armed the first hand grenades. I summoned up all the soldier Russian I knew and asked in despair: *"Schto takoj?"* — "What's wrong?" He gave another shrug and went on fiddling. Then he put the plugs back in and hit the starter, whereupon the engine roared to life. The Ukrainian was beaming from ear to ear. We moved on and found ourselves moving steadily deeper into the enemy formations. It gradually grew light and correspondingly more uncomfortable. Even though we stuck to forest roads and country lanes, the whole area was teeming with Russian infantry.

While this was going on, a tremendous drama was being played out far away to the east in the area round Rutky and Brody. Ukrainian troops, fresh from the training area where the division had been formed had been put into the front line. Initially, it had only been intended to pull security duties behind the front or conduct anti-guerrilla operations. Their first experience of war was one of broken and retreating German soldiers, the soldiers on whom they had built their whole future, their lives and the safety of their country. Nothing could have been better calculated to destroy their morale. Those

Galicians of the western Ukraine, moreover, lacked the hardness of the Russians, being closer in thought and feeling to the West than the East, largely as a result of their ties with the old Austrian monarchy. The Russians launched a massed attack. The senior command under *General* Lindemann and, presumably, our divisional commander, who had been a police general in peacetime, lost their heads to the same extent. In a very short time, the Bolsheviks had succeeded in encircling a whole army corps with comparatively weak forces.

The Ukrainian officers received little or no help from their German brothers-in-arms, for reasons which any soldier, would quickly appreciate. Whenever a new division was formed, existing divisions were required to transfer to it a number of their officers to provide a cadre. Naturally, no divisional commander was ever prepared to part with his best officers. Consequently, those transferred were either those who were not seen in a favorable light or who were known to be of lesser quality. In short, those whose presence could easily be spared, even if the divisional commander did not exactly wish to be rid of them.

Consequently, it happened that leadership was at its worst in these new, non-German *SS* divisions. There were exceptions of course, but they did no more than prove the rule. Anyway, it was certainly the case with the Galician division. To make matters worse, the division commander had flown off to talk over the situation with the Commanding General, and the division had been left under the temporary command of a young and very brave officer who, at that late stage however, had no hope of making good the errors that had been committed.

It was not long before word went around: "Every man for himself!"

The Ukrainians, officers and volunteers alike, picked up their pistols and guns, not to fight it out to the last drop of blood, but to commit suicide.

After that failure of the command, a few determined young officers took matters into their own hands and attempted to break out with small groups of men. Their attempts were successful. What, one might ask, would have become of the encirclement, if the command had kept its nerve and resolution?

As it was, less than 10,000 out of the 100,000 men of *XIII. Armee-Korps* escaped from the ring. The Ukrainian division suffered particularly heavy losses.

Meanwhile, high up in the Carpathians, the *Banderovzi* were trying to raise men for their army of irregulars. They rounded up and disarmed the fleeing German troops—without doing them any harm—and used the arms they thus acquired to equip their volunteers in the fight against Bolshevism.

In the general flight, I also made my way with a detachment of Ukrainians back to the foothills of the Carpathians, where we suddenly found ourselves face-to-face with a group of heavily armed irregulars, their rifles pointed at us.

"Where are you going?"

"Ungvár."

"We are *Banderas*. Hand over your rifles."

My Ukrainians replied that they were also fighting against the Bolsheviks. The partisan leader was completely taken aback to find himself talking to his own countrymen and tried in a torrent of words to persuade the Ukrainian *SS* men to join him. But my men refused and, in the end, the partisans simply let us go on. In Zserdny, I found the division's contact point and reported to the commander. The general mood was as might be expected, the German officers rivaling each other in cursing the Galician volunteers, probably for not doing what they themselves should have done. The commander of the division finished up by receiving the Knight's Cross from Himmler—for gallant conduct. Those in the know had a good laugh. There was nothing else we could do.

To my great relief, I was reassigned just as the tattered remnants of the division were being reconstituted at the training area.

The fatal 23rd of August 1944 found me in the Carpathians. Rumania was lost. That was all I could gather from the first confused radio reports. The Rumanian Army was in a state of complete disintegration, the 3rd Frontier Guard Regiment having enjoyed the dubious honor of being the first to go over to the Russians. A vast rabble of the Rumanian Fourth Army under the command of the inglorious General Rakovita was pouring back from the line with only one thought: To get out of the war and go home. The German troops were betrayed and left in the lurch. Many of them stayed on and fought to the end in hopeless positions.

Only a few days before, in defiance of reason, the German ambassador in Bucharest had still been reporting to Hitler that the warnings given by the German Armed Forces and German Secret Service about a Rumanian plot were completely without foundation. Shortly afterwards, he shot himself in the besieged German Embassy at Bucharest.

Of course, the capitulation brought no peace for the Rumanian soldiers. They had to march—once again back to the east—but this time disarmed, an army without hope. Altogether, a million and a half Rumanians went east as slave laborers of Bolshevism. Vast numbers of officers were arrested and shot, and Ana Pauker[56] operated in the background of the Rumanian plot to capitulate.

Moscow's puppet regent, Macici, now delivered up his peace-hungry fellow countrymen to the Soviet slaughter machine and, in the "Trudor Vladimirescu" Division, they were committed as cannon fodder against the rifles of the desperately fighting German divisions, where they died like cattle in a slaughterhouse.

With the Rumanian capitulation, all resistance to the Red Army collapsed in the Dobrudja and Walachia areas, and two mechanized corps of the Red Army then advanced on Bulgaria, a country with

---

56 Translator's Note: Ana Pauker was a Jewish Rumanian Communist, who spent much of the war in exile in the Soviet Union later returning to assume positions of responsibility within the re-emergent Rumanian Communist Party.

which Russia was not even in a state of war. After a perfunctory declaration of war, the invasion began. A brief Kerensky act was put on with the aid of a renegade general and the left wing Prime Minister Georgieff.

The army was the first victim. Its officers were shot in a steady stream as "fascists" or else escaped the firing squad by committing suicide.

The stage was then set for the fighting for the Hungarian plains.

***

By then, the outcome of the war had already been decided and nothing could have saved us, nothing short of that great German miracle for which so many millions fervently hoped and prayed. This mass faith in the coming miracle was being artificially fostered by the spread of mysterious hints and rumors.

"He'll pull it off all right; he could finish off the world, if he wanted to. He's just biding his time. Our moment will come, you'll see." That was the sort of thing I was hearing again and again from both officers and men, said with the utmost sincerity. My doubts were laughed aside.

People believed in a miracle, because they wanted to, because they simply could not face a collapse. They took refuge in unreality, because reality was written so terribly clearly on the military horizon. Often, I felt myself in a world of fools and heroes. Though the situation was long beyond all hope, deeds were performed through this faith in the coming miracle, which can hardly be matched in the entire history of warfare.

This tide of faith in the secret weapons and the coming miracle sometimes ran so strong as to sweep us along with it, even the most critical and realistic of us: We drugged ourselves in an opium smoke of wishful thinking, but when we awoke and came to our senses, our dreams vanished as quickly as the smoke, leaving behind nothing but a terrible hangover. Despite that, I envied the mass of the people and their faith.

To march to one's doom with eyes wide open put you in such a pit of despair that everything else was easier to bear.

***

On 21 June 1941, Hitler had broken through the Russian defenses of 155 divisions and virtually annihilated the Red Army's armor with his 121 divisions and 3,000 tanks. His plan was bold, bordering on a gamble. But the very boldness of it and the novelty of his tactics and, of course, the supreme courage of his forces fighting in the East, nearly gave him victory in the first round.

Seen against the background of Hitler's strategy, Stalin's generals at that time were not much more than comic-opera soldiers and not a single one of them was up to the task of resisting Hitler's attack. How else to explain the fact that, notwithstanding the dogged and death-defying struggle of the Red Army soldiers, *General der Panzertruppen* von Kleist was able to attack and soundly defeat the 2,500 tanks of Marshal Budyonny with 600 tanks of his own?

At this moment of brilliant German victory, at the height of the triumph of his revolutionary art of war, Hitler committed the two dramatic mistakes of his war. In the first place, instead of acting on the advice of that genius in tank warfare, *Generaloberst* Guderian, and making an immediate and rapid full scale thrust to Moscow, the heart of Bolshevik Russia, Hitler accepted the counsel of his old-fashioned generals who, daunted by the vastness of the Russian space, saw before them the specter of Napoleon and wanted to start by out-flanking, surrounding and destroying the enemy's forces in order to secure their rear.

This showed, of course, that they knew nothing of this new total warfare, with its partisans and guerrilla bands and total mobilization of the whole strength of the people, and that they had even less understanding of Hitler's antipathy to the concept of the "nation." Hitler had long been trying to replace the idea of "nation" by that of "race", and it would have been impossible, even if goodwill had existed, to incorporate the Slavonic, Kalmuck and Tartar peoples of the Soviet Union into Hitler's world. Consequently, the war against

Bolshevism was fated from the start to become a war against the Russian people. That was what led to all the disastrous mistakes that Germany committed in her handling of the Russian peoples: Mass executions, deportations and oppressive administration were simply a natural consequence of Hitler's theory of Nordic superiority.

This in its turn gave rise to Hitler's second major error—fatal for Germany and Europe alike—the creation of the conditions by which Bolshevism could be reborn as a national, Pan-Slavonic force. Everything that followed thereafter flowed inevitably from that major development in political history.

Time, precious time was lost. The autumn of 1941 came, but the German armies had still not reached Moscow. The battle of Vyazma was won by us, but it was a Pyrrhic victory: The roads were already blocked by rain and snow and we had given the enemy time to bring up his Asiatic reserves. Moreover, the German attitude towards the *Untermenschen* was already beginning to have its effect in the attitude of the *Russian* people towards us.

Much has been written, much will be written and yet more talked about what would have happened if Hitler's armies had crossed the marshy, waterlogged and snow-covered steppes on tracks instead of wheels: It might certainly have brought us very much closer to the expected great victories, which already seemed in our grasp. But whether it would have turned the issue remains unknown. The mistakes in our policy towards the Russian people would probably have been too great.

Fate gave us one more chance. Again it was Kleist's armor which, when we reached the western Caucasus and stood before Tuapse and Ordschonikidse, only just failed to swing the scales in our favor. That time it was neither weather nor tracks that stopped us; the war itself was beginning to grow old. Our supply lines no longer worked properly, and Stalingrad, where the *Führer* was convinced our fate would be decided, drained off forces from the Caucasian front which might have signed the Red Army's death warrant.

In the end, Hitler was right. Stalingrad did decide our fate, though not in the way that he or any of his officers and men had imagined.

Our decisive opportunities, two military and one political had been gambled away and wasted. Why and to what end, God alone knew. We certainly did not. Few of us even so much as suspected what had happened. Those of us who did secretly know or thought we knew marched on, fought on, and in many cases died, because we could see no other road open to us.

I myself lived through what followed as if in a dream. A wild and terrible nightmare, from which there was no awakening.

Chapter Eleven:
Battle For Budapest

A short while later, I received my promotion to *SS-Untersturm-führer* and was ordered to go to Budapest on a special mission.

The situation there was gradually becoming impossible. The Regent, Admiral Horthy, had realized that Hitler's account could not possibly balance, and was ready to contract out of the business in order to save his country and his own skin.

To this end he began making cautious overtures to the British, trying first and foremost to receive guarantees against Soviet Russia. At the same time, however, his younger son Miklas, or Miki as he was called, the *enfant terrible* of the Horthy family, also began to dabble in high politics.

Miki's name was none too good with the Hungarians, largely because of his dissipations and wild orgies. Budapest gossip was as much concerned with his extravagant parties on St. Margaret's Island as with his affair with the young Goldberger girl, daughter of the fabulously rich and world-famous Hungarian textile manufacturer.

Idle tongues even went so far as to say that he had not been right in the head since the motorcycle crash in which he had been so badly banged up. That was perhaps an exaggeration. Nevertheless, it was true enough that Miki's father had had to send his black sheep son to Brazil on a "diplomatic" mission long before the war started, in order to allow some water to flow beneath the Danube bridges and over Miki's exploits.

After his return from South America in 1942, Miki had made contact with liaison officers from Tito and had begun to negotiate on the possibility of Hungary getting out of the war, with absolutely no authorization from either the Hungarian people or the Hungarian Government. In time, this information came to the ears of the German Intelligence and a counterstroke was promptly prepared. On the German side, the first steps were taken by *Dr.* Vesemayr, the former German ambassador in Budapest, and *SS-Obergruppenführer* Winckelmann, the Senior *SS* and Police Leader for Hungary. Negotiations were opened and developed with the Hungarian opposition party, the "Crossed Arrow" organization. Its leader, Szálasi, was taken into protective custody, while the other members of the organization began to make preparations for their seizure of power, an event which took place in front of a backdrop of burning Hungarian villages and the cries of Hungarian women raped by the Soviets.

In any event, a stupid incident almost put an end to the whole plot at the last moment. The Germans had arranged for the whole of the Crossed Arrow propaganda material to be printed at a big print shop in Vienna, because the danger of leakage would have been too great in Budapest. The fly bills were to be sent from Vienna to Budapest by truck convoy under the guard of a detachment of Vienna police. And what happened: A bundle of pamphlets dropped out of one of the trucks right in the middle of Budapest and ripped open in the street. On top of everything else, as luck would have it, it was the very parcel that contained Szálasi's proclamation of his assumption of power and his appeal to the Hungarian nation.

The parcel was found by a policeman a week before the historic events were to take place, and he took it to the Hungarian State Police. Then luck stepped in again, on the German side this time, as the official who took charge of the parcel was himself a member of the Crossed Arrow movement. He realized what was at stake and handed the salvaged proclamations to the German Security Service, without mentioning the matter to his superiors.

Meanwhile, the Bolsheviks had succeeded in crossing the Carpathians, despite the desperate resistance of the German forces there and was flooding down into the Hungarian plains. Tension in Hungary grew to breaking point and rumors were soon flying about Budapest that the "Castle" was preparing to cut loose from the Germans. The people were divided; most of them wanted nothing more to do with the war, but even less to do with Bolshevism. So, torn between conflicting emotions and decisions, they let the time for action go by.

Germany, on the other hand, made good use of the Miki Horthy affair. Two *SS* officers, both good linguists, were sent to him, masquerading as two of Tito's generals come to continue negotiations. Miki promptly fell into the trap, probably thinking that Tito was favorably considering his proposals.

During the course of the discussions, which took place in a palace on the Petöfiter, one of the fake Tito generals gave a pre-arranged signal, whereupon German troops, both uniformed and in civilian clothes, stormed into the building. Miki, who had fallen victim to his own intrigue and unlimited naïveté, was arrested and quickly rushed across the frontier into Germany.

In the person of Miki, the German Government then hoped to hold the trump card over the old admiral, who was all the more attached to his problem child since the death in action on the Eastern Front of his favorite son Stephan, an air force pilot.

But this proved a miscalculation. On 15 October 1944, Horthy issued his famous proclamation stating that he wanted to make peace and called on all Hungarian troops to lay down their arms. The hour of decision had come and German troops, led by Skorzeny, the liberator of the Duce, stormed the castle at dawn on 16 October 1944, with only minor casualties on either side. The radio broadcasting station and transportation facilities were swiftly occupied by German forces. A few hours after Horthy had spoken his fatal words, millions of pamphlets rained down over Hungarian cities and villages. The new Hungarian Government of Ferencz Szálasi appealed to the Magyars to fight to the last against the hated *Orosz,* the Russians, and to do everything in their power to defend their homeland.

A few hours after he had called on his people to abandon the Germans, Horthy and his wife, together with the Prime Minister General Lakatos, voluntarily placed themselves "under German protection". In honor of the occasion, Lakatos even put on the Knight's

Cross that Hitler had awarded him as a Commanding General on the Don.

All this, of course, was pure comic opera. But there was nothing comic about what happened at the front. The fighting spirit of the Hungarian troops, never very high at the best of times, collapsed completely after Horthy's appeal. One of the first to get out—in six staff cars and with his mistress and the field army's funds—was the Supreme Commander of the Hungarian troops on the Carpathian Front, Colonel General Miclos Béla; he simply drove straight over to the Bolsheviks. He was stopped neither by his Knight's Cross, which Hitler himself had fastened round his neck, nor by the untold suffering that was then to befall the Hungarian people, especially the women, in the districts the Russians occupied.

What took place in the streets of the Hungarian cities was no less than a comic opera. The followers of the Crossed Arrow movement, long suppressed by the Horthy regime and disappointed in their hopes even by the Germans, had a free hand at last and were determined to exploit their power to the utmost. Their seizure of power was made all the more hysterical and savage by the fact that it took place in the shadow of a gigantic collapse.

The company I commanded had the mission, among other things, of storming the Budapest Broadcasting Station in the Föherczeg-Sandor utca. It was actually more in the nature of an occupation than an assault, as the supporters of the old regime had all disappeared by the time we arrived. Instead of them we had the Szálasi followers around us, all of course falling over each other to get to the microphone.

I had barely sat down in a chair, when my noncommissioned officers reported that a number of extremely suspicious looking Hungarians were talking into the microphone. I promptly ordered everyone off the air, whereupon a whole succession of people began to file into my office all wanting permission to broadcast. My Hungarian was limited to "How are you? " and" Thank you", and I was completely unable to get in touch with my superiors. One young man, from Budapest, carrying no official credentials, was blandly determined to call on the population to murder all the Budapest Jews that same night—a Budapest night of the "long knives".

I was faced with some very difficult decisions. These were all really questions for the Hungarians and were no concern of mine, a junior lieutenant of the *SS*. I decided to take a tough line and had all the microphones put under control, permitting only the official news and government announcements to be broadcast by ethnic Germans under my command.

Some time later, I learnt that an acrimonious complaint about my action had been lodged officially with *Obergruppenführer* Winckelmann, as Senior *SS* Commander in Hungary. Not that I was particularly worried by being officially in disgrace. The guilt for this blood bath would not have been laid on Hungary, but on Germany, on top of all the rest, and not a single soul would have believed that we had had nothing, literally nothing, to do with it.

When, some hours later, I finally managed to get through to Winckelmann and Vesemayr, they completely endorsed the action I had taken. It turned out that I had even stopped the new War Minister, General Berger-Beregffy, from going on the air. However it was better to have been on the safe side.

***

In any case, I was very glad to get away from the broadcasting booth. The Hungarians were beginning to quarrel amongst themselves. The German Government did its best to bring about a coalition of all the right-wing groups, but Szálasi quoted back at them the demand that Hitler himself had made to Hindenburg in 1933—when he had insisted on all or nothing—and, as a result, managed to get away with having only a few outsiders—Count Palffi Fidel, for example, as Minister of Agriculture, and the well-known journalist Ferencz Rajniss as Minister of Culture. All the important ministries went to his own men.

Great dissatisfaction existed among the various groups that had collaborated with Germany, particularly in the *KABSZ*, the Hungarian Legion of East Front Veterans. This organization, which was led by Dr. Karl Ney, a former lieutenant in the Hungarian army and a Budapest lawyer, contained tens of thousands of anti-communist officers and men who, during the eastern campaign, had renewed that acquaintanceship with Bolshevism, which had begun so unhappily with the affair of Béla Kun[57]. These were men prepared to stop at nothing to prevent their country becoming another "Workers' and Peasants' Paradise".

But Dr. Ney and his friends were unacceptable to Szálasi, largely because of their association with the former Prime Minister Imredy, who had been dropped because of doubts about his ancestry. Ney tried many times to offer his services, but the Germans had decided to play other cards, and left him in the discard pile. Szálasi, of course,

---

57   Translator's Note. Additional information concerning this rather obscure Hungarian Communist comes from Wikipedia (http://en.wikipedia.org/wiki/Béla_Kun):

Béla Kun (February 20, 1886 – August 29, 1938), born Béla Kohn, was a Hungarian Communist politician, who ruled Hungary, as the leader of the Hungarian Soviet Republic, for a brief period in 1919...

... It is difficult to overstate the impact of Kun's brief and failed regime on Hungarian history. Though the executions meted out in the Red Terror were, by contrast to other such upheavals, relatively few, shock and horror at Kun's excesses remained deeply imprinted on the Hungarian consciousness for years to come.

One bitter repercussion was the association of Hungary's Jews with the suffering inflicted by the Communists; as Kun and many of his colleagues were seen as Jewish, it was easy for anti-Semitic activists in Hungary to fuel fears of "Jewish-Bolshevist" conspiracy.

Another was the severe rightward direction of Post-Kun Hungary. The election of admiral Miklós Horthy, the chief of the reactionary National Army, as Hungary's regent was a stark political about-face, and the heat of Horthy's anti-communist feelings was legendary. It was partly to keep the "Asiatic barbarians" of Soviet Communism at bay that Horthy gradually helped steer his country into an alliance with Communism's greatest foe, Adolf Hitler. It was a fatal partnership; Hitler would eventually crush Horthy's regime, invade Hungary, and install a puppet government, which helped the Nazis deport more than 400,000 Hungarian Jews to the gas chambers at Auschwitz concentration camp.

Ironically, Hitler's stranglehold on Hungary was finally loosened by the army of the dreaded Soviet Union. After the war, Horthy remained in exile, while the Soviets inaugurated a 50-year Communist regime under the leadership of Mátyás Rákosi, one of Kun's few surviving colleagues from the 1919 coup.

was not prepared to advance the interests of a possible rival in any field, and the result was that valuable Hungarian elements were left completely unused.

But for all these troubles, the Hungarian affair remained our last big success. We had once again been quicker. We had prevented Horthy from waiting until he had received notice from Faragho, his agent in Moscow, that Russia had agreed to the date for Hungary's withdrawal from the war, and had forced him to act prematurely and hence unsuccessfully. We had once again forced our initiative on the course of destiny, and this last bright gleam had illumined the evening sky of our sinking day and thrown a brief rosy light on our fortunes. What followed was nothing more than the prelude to the closing tragedy.

***

The next day the rumor circulated that *SS-Obergruppenführer* Phleps, one of the best *SS* generals, had been killed. At first, no one wanted to believe that.

A few days later, however, I happened by chance to be visiting *Obergruppenführer* Winckelmann's adjutant and found myself holding Phleps' paybook, shoulder boards and Knight's Cross in my own hands.

The story was that this brave and skillful general had, on the *Führer's* orders, left his ethnic German division[58], which was then fighting in Croatia, and had rushed up to Hungary accompanied only by his adjutant. and a driver in order to take over the defense of the southeastern part of the country. Misdirected by a command post,

---

58 Translator's Note: The author is referring to the *7. SS-Freiwilligen-Gebirgs-Division "Prinz Eugen".* According to Veit Scherzer in *Ritterkreuzträger* (Knight's Cross Recipients)(Ranis/Jena [Germany]: Scherzer Militaire-Verlag, 2005, p. 566), Artur Phleps was executed after being taken prisoner at Arad (Rumania) on 21 September 1944. An ethnic German from Transylvania, Phleps was a recipient of the Oakleaves to the Knight's Cross, attained the rank of *SS-Obergruppenführer und General der Waffen-SS* and last served as Commanding General of the *V. SS-Gebirgs-Armee-Korps.*

the party had run straight into the hands of a Russian armored reconnaissance unit and been taken prisoner.

But, as luck would have it, before the surprised Russians had had
time to realize their incredible good fortune, a few German aircraft
had made a chance attack on the Soviet armored column. The Soviet
commander apparently lost his head, and fearing that the German
general might escape in the confusion, shot the defenseless man and
then moved out with his unit.

Some time later, a party of Hungarian gendarmes who were doing a motorcycle reconnaissance of that district were told by some
villagers that they had buried a German general in the neighborhood
a few hours before. Following their directions, the gendarmes went
to the spot described by the villagers and there exhumed the body of
Phleps, which they then reburied after removing his paybook, shoulder boards and Knight's Cross.

And so, after a soldier's life rich in battle and victory, Phleps had
come to a senseless and useless end: As early as the First World War,
Phleps had distinguished himself as a first-class General Staff Officer
in the Imperial Austrian Army. After the collapse of the Hapsburg
Monarchy, Phleps, a native of Transylvania, which was one of the areas handed over to Rumania, was given the task of reorganizing the
Rumanian mountain troops. As a general officer, he later became an
instructor of tactics at the military academy in Bucharest. Then, in
1940, Phleps, as an ethnic German from Transylvania, put himself
at the disposal of the *Waffen-SS* and was given command of a regiment in the East. His thrust into the Kamenka—Dnjepropetrowsk
area made a decisive contribution to the creation of an bridgehead to
the East. From there, he was recalled to take command of the *Prinz
Eugen* division in Croatia, where he later commanded the *V. SS-Gebirgs-Armee-Korps*.

His orders had included a directive to report to the *Führer* on
conditions in Transylvania and Hungary, the area of his new command, and he had therefore decided to personally obtain for himself
the most detailed information, especially about the situation round
Arad and Klausenburg. His intention was to go on the next day by

air to give a factual account of the situation as he found it to the man who not only made the final decisions, but also bore the final responsibility. In the course of his journey, the general who had fought in a hundred battles and skirmishes, died from a commissar's bullet in his back.

***

Meanwhile, the Red Army's operations were being conducted with relentless precision over a very broad front. Marshal Malinovsky, who was one of Stalin's most ambitious generals, was concentrating every man and every unit he could lay his hands on in order to pin a quick victory to his colors. Army upon army of Red Guards—including the Sixth Guards Tank Army—were concentrated in the Second Ukrainian Front; divisions were even brought up in forced marches from the Fourth Ukrainian Front in this bid for a quick decision.

Against this overwhelming superiority, the battered German formations maintained a tenacious and determined resistance. Armored formations from Wuerttemberg, Lower Saxony, Thuringia-Hessia and East Prussia, Alpine troops from Austria and Bavaria, infantry from the Sudetenland and Brandenburg, an *SS* cavalry division and the remnants of the *Luftwaffe*, under the renowned one-legged fighter pilot and tank buster, Rudel, hurled themselves in wave after wave against the oncoming Soviet flood.

But it was all in vain. The ring round Budapest grew steadily tighter.

In the early afternoon of the 29 October, Malinovsky launched his first infantry attacks over a broad front between the Theiß (Tisa) and the Danube, and the battle for Budapest was on.

My unit was holding a sector at Soroksa and Dunaharasti, just outside Budapest. The enemy had already reached the outer suburbs of the city, where his attack had bogged down and he had stopped to recover his breath for the killing blow. We could sense it coming. Behind us, in the lovely city of Budapest, there began a last avid bid for life, a frantic search for pleasure. Despite the Russian shells already dropping in the city and the Russian bombers unloading their deadly freight night after night, every bar and cabaret was standing room only. Rivers of wine, sparkling wine and *barsky* flowed in the luxury hotels along the Danube: The Gellert, the Carlton and the Hungaria. Women gave themselves freely without a thought, and men took what they gave. Anybody who wanted took a 50 *filler* streetcar ride to the front, because the public transportation went on running right up to the end. They could get off only a few hundred meters behind the main line of resistance. The German troops also took advantage of the streetcars when they came out of the line to take a trip to town, bathe, drink or try their luck with the pretty women—or all three at once. It was a war such as we had only seen so far in pulp fiction. But it would be a lie to state that we did not prefer it to the bleakness of the steppe and the icy snowstorm.

***

One morning, we were told by some civilians of a ghastly horror which the Russians had committed in a village just outside Dunaharasti. At the time when the Red Army penetrated, the local watchmaker of this village had had a number of peasants' watches in his house for repair. Despite his entreaties, the Russians took the watches from him and began to look for more, but they found no more because there were none. They threatened him and questioned him, but he could not confess, because he had nothing to confess. So they stripped him of his clothes and sat his naked body on the red-hot stove. He still could not tell them where the treasure was hidden because he had none. So they let him burn, and he died.

We sent out a patrol. They found the village, now deserted, and discovered the body of the watchmaker lying in his plundered kitchen, the flesh of his hands and buttocks charred and hanging off the bones.

Bolshevik culture was on the march into Europe.

The fighting took on even more bestial forms.

In a quiet hour during this Budapest dance of death, I happened to read in a Viennese paper of the mysterious death of my friend

Ernst Handschmann, press chief of the Austrian "illegals" and the gravedigger, in the journalistic field, of Schuschnigg's Austria.

An icy shiver chilled me. I was gradually getting to the point where I had no more living friends. I felt myself encompassed by a ghostly circle of the dead. Other people told me that they had had the same experience. Those of us who were still alive were like dead men on furlough.

It was therefore with no surprise that I heard shortly afterwards of the death of *Gauleiter* Josef Bürckel.

With this man, the last pillar of revolutionary National Socialism was gone. Now that he was no more, I heard again, as if in a vision, his farewell words to me in 1943: "Once we're through with this war, then we must make an end of this miserable substitute for socialism, or..." His eyes had held a fanatic light.

Was it perhaps for the sake of his great ideal that God had spared this man, this German rebel, from the bullets of a French execution squad?

It was with deep emotion that I read the accounts of his funeral, where the major figures of National Socialism showed themselves yet again and for the last time before the public eye.

"*Totentanz* — Dance of Death," reverberated in my ears. "*Totentanz* — Dance of Death" screamed the rounds of the advancing Russian tanks. "*Totentanz, Totentanz*," thundered the bombs of the American bomber formations.

* * *

The enemy crossed the Danube considerably further to the south, threw back the *Hoch und Deutschmeister* division[59] and wiped out

---

59   Translator's Note: = Die *44. Reichs-Grenadier-Division "Hoch- und Deutsch-meister"*. The honorific was a reference to the Grand Master of the Teutonic Knights, with a number of military formations given the title over the centuries. The original *44. Infanterie-Division* was destroyed at Stalingrad. When it was reconstituted, it was redesignated with the honorific and its members were entitled to wear a so-called "Stalingrad Cross" cipher on their should straps and boards.

the 33rd *SS* Division[60], which was still in process of being formed from Hungarians of German ancestry and had so little of its equipment that it had been nicknamed the "Hat" Division. The Red Army was to all intents and purposes in our rear, with the result that our defensive works east of Budapest, which were well constructed and in considerable depth, were rendered completely worthless. It was enough to make a man despair, and I began once again—the first time in months—to think about the way things were being handled. Fellow officers with whom I discussed it were equally shocked by the way the defense of Budapest was being run.

Even the Turks had known that Budapest could be outflanked and that by putting artillery on the hills west of the town, on the Schwabenberg for example, the city could simply be shelled to ruins without risk to the attacker. They had realized as well that a defense that had to fight uphill could be no defense and that in any battle for Budapest it was vital to command the hills and mountains to its west.

The Turks had known all this and acted accordingly. But we did not, and so Budapest was without defenses in the west. There was nothing. One day, I had to conduct reconnaissance in the direction of the and was shocked by what I did not see. It all reminded me so terribly of the Dnjepr. My God! The Dnjepr. That had only been a year earlier, and here we were at the gates of the *Reich*.

Our defensive lines were east of Budapest. But the Russians had read their history books and paid little heed to our defensive lines. Instead, they crossed the Danube in the south and pushed up the west bank, arriving, of course, at the very heart of our Budapest position.

---

60   Translator's Note: The author is mistaken here inasmuch as the 33rd division was the *33. Waffen-Grenadier-Division der SS "Charlemagne" (franz. Nr. 1)*, a formation formed from volunteer Frenchmen and which gained fame as one of the last formations to go down fighting in the Battle for Berlin. The author is most likely referring to either the *25. Waffen-Grenadier-Division der SS "Hunyadi" (ungarische Nr. 1)* or, less likely, the *26. Waffen-Grenadier-Division der SS*, both of which consisted on Hungarian volunteers with a German cadre.

My company was positioned on the Gellerthegy, known in German as the *Blocksberg*. We spent our time practicing immediate counterattacks suited to that terrain. If the enemy's first deadly wave was to be thwarted, then it had to be there. The *Blocksberg*, the castle. The eastern bank could be written off.

Suddenly, an order arrived from out of the blue: "Company to move off in an hour, direction west, along the Vienna road." I passed on the order automatically, my brain reeling. The company *Spieß* was beside himself. It was Christmas Eve, 24 December 1944, and he had arranged for an entire pig and all manner of delicacies—wine, *schnapps*, cake. A fierce low-level air attack burst in over our frantic packing and loading. Machine guns rattled and women and children ran screaming into the cellars in the houses close by. "You'll have to get used to a hell of a lot more of that," I thought sadly. Then we moved out.

As we moved up the broad road, we encountered an *Obergefreiter*, all dolled-up, white gloves, huge bunch of flowers. I called a halt. "Where the hell do you think you're going?" I asked. He grinned broadly. "Going to see my Hungarian mama!"

"Enjoy yourself," I wished him. "Do you know what time it is ?" He looked at his watch and reported in his best parade-ground voice: "Twenty minutes past one." The whole company roared, but it was the humor of the gallows. We had just heard that the city was all but surrounded and that we'd have to run the gauntlet along the Vienna road within the hour. It was still being held open by our tanks, but only with some difficulty.

We had unbelievable luck. A few minutes before we passed the critical spot, low-flying aircraft had caught a Hungarian battalion on the march and knocked the hell out of it. Dead and wounded were everywhere. But when we raced through, it was as quiet as a mouse. Our tanks had thrown back the Russian counterattack, although we did not know it at the time. But it was only to be for a short while. A few hours later, Budapest was surrounded for good.

***

Our new area of operations was the Gran Bridgehead, but not many days had passed before we were pulled out of the line again. Preparations were being made in the greatest secrecy for a new German counteroffensive in Hungary. The well-proven *SS-Gruppenführer* Gille had been pulled out of Russia with the *"Wiking"* and the *"Totenkopf"* divisions[61]. Budapest was to be saved at all costs. We carried out our orders automatically—like robots; we attacked, we held our line.

One morning, the "Viking" tanks broke through near Tarjan and Bitschke and threw the enemy far back, the thrust finally fizzling out in the hilly country north of Lake Balaton. It was a mining district where sympathy had been strong in some sectors for the Bolshevik cause. When the Red Army had been approaching this district, the local communists in one village had formed a procession—Red flag flying high and their wives all in their Sunday best—to go out and meet them. The first thing the Red Army men did was to take away their Red flag and beat up the men for having been "such bad communists and having failed to do anything against the fascists". Then they had looted all their belongings.

The Red Army's morale and discipline being what it was at that time, it goes without saying that the women were also raped there and then on the snow-covered road.

The mayor of the small farming town of Tarjan decided to try his luck with a white flag. Shouldering his responsibility for the community, he went out alone to meet the oncoming Russians. But the Red Army men took off his best Sunday boots and his best Sunday coat and forced him, bootless and in his socks, to trot miserably back through the snow by the side of the Russian captain. On reaching the town, he rushed home, put on his work boots, and immediately

---

61   Translator's Note. The author is referring to *SS-Gruppenführer und General-leutnant der Waffen-SS* Herbert-Otto Gille, the Commanding General of the *IV. SS-Panzer-Korps*, which consisted of the *3. SS-Panzer-Division "Totenkopf"* and the *5. SS-Panzer-Division "Wiking"*. Gille was one of the most highly decorated general officers of the *Waffen-SS*, ending the war with the award of the Diamonds to the Knight's Cross. He also survived the war, living until 26 December 1966.

reported back to the Soviet military administration to continue his duties as mayor.

Before he was allowed in, however, the sentry made him wait while another Red Army man was called, who promptly deprived the unfortunate man of his boots for the second time.

When, at last, the Russian captain deigned to receive the mayor, once again reduced to his socks, he instructed him in the duties he was required to perform. The mayor, who by this time was almost in tears, begged for his boots back, whereupon the captain gave a brief order. A few minutes later an enormous pair of boots arrived, far too big for the poor man, but which he nevertheless put on with a sigh of relief. Afterwards, he found out that a Red Army soldier had simply stopped another Hungarian in the street and taken his boots off him.

"Don't make any mistake about it," the mayor said, serious again after we had laughed ourselves hoarse over his story. "There's no hope of reasoning with these Russians. They don't regard us as human. We're animals, *burshoi,* capitalists, fascists—anything but human beings."

The morale of the Red Army was, in fact, extremely low at that period—and for very good reasons. The vast majority of these Russian factory hands and peasants were sick to death of the war, of its terrible hardships and slaughter. The great morale booster was no longer valid: "Throw the Germans out of Mother Russia" The enemy was gone; the homeland was free. Stalin's "patriotic war" was over.

The ordinary Red Army soldier simply wanted to go home. For years he had been carrying his life in his hands and enduring terrible hardship, and now, as with our own German troops, all he wanted was to be back with his wife and children, back in his home, however primitive it was.

New problems, new methods. The Red Army man had to have his fervor roused, and so the Bolshevik leadership began to play on his human weaknesses. First, greed: "You see that town in front that we're going to attack tomorrow? It's a notorious hotbed of fascism, but there are pretty women there, plenty to drink, good boots, and lots of good food. It's all yours if you go and take it."

In Budapest alone, the invading Red Army men were given a whole week to plunder and rape.

Then hatred: "You see those beautiful houses, those lovely residences and lovely clothes? That's how those capitalist, fascist criminals live. Just think what modest lives your wives and children are leading in the Soviet Union. And how you have to work. And why? Because we had to make arms and yet more arms instead of things for your houses, all because these fascist beasts were going to attack us. They're all alike, all of them: British, Americans, and above all these filthy Germans and Hungarians and their henchmen. We must defeat them. Only then will our wives and children be able to live as well, or even better, than these capitalist swine."

Lastly jingoism: "Now we must make a last effort to fight and win. We've got the whole world before us. We'll rule the earth, nothing can stop us. Let us prove ourselves worthy of our dead comrades, worthy of the October Revolution and the sacrifices that have been made since then. The world, comrades, the world. Forward, Red Army men."

There is no other people on earth so susceptible to propaganda as the Russians. And no other army in the world has such a fiendishly clever propaganda machine.

It whipped up the lowest animal instincts, only to condense them into a death-defying aggressive spirit. It roused a nationalist fervor in the slaves of Stalin's collective farms and then exploited it for the ends of Bolshevist world revolution. It used Leninist ideology for its own nationalist purposes. It twisted and distorted God and the world and finally achieved its aim: The Red Army was kept in line and went from victory to victory.

How essential this shrewd Stalinist propaganda was to the Red Army, I was able to see from two small examples that came my way in the vast mosaic of events during those critical days.

One night, a Russian infantry battalion took up quarters in a small village just outside Tata. The frightened occupants of the house, which had been selected for the battalion commander, were crowded together into an outbuilding room with all their children and property. Then the Russian major moved in, together with his mistress, a battalion surgeon, and his enlisted aide.

That evening, the three of them—major, mistress and enlisted aide—drank together from the abundant wine cellar of the house. Whether the enlisted aide knew too much about his major's affairs or whether the dear battalion surgeon had a heart for both the gentlemen, the people of the house could not say, but what they could and did tell me after we re-occupied the village, was that during the evening a quarrel started between the major and his enlisted aide, which soon developed into a violent brawl.

One can imagine the terror of the Hungarians when a little later a loud knocking came at their door. Shivering with fright, they opened the door. They could only stifle their laughter with difficulty. There, outside the door, shivering not with fright but with cold, stood the Red Army major in his nightshirt, begging for a place to lie down for the night. Cursing, he rolled himself in a blanket and lay down on the floor. The enlisted aide had thrown him out and was now triumphantly ensconced in the house alongside his major's mistress.

The next morning, the major was forced to send the house owner to negotiate for his uniform, as he could hardly present himself to his battalion in his shirt. To the householder he remarked angrily: "Discipline not good with us...damn it, war's lasted too long."

In a somewhat more serious vein was an experience I had near Tarjan, where a Red Army lieutenant suddenly deserted to my company. He was sullen and, unlike the usual deserter, did not want to say any thing to me. But in the end, he admitted to being a wholehearted supporter of Stalin and firmly convinced of final Russian victory. In my amazement, I asked him why he had deserted. Gradually it emerged that he had done it to save his own skin. Because he had held a tight watch over his company, he was so hated by his enlisted men that they had already tried twice to shoot him from behind.

He had no illusions about surviving the third attempt. His battalion commander had turned down his request for a transfer. So there was nothing for him but to desert.

He told me that at night all the officers of the battalion slept together in one billet whenever possible, as otherwise they could never be sure that they would not all be finished off by their ill disciplined enlisted. "I'm finished either way," he said when he had ended his story. "It makes no difference."

The fact that fighting discipline was in general maintained, in spite of these incidents, which prisoner interrogation showed were by no means exceptional, was entirely due to the political commissars and their propagandists.

Conditions were, of course, very different with the elite forces of the Red Army, with the armored formations, with the NKVD battalions and with the *Komsomolz* formations. But with the ordinary infantryman in the line, things were very shaky. At that stage, they would not have been able to resist a really large-scale counteroffensive. But such an offensive could no longer be mounted, at least not on the necessary scale. American bomber squadrons, by blasting our arms and ammunition dumps and our supply bases, had seen to that only too thoroughly.

It was not long before we were pulled out of this sector, where things were relatively quiet. Our positions were taken over by Army cavalry formations, which equally unable to earn any laurels in the heavily wooded hill country.

***

Our next destination was the frozen Lake Balaton and for a time, all too short, my company found wonderful quarters at Balaton Kenese, where we spent some quiet and peaceful days practically undisturbed by the Red Air Force.

***

And then one morning, German artillery fire of almost forgotten intensity broke over the surprised Russians and the four armored divisions of SS-Gruppenführer Gille's *IV. SS-Panzer-Korps*—*"Wiking"*, *"Totenkopf"*, the *1. Panzer-Division* and the *3. Panzer-Division*—crashed deep into enemy territory. Within a few days, Stuhlweißenburg was back in our hands and we had even reached the Danube and Lake Velencz in places.

This advance gave us the chance to see for ourselves what was in store for Europe. The portrait that Hungary offered was so infinitely horrible that it is impossible to give more than a limited account of it.

The Soviets had not only taken from the populace all foodstuffs and drink, which, for an army that lives almost entirely on the land is perhaps pardonable in wartime, but they had also gone systematically through the homes of all the small peasants and workers for whose "liberation" they had invaded Hungary. They looted all they could lay their hands on, not only valuables such as rings, bracelets and watches, which they took as a matter of course, but even such things as clothing, linen and footwear. Anyone who resisted or even protested was shot out of hand.

In the village of Lepseny, the Bolsheviks had not been content to stop at the living, but they had even ripped open coffins and torn rings from the bodies. Any difficulty had been overcome quite simply by cutting off the fingers.

In one of the burial vaults, some of which had obviously been used as dugouts, the coffins had been heaved out and the shelves covered with straw. I found several torn brassieres and a pair of women's undergarments, ripped to shreds, alongside a large heap of broken vodka and wine bottles.

Calling cards of Communist culture and the new era of Moscow's mercy.

Sprawled in the snow by the outer wall of the church, we found the frozen bodies of two men, their hands clenched, even in death.

I was about to inquire how it was that the bodies were lying there, when I noticed two children, a girl of about seven and a boy, perhaps five, standing close beside them, crying. The bodies were those of two young peasants in the full vigor of health, who a month before had deserted from the Hungarian army to go home. They had had enough of war and death, and the land and the women were waiting.

But the war and death they had left behind in the Carpathians had followed and overtaken them.

Death had come in the shape of the pale and haggard Commissar Osipoff. When the Red Army had marched in, this man had had Ferencz and Istvan shot as an example, because they had been wearing the greenish grey trousers of the Hungarian Army for their work on the land. To make the example effective, he had refused permission for them to be buried, and so there they had stayed, lying at the side of the road along which their wives, mothers and children had to pass every day.

The women of Hungary were simply fair game for the dehumanized Soviet rear-area soldiers. In Polgardi, a 53-year-old woman told me in the presence of her mortified husband how a Red Army major had raped her, and then before going to sleep, had tied her, still naked, by a strap to the waistband of his trousers, so that he could be sure of having her handy for the morning.

In Stuhlweißenburg, we found the naked body of a beautiful fair blonde of about 19 down a well. The people told us with tears in their eyes how a Soviet detachment had installed itself in the house on the other side of the road, probably on guard duties. The 16 men who made up the detachment had rounded up two young girls, both of them under 20—Maria, an ethnic German, and Ida, a Hungarian. They had taken the girls back with them to the house, stripped them of their clothes, which they then burnt in the stove, and set out a bucket for their bodily needs. And there they kept the two unhappy creatures, confined like beasts in a stall, for their pleasure. As each man came in off watch, he would satisfy his wants, all in good order: First food and drink, and then the two women.

On the third day, Maria was no longer able to bear what was happening and ran stark naked into the street where she threw herself into the well in order to escape her torture. After the precipitate departure of the Russians, the other girl was rescued by the neighbors and taken back to her home, gravely ill.

Terrible accounts came to us from all over Hungary. It was impossible to take it all in, let alone to relate it, not even now, so long after the event.

In the village of Napkor, drunken Red Army troops shot every single horse belonging to the Hungarian peasants, simply for the fun of it. The women who had stayed in the village were raped by force or under threat of force. Twenty-two year old Helene, who managed to escape, was fired on by two drunken Russian snipers as she ran, but they missed her. She told us, in tears, that the young Red Army men had behaved the worst. It was perhaps telling that after our retaking of the village, it was the people who had formerly considered themselves communists who were the first to flee to the west under the protection of the German Army.

In Nagykallo the Soviets had also behaved worse than animals. The mental hospital had been a particular target for their entertainment, and the doctors who had stayed through it gave us a unanimous account of how a Red Army headquarters had forcibly violated almost all the deranged women patients between the ages of 16 and 60.

The Bishop of Nyiregyhaza had been robbed of everything' he possessed, and when the German and Hungarian forces returned, his only remaining belongings were the clothes he was wearing. In addition, every member of the female sex who had showed herself, irrespective of age or condition, had been raped at the point of the pistol.

The Soviets had also succeeded in entering Kisvarda. As was their custom, they emptied every home. In Homokkertutca, a mother of four children had been raped in the presence of her husband and his farm helper by three Russian soldiers, one after the other. Three sisters—Jolan, Ida and Berta—who had also been attacked, were the only women, who had managed to fight off their attackers and escape by their vigorous and courageous behavior. In Rakocziutca, a doctor whose husband was fighting on the Carpathian front had been attacked by Russian soldiers at three o'clock in the morning, raped and cleaned out of all her possessions.

A man named Istvan from the Margitta district told us that his neighbor, a 30-year-old woman named Peterné, had been raped at the point of a pistol by eight Bolshevist soldiers only a week after she had given birth to a child. Her husband had been forced to stand by and watch. The 38-year-old wife of Imre Szabo had been shot, because she would not consent.

All this was only an infinitesimal part of what Hungary and its unhappy people were being forced to suffer. Thousands upon thousands of people—men, women and children—were rounded up indiscriminately and herded off to the east in the most inhuman conditions imaginable. The "liberation" of the *Puszta* had begun.

Over on our side, things were also happening that no one could have imagined. In front of us was Budapest, and inside it there were no fewer than 45,000 half-starved German troops and at least as many Hungarians. *Gruppenführer* Gille's intention was to break the stranglehold that the enemy had on the city and liberate the men inside, but General Balck, Commander-in-Chief of the *6. Armee*, did not give his consent. Instead, he issued orders that we were first to attack and destroy the Russian divisions operating to our north.

Gille pointed out the urgency of relieving the Budapest garrison and drew attention to the excellent military situation that our surprise advance had created. But all in vain; even an appeal to Hitler failed. So Gille's corps had to be regrouped for a move up north to surround the 10 Russian divisions said to be located there.

In vain, *Gruppenführer* Gille pointed to the danger inherent in the open flank of the *IV. SS-Panzer-Korps* and to the impossibility of ever having another such chance. His four armored divisions were already in sight of the Budapest airport at Buda-Örs, and the Russians had no hope of stopping them. Together with a simultaneous breakout effort by the encircled divisions at the castle, the Russian front lines would be smashed and the starving German and Hungarian forces would be relieved.

After hearing from Balck of the *Führer's* decision, however, Gille grit his teeth and reluctantly issued orders for the regrouping. Precisely 24 hours later, what Gille had predicted came true: Ivan crossed the Danube with hundreds of tanks and thrust deep into our flanks.

As was to be expected, the Russians had made good use of the time we had lost in regrouping and had now committed a fresh corps, the III Mechanized Corps, which they had just brought up. That night saw a real tank battle, the last one of those four bloody years on the Eastern Front. The *"Totenkopf"* Division alone scored almost 200 kills of enemy tanks. But it saw the end of Gille, because the Russians made a practice of shooting back.

This action finally sealed the fate of Budapest.

Of its garrison of close to 100,000 men, less than 800 managed to break out and reach our lines, more dead than alive. What they had to say about *SS-Obergruppenführer und General der Polizei und Waffen-SS* Pfeffer-Wildenbruch[62], the defender of Budapest, and about the tactical defense in general, does not constitute one of the most glorious chapters of German military history.

Then our spirits rose again, for the last time, when *Generaloberst Dr.* Lothar von Rendulic took over the command of *Heeresgruppe Süd*, which had been commanded, in quick succession, by first *Generaloberst* Friesner and then *Generaloberst* Wöhler. Rendulic, who was one of the ablest of the Austrian generals, had earned his laurels as Chief-of-Staff to Dietl, the popular general of Alpine troops, and as Commander-in-Chief of the *2. Panzer-Armee*.

---

62   Translator's Note: More recent accounts have been kinder to Pfeffer-Wildenbruch. See, for example, Georg Meir's *Drama zwischen Budapest und Wien*, which has been published in English as <u>Drama Between Budapest and Vienna</u> by J.J. Fedorowicz Publishing of Canada. He ultimately received the Oakleaves to the Knight's Cross from Hitler for his defense of the city.

Now, everyone thought, the change would come. Now things would begin to happen. Rendulic was the man to prevent disaster reaching the *Reich* frontier and Vienna.

But none of that occurred. We had to retire back to our Stuhl-weißenburg positions.

While in the wine-growing hill country of that district, I had a curious experience. Two deserters came in one evening, both of them officers, who had had their fill, but for exactly opposite reasons. One was a young Ukrainian, who had known the Germans in his native Ukraine and no longer thought much of the Bolshevik magic. He was simply longing for the west, for quietness and culture. The other, a young Uzbek, was a fanatical communist. He said he was through with the war, because Stalin was no longer a communist: He had become an imperialist. He said that Stalin had betrayed Lenin and Karl Marx.

However much they may have differed on politics, they were unanimous on one point: That some 3,000 Russian vehicles were concentrated near a village between Mor and Stuhlweißenburg and that a new and dangerous thrust was threatening us in that area.

I promptly took hold of the two of them and carted them off the same evening to the intelligence officer, who, to my disgust, ordered me to take them straight on to the field-army headquarters. I arrived at those headquarters at about midnight, frozen stiff, but in view of the importance of the information, was immediately sent on to the field army group headquarters at the Esterhazy palace. Half-frozen and punch drunk from the lack of sleep, I arrived at the headquarters in my *Kübelwagen* at about 0800 hours. After getting past the sentries, which was no easy task, it was with some awe that I walked into the interior of the palace. This was the first time during the whole of the war that I had found myself in a field army group headquarters, the place where decisions were taken that might have meant life or death, not only to the enemy but for us as well.

After a lot of asking, I eventually found my way to the offices of the intelligence officer, an *Oberstleutnant Graf* Rittberg. The first room was empty, the second and third as well. Finally, a sleepy sergeant asked me, with surprise in his voice, what I wanted. I said I wanted to see the *Oberstleutnant.*

He gave me a bored smile and informed me that it was quite impossible for me to see the Count before 1030 hours, not even if I had come to announce the end of the world. I therefore left the palace, went first for a shave and then had breakfast with the two Russians, arriving back again at exactly 1030 hours. This time, I was admitted.

Oberstleutnant Graf Rittberg received me very cordially. He said he had already been told by the field army during the night that I was coming and offered me a variety of drinks. Then he listened with great attention to what I had to say. He took me to see the aerial reconnaissance map and compared the prisoners' statements with the results of our air reconnaissance. They coincided exactly.

"Most interesting," said Rittberg. "I must tell the Commander-in-Chief over lunch. I'll tell you what, come back immediately after lunch and I'll probably be able to give you a message for Gille by then."

I clicked my heels and left. After handing over the two deserters to the interrogation office, I made my way out of the palace again. I had lunch at the officers' mess and, in chatting with some friends I ran into there, completely forgot the time, with the result that it was after two when I rushed back in some alarm to see the *Oberstleutnant.* The morning's little game was repeated. The first room was empty, the second, and so on. At length my friend the sergeant showed up again and instructed me that afternoon meant half-past four. At the moment, I was informed, the Count was out riding, after that there was an hour for chess and that was to be followed by some tremendous birthday celebration. But he could assure me quite definitely that the Count would be back by half-past four.

He was, at five. He even remembered me in spite of his many activities and said gaily:' "The general was extremely interested. Extremely interested. Please extend regards to Gille."

I stood there looking stupid.

226

"Is there anything else? " he asked, his tone slightly impatient.

"But what's going to be done about it?" I asked. "What am I to report? After all, this is an extremely dangerous threat to our flank."

"Calm down," he said, smiling. "For starters, you've got the Hungarian 25th Hussars there. They'll have to hold up the Russians for an hour or so, and by that time Gille will have sent up the fire brigade…"

"The Hungarians," I hesitantly broke in, "with two machine guns per company? You expect them to hold up a force of 3,000 vehicles for an hour? "

"Everything's under control," he said testily, by way of dismissal. "Army Group will do all that's necessary."

I left in a state of considerable depression. This was the first and last time I ever talked to a senior German General Staff Officer. A few weeks later Count Rittberg was executed by the secret military police based on the verdict of a court-martial. We never found out why.

***

Back with my company, I found another surprise awaiting me— we were under orders to move again, this time to the *6. SS-Panzer-Armee* of Sepp Dietrich.

When we arrived at Lake Balaton, I had the shock of my life. I found that an offensive was being prepared there on the grandest possible scale. Nineteen divisions had been assembled for an attack in the enemy's flank, which was to carry us across the Danube, through Hungary and as far as Ploesti.

The watchword: Present the *Führer* with the Rumanian oilfields in time for his birthday on 20 April 1945. That would enable the *Luftwaffe's* new aircraft to take the air against the US Air Force and sweep the German skies clear. Once this pressure was off our minds, we would be able to concentrate all our strength against the Soviets and chase them clean out of Europe!

I was aghast. Had I observed everything incorrectly? Had all my observations, my calculations been wrong for all these years? Was I so completely immersed and imprisoned in my own ideas that I could no longer see straight?

I was at a loss. Around me, division after division: Tanks rolling, battalions marching, cavalry regiments galore drawn up for the pursuit once the tanks had broken through. Everything pouring forward.

Dear God, I prayed, let the miracle happen. Though we have done much wrong, don't let Bolshevism sweep over Europe, and over our poor, stricken and bomb-ravaged country.

***

Our offensive began slowly, being held up by the bad weather. Then, just as the fighting was beginning to grow heavy near Simontornya, the last stage before the Danube crossing, the enemy counterattack burst on our flank at the precise point where our aerial reconnaissance and the two Russian officers had said it would come. The Hungarian Hussars were swept away within a matter of minutes, and Gille's formations became involved in heavy fighting against fantastic odds and had to fall back.

Our grand Danube offensive threatened to become a grand trap for our armies. The retreat started.

The retreat from which the German Army in the southeast never recovered. Nineteen divisions streamed back through the long pocket: Tanks, infantry, cavalry and still more cavalry. It was more flight than retreat. Nineteen divisions. Never before, throughout the entire war, had I seen so many in one small area.

The Russians rapidly outflanked Stuhlweißenburg and were then on the road from Inota. Then they pushed down as far as Lake Balaton from above. Soon they were in front of Raab. We tried to stop them on the road from Raab into Styria, but they broke through again and went on.

For the first time in the war you then saw whole columns of fleeing German troops, with or without officers, all making for the *Reich* frontier. They had only one thought: To get back to the *Reich*.

***

I was pulled out of the line and ordered to form a catch line for deserters between Lake Neusiedel and the frontier station of Kittsee. My orders were to shoot every man who arrived without arms.

In one day, I stopped 900 men. There could be no more question of shooting, though I had a difficult struggle with myself: On one hand, a military order and, on the other, the command of conscience. I had them formed up and they looked at me grimly. They could imagine what my orders were.

I talked to them calmly: "Comrades, you've lost their heads... you're being formed into new *Kampfgruppen* and will be sent to Neusiedel, where you will be rearmed and committed again."

A young *Unterscharführer* jumped forward out of the ranks. He was a recipient of the silver wound badge, the bronze close combat clasp and the Iron Cross, First Class.[63]

Untersturmführer," he cried out with his high-pitched child's voice. "You know as well as we do that we're finished. What's the good of all this now?"

I said nothing for a moment. According to all the rules of the game there was only one thing for me to do, to draw my pistol and shoot him down, regardless of would then happen next.

The eyes of the 900 bored into me.

---

63   Translator's Note: There were three classes of wound badge (*Verwundeten-abzeichen*), each with a different color. A black badge was received for one or two wounds; a silver for three or four; and a gold-colored one for five or more wounds. Similarly, there were three classes of the Close Combat Clasp (*Nahkampfspange*): Bronze for up to 15 days of close combat with the enemy; silver for up to 49; and gold for 50 or more days. The Close Combat Clasp was one of the most highly respected German combat awards.

"Do you have a mother?" I asked the mutineer.

He dropped his eyes. "Yes," he said slowly. "What's that got to do with anything?"

"You've seen enough of the Red Army's methods with women. Do you want to see your mother in their hands?"

"No!" he said excitedly. "No!"

"Well, then. So that our mothers in the rear can save themselves, we will fight to the last man, no matter how the war turns out." My voice boomed out across the area: "Formation...Attention! The most senior NCO's each take 100 men. Take charge! Move out towards Neusiedel!"

They sang as they marched off, those last assault columns of Germany. But I did not feel like singing.

However, the expected court martial for failing to shoot deserters did not materialize. It had been realized after all that this was the better way.

Easter came, and on Easter Sunday my wife came out from Vienna in a ration truck. She was dressed in ski trousers and mountaineering outfit. I handed her a small private-purchase automatic as a present. We looked at each other, and she understood.

A few hundred yards behind us was the southeastern defense wall, the *Reichschutzstellung* — Defense Wall of the *Reich*.

It was quite good, although it had never been completed. Still, it did have trenches and pillboxes, artillery and antitank positions. If we had only had had a line half as good on the Dnjepr!

In spite of the hopelessness of the general situation, I felt quite happy about things in our sector. The Russians wouldn't drive us out of these positions so easily.

But next day a rumor went around that in the whole of the German defense wall there were no more than a few companies of the

Volkssturm[64]. Confirmation quickly followed when the Russians broke through in the south and penetrated into eastern Styria. On the next day, they were in Lower Austria and we received orders to fall back to the Vienna Woods.

Everything then flowed west and our beautiful wall remained unused—debris of the collapse, which could now no longer be disguised from the simplest man.

Infantry, tanks, camp prisoners...women and children with their scanty belongings piled on peasant carts...entire military hospitals with badly and severely wounded soldiers. Everything was pulling back.

Only the food and clothing stores were left behind, vast accumulations of boots and clothing that a senseless bureaucracy had gone on piling up until the last moment. Suddenly there was fuel for everyone, oceans of fuel, where a week before it had been unobtainable for even the most important operations.

Wherever I passed, I had the stores thrown open to everyone. Not many others did that, unfortunately, with the result that abundant supplies fell into the hands of the advancing Soviets. But they got nothing, not a single can, not a boot, where I had been.

---

64   Translator's Note: The German Home Guard.

Chapter Twelve: The Great Delirium

An appeal by Schirach and a statement by Sepp Dietrich on the defense of Vienna were broadcast. I could have vomited. I knew too well what had *not* been done for the defense of the city. The one *"Totenkopf"* regiment and the few dozen *Volkssturm* men and Hitler Youth were sacrificed purely for the sake of prestige—a consideration which should have just been dropped.

Schirach himself had "repaired" to the Army, which was far enough away from Vienna to prevent the call of duty reaching him— the duty which required him to either declare Vienna an open city, in contravention of even the highest orders, or else die in its defense, and thus redress some of the many blunders he had committed there by means of an honorable death.

***

For all practical purposes, Sepp Dietrich had ceased to have any part in events. He had received orders from the *Führer* that his field army was to remove all its orders and decorations and also its cuff titles from living and dead alike, because of its cowardice before the enemy and the failure of the great Hungarian offensive. The men of the *6. SS-Panzer-Armee* were to fight on in order to win back the orders and decorations for their dead comrades.

This was too much for the old warrior. It hit him even worse than the now irrevocable collapse.

***

We then fought a hopeless but bloody battle as small combat teams through the villages and hills of the Vienna Woods. Among whose flower-bedecked meadows and slopes, the final act of the greatest tragedy that has ever befallen the German people had opened.

Often, the artillery had no more than six rounds a day per gun. Riflemen and machine gunners were issued ammunition bearing green slips on the cases: "Warning! Ammunition expired. To be used for training purposes only." We had to fire with it.

Or sometimes we received Czech ammunition that was too heavily waxed for our weapons and caused frequent burning. But we had to fight with it all the same.

The civilian population no longer looked on us as a protection but as an unnecessary and dangerous nuisance. Women of communist sympathies were continually leading Soviet troops behind us. On one occasion, they even threw out some of our wounded whom we had put into the temporary safety of house entryway. Others—but only a very few—joined our ranks and fought and died beside us.

Most of civilians acted as though paralyzed, all thought and feeling obsessed by an irrational fear of the Bolsheviks, while we, for our part, were a forlorn and outlawed band, holding a hopeless position that had already been given up for lost.

There was no longer any question of political leadership from above. One day, I had to carry dispatches to the rear; it was the day that Munich radio broadcast the story of *Hauptmann* Gerngroß'[65]

---

65   Translator's Note: For those not familiar with the relatively unknown resistance leader, who survived the war and lived into the late '90's, here is additional information from Wikipedia (http://en.wikipedia.org/wiki/Rupprecht_Gerngroß):

Rupprecht Gerngroß (21 June 1915 - 25 February 1996)was a German lawyer and leader of the *Freiheitsaktion Bayern*, the *FAB*, (English: *Bavarian Freedom Initiative*), a group involved in an attempt to overthrow the Nazis in Munich in April 1945...

...In the final days of the Second World War, Gerngroß was serving as a Captain in an interpreter company in Munich. On the morning of 28 April 1945, he ordered the occupation of the radio transmitters in Freimann and Erding and he broadcast messages in multiple languages, encouraging soldiers to resist the Nazi regime. He proclaimed a *hunt for the golden pheasants* (German: *Jagd auf die Goldfasane*),... [translator's note: a reference to the highly decorated party officials, who wore light brown uniforms]...and encouraged people to display white flags from their homes as a sign of surrender. His group also occupied the Munich city hall and attempted *Putsch*, which I had heard in the early hours of the morning before I started. On my way, I happened by chance to hear that *Dr.* Jury, the *Gauleiter* of Lower Austria, was spending the night in a small inn farther along my route. I had him awakened and told him about the Munich uprising. He was as clueless as a small child. "That's impossible," he kept saying, "it can't be true." Instead of replying, I turned up the nearest loudspeaker. *Dr.* Jury's haggard features took on a frightening look of decay. It was as if the Angel of Death, who actually did come for this man a few days later, had lowered his wings over him.

We parted silently.

***

The fall of Vienna made little impression on us. Hitler's death, on the other hand, came as a terrible shock. Victory or defeat, criticism or blind faith, he had been the idol of all of us, and we had sworn loyalty to his creed.

The total capitulation somehow brought relief.

A few days before it came, we had launched our last counterattack and had driven the Russian battalions back to the east. It was amazing how close they were to the end themselves at the time. If we had only had the strength to launch even a small number of armored and mechanized regiments in a serious counterattack, who knows what the astonished world might have witnessed: The spectacle of a Russian Army in rout? But we had no regiments, all we had left were a few companies and "battle groups".

During that final fighting, I had an experience, which has remained fixed in my memory ever since. At the height of our attack, I suddenly had to counter an enemy threat to our flank and decided to move far forward with a machine-gun section that had been placed under my command. Ivan was using explosive bullets, a weapon that

---

the headquarters of the *Völkischer Beobachter* and *Münchner Neuesten Nachrichten*, two newspapers vital to the Nazi propaganda. The claim that the *Freiheitsaktion* had taken control over Munich was however premature and led to other uprisings against the Nazis in the region, which were often brutally suppressed by the *SS*...

was greatly feared by our men. The leader of the machine-gun section, a man from Hanover, who had already been lightly wounded, was slow to obey my order. I lost my temper and let loose at him.

He knelt on the ground, wiped the blood off his face, and said slowly: "What a miserable, accursed people we are...my grandfather killed in 1870, my father in 1918, and now we're finished again...all to no purpose. Three of my brothers have been killed, and now this." He stood up with an effort, led his section to the designated place and turned back the enemy counterattack.

I stood there silently. There was nothing that could be said at that point.

***

The Ennstal Mountains shimmered like silver in the sparkling radiance of thousands of stars. It was a vision of majestic beauty and solace. It was only among us along the broad highway that unrest, noise and fear predominated. We were unable to move forward or backward. I probably tried abut 10 times to find out the cause of the congestion, but all my attempts were in vain. You were barely able to make your way through the jammed-together staff cars, trucks, *SPW's*, motorcycles with sidecars and four-barreled *Flak* on self-propelled mounts.

One rumor followed the next. The lead Russian armored elements were said to be only 10 kilometers behind us. Any officer above the rank of *Hauptmann* and any and all *Waffen-SS* were being shot on the spot. It was said that the Americans had established a permanent passage point at Radstadt and whoever did not pass it within the next 24 hours would not be allowed to pass. American tanks had already directed their guns on the road.

"Perhaps we should just take off with a few groups across the mountains," Franz, the junior noncommissioned officer from South Tirol suggested. "They'll never take us alive."

I kept quiet, depressed that I was completely at a loss for ideas. You could still fire against Ivan, negotiates with the Yanks, force soldiers to rebellious soldiers to perform their duty, but I was completely helpless in the face of this exhausted resignation.

In the years gone by these men, the tens of thousands of them that were gathered here in this great trek westward, had endured much more difficult and harder deprivations, far greater missions than simply moving along in such a gigantic column. How often had we felt the icy whiff of the word "retreat" in the unending expanses of the East, and yet everything worked out somehow in the end. Everything worked, even though bombs rained down from the heavens night and day and our flanks were being threatened by the lead elements of enemy mechanized forces or by Red partisans. But now, at the moment of our retreat into total capitulation, there was something different going on. We had been chased back more than 3,000 kilometers from the fruited plains of the Ukraine, from the unending forests of the Caucasus and from the Ginster-covered[66] coastline along the Gulf of Finland, but we had always fought and left behind dead and wounded. It had been a long journey to this collapse. Our fears were no greater than normal and there was no dread. Just an enormous indifference and a paralyzing exhaustion.

Gruppenführer Gille, it was said, had surrendered his "Vikings" in good order. The Yanks had received them with honors and provided a banquet. That particular rumor provided tens of thousands with both new hopes and new illusions. Just wait, just hold out until the advance guards of the Americans encounter those of the Soviets.

An *Oberleutnant*, who was trying to make it through on foot with his last six men, told us something different. In Bohemia, even in upper Austria, the Americans had turned over all of the German divisions that had checked in with them to the Soviets after a short period. The reality was apparently different than Minister Goebbels' final false hopes.

Suddenly, red signal flares shot up into the sky behind us. The sound of fighting could be heard.

---

66   Translator's note: The ginster is a relatively small plant with many small branches, small leaves and many yellow blossoms.

"They're here!" Toni screamed. Two dozen eyes were riveted on me, full of questions.

"Get ready to move out!" Strange, but my voice sounded normal. In a flash, the remaining machine guns were in position. Franz got a few *Panzerfäuste*[67] ready to fire. Officers and men jumped down from the neighboring vehicles, submachine guns and carbines at the ready. There wasn't a lot of discussion; these were all old hands from the Eastern Front. In the blink of an eye, a skirmish line had been established behind a small swell in the ground; it was our last mainline of resistance.

Over on the opposite edge of woods there was movement. I was able to make out a group of men through my binoculars. Were they Russians or Germans?

All at once, the entire column came to life. Orders echoed, women's voices shrieked among them and children began to cry.

A miracle occurred: The congestion in front of us disappeared and the vehicles started up. The exchange of fire that we had heard had not come from Red Army men, who were only following hesitantly. Instead, it had come from a few groups of men, who were not about to let plunderers rob them of their rations.

We also started to move out. But where were we going, really? Our future was also riding with us. Only yesterday we had heard Montgomery, the big British general, on the radio: "20 Years for every rifleman of the *Waffen-SS*; 20 years for every staff officer; life for every member of the general staff."

Vehicles jammed up again in a small village. My enlisted aid, Arthur, was able to quickly secure hot water, which meant coffee.

An old general sat next to the road in his *Kübelwagen*. Both of his drivers had vanished hours ago without saying anything and burned

---

67   Translator's note: The *Panzerfaust* was a hand-held, self-propelled, unguided rocket with a hollow-charge warhead. It was a single-shot weapon. Although it had a limited range, it was effective against all known armor at the time. It was the precursor of the internationally famous reverse-engineered RPG-7.

their identity books. They couldn't help it, after all, that they had been detailed to a general staff.

I still had enough drivers, so I went over to the elderly gentleman, talked to him for a while and then proposed that one of my men drive him.

He looked at me surprised, silently shook his white head and suddenly shook my hand so firmly that I was startled.

"I was never able to stand you people in the *Waffen-SS*," he said with a cracking voice. "You always thought you were the better ones." A bitter smile crossed his lips. "Perhaps you are."

I was embarrassed. I wanted to say something, but the old man, whose homeland was East Prussia and whose only son had been killed in the war, turned away silently. When the first cup of hot coffee arrived, I stood up, filled up a mess tin and carried it over to the vehicle. The general was bent slightly forward and paid no attention to me.

"Something hot to drink, *Herr General*," I literally said, "always does wonders."

The old man did not answer. Sensing something wrong, I walked closer. I then saw that he had shot himself. Right in the temple. Right in the middle of the entire gigantic column with tens of thousands of people, and not a single one had noticed it or cared.

We quickly dug a grave with our entrenching tools next to the road. During the four years in Russia we had become practiced at it. The old man laid in the shelter half and looked like he was peacefully sleeping.

The *Kübelwagen* was quickly driven into the roadside ditch. When I turned around, I saw how a group of children in tattered clothes were already plundering the suitcase of the dead man and the vehicle. One of my men raised his pistol, ashen white. I pushed his hand away. It made no difference, after all.

We moved out. After we had traveled a bit, it occurred to me that I had failed to secure the paybook of the general. But who was I supposed to give it to, anyway?

We were stopped in Wagrain. Apparently, the Americans had forbidden any further movement west. We stood next to a larger building, which was obviously occupied by poor people. I sent out two men. Perhaps it was possible to find quarters somewhere in the locality.

They returned, filled with bitterness and anger. "They don't have any room for us," Arthur said. Franz said in a monotone: "The fat bastards don't want to be reminded of the war by our uniforms. For them, peace has already broken out."

Toni, the man from Buchenland[68], laughed a bitter laugh: "That's the way it is. We're superfluous!"

It started to turn dusk, and it soon started to rain softly. An old woman, who had fled Vienna with her family, hesitated as she passed our column and approached me. She had recognized me. She pulled out a bottle of *Enzian schnapps* from one of her pockets. It was the last thing she had, and she wanted to give it to me. I had to turn her down.

"What's going to happen to our old Vienna," she asked hesitantly? "Our street was on fire when we left the city."

For the first time, my voice failed me. I was unable to answer her.

We were finally allowed to continue moving. We still did not see any American armored vehicles. A jeep with a gigantic Stars & Stripes, driven by a coal-black Negro, was the first we saw of the armed forces of the USA. On it were two cameramen in uniform, who seemed not to get tired filming us.

---

68   Translator's Note: The Buchenland is a portion of the Ukraine in the Carpathians.

239

There was still discipline and order at St. Johann. *General* Pork had set up a capitulation detail there. It was said that whoever joined the group would be among the first to be discharged. I reported in immediately, of course. And, in actual fact, a general inspected us a short while later. Although he wore the red stripes on his trousers and the shoulder boards of a German general, he had no war decorations. He had us form a semicircle around him and informed us what the general rules of behavior were. Of course, we asked a lot of questions, which the good man could not answer. In the end, I wanted to know when the trains in the *Ostmark*[69] would start operating again.

The general looked me over critically from head to toe. "That's Austria, mister!" he informed me smugly, "and not *Ostmark*."

But he still could not tell me when the trains would be running again.

The men around me were boiling mad. Franz, who was standing right behind me, said quietly: "Should I shoot him?"

I waved him aside. I was too tired to dress down the excited man.

The general told us then that we would be taken to Bad Aibling by rail. The discharges would take place there. Then he quickly disappeared.

But we then waited for days on end. A kilometer away from us, *Obersturmführer* Valentin Schuster, who had written exciting newspaper articles and reports under the pseudonym of "Mungo", shot himself. His adventurous life did not want to hang around to enjoy the defeat.

Soviet prisoners from a near-by camp and concentration camp inmates with their stripped uniforms crisscrossed the countryside. Woe be on to the lonely farmer's house where such a group showed up! Again and again, the farmers asked us for help, and even though

---

69   Translator's Note: The reader is again reminded that *Ostmark* was the name given to Austria, when it was annexed into Germany.

we were forbidden to move outside of the open-air camp with arms, we did what we could.

One afternoon, I was sitting around at a near-by farmer's house and saw Americans for the first time up close. Up to that point, I had only seen them from a distance. Two very tall and exceptionally good-looking sergeants entered the farmer's courtyard in a jeep and, gesticulating energetically, asked for eggs. The farmer's wife offered them a dozen with shaking hands, and they tossed her a pack of cigarettes. Just as they were abut to drive off, they caught sight of me. They approached me. One of them stood in front of me and grabbed my Iron Cross, First Class. "Invasion?" he asked, as if to set me up.

I shook my head.

In a playful move, he removed the Iron Cross from me. I was incensed. I still had my pistol and pistol belt on me.

The second one looked at me attentively, suddenly took the Iron Cross out of the hands of his comrade and handed it back to me. He said something to his compatriot, which I did not understand, who shrugged his shoulders in an embarrassed manner. They then jumped back into their jeep and raced away.

We entrained the next day. We were transported as far as Feldkirch, near Bad Aibling. We were then sorted into groups, after spending a few days in an open-air camp: The politically suspect, members of the intelligence, general-staff officers and, of course, the entire *Waffen-SS*. Transportation was then arranged. The 41 officers of our group were squeezed aboard two small trucks. All of a sudden, there were American guard forces present, who escorted us with submachine guns and carbines.

The day was beautiful and the sun was shining brilliantly. People were working everywhere in the fields; it was a peaceful scene we had almost forgotten. All f a sudden, our two trucks turned off the highway and onto a lonely forest path. Was that where our camp was located? After a short while, the path widened out to a clearing, where peat moss had been processed a long time ago. The individual outbuildings there were in bad shape. It was at that location that we halted.

"Dismount! Let's go!" The Americans yelled.

"If we were with the Ivans," I whispered to an older *Major* next to me, "I'd know what was going to happen next."

The *Major* did not answer. We had to form up in two ranks. The guards gestured with great deliberateness with their sub-machine guns. We looked at one another.

Then a sergeant appeared and said in fluent German: "Knives, binoculars, scissors, razors, razor blades, watches and rings, as well as, of course, all weapons, have to be turned in immediately."

We had to open the containers our personal belongings were in and everything was searched with an admirable dexterity that probably came from a lot of practice.

"Not watch?" The GI next to me said with irritation. But not all of them were so unsuccessful. As we mounted up again later, I saw how some Americans were showing each other a few golden watches.

Suddenly, the Americans were in a hurry and we had to mount up hastily. We then drove back to the highway and raced off in the direction of Bad Aibling, which we soon passed. We stopped at the airfield, where 80,000 German prisoners had been forced into a small area behind hastily erected barbed wire.

Our escorts transferred us to the new guard force. We were then told to double time into the interior f the camp. The elderly *Major* from the militia evidently had heart problems. He was not able to keep pace, and he lagged behind, gasping. But none of that helped him. As quick as lighting, a GI turned around and hit him in the head with a fence picket, which he had in his hands, without saying a word. He collapsed, blood flowing. We were driven forward with submachine guns, which were on prominent display.

We were in the middle of the barbed wire. Our situation was more than desperate. We received practically nothing to eat. There was only one loaf of bread for every 20 men. At noon, we received 6-10 tablespoons of soup and, in the afternoon, about 5 grams of sausage. It was a single thin slice. Early in the morning, there was a mug of real coffee. Soon the desire to eat dominated everything.

In addition, it rained mercilessly down upon us; it appeared to never want to stop. Water oozed out of the ground constantly. Despite that, we had to spend our time sitting on the wet soil during the day and lay there at night. Those who no longer had a blanket or a shelter half didn't have a chance. The only thing that was arranged for us was loud music played over the loudspeakers and "culture" events consisting of some poetry in the morning and again in the evening. Otherwise, we lay on the wet ground, starving and freezing, and tried to come to terms with our fate.

The prisoners fell into three groups: First, those who forgot everything—their country, their social standing and even their honor—as a result of the physical deprivations and the hunger inevitable in any captivity. There were plenty of them. Then there were those who held stubbornly to the belief that betrayal and sabotage alone were to blame for the national disaster. Finally, there were the few who sought day and night to get at the underlying causes of the military and, ultimately, the moral collapse. I soon found myself with the last group.

Strangely enough, the shock of the catastrophe passed more quickly than we had thought possible. We knew that everything had its origin in the mind. We stood or sat round together, or when hunger made us too weak to stand, lay on the ground and talked the hours away. The arguments were fierce and passionate. It was the last grind of the great steamroller that had passed over us. But it was also a new beginning in our hour of greatest moral and physical distress.

The subjects which initially caused the greatest heat were the mistakes we had made in our eastern policy and in our foreign policy as a whole, the concentration camps, and the *Gestapo*. It was especially the officers and soldiers from the front who heard of things—often for the first time—we had never dreamed possible. Yet, at the same time, questions and doubts began to form in our minds: How much was truth and how much propaganda? Then we began to dig down deeper, and the *Führerprinzip* itself, the absolute State, became the main topic of discussion. From that we went on to the persons such as Himmler and Göring and, finally, the hardest nut of all to crack, the *Führer* himself.

"Do you know when the beginning of the end started?" a grizzled old *Major* said to us. We knew he had been former high-level *SA* leader, one of the real old guard. "It was on 30 June 1934. It was not only the old *SA* leaders and Röhm who died in front of the firing squads that day, it was everything that National Socialism had meant to us, everything we'd dreamed of."

A stream of denials and contradictions met his words, but he went on undeterred: "Adolf Hitler, in the period after he first took power, was faced with the greatest decision of his life: Either to work with the revolutionary masses of the *SA* or with the Army General Staff. On the one side...a the people's army, similar perhaps to the Red Guard of a Trotsky—that way promised a long and difficult passage, but a passage that would finally have led to the end of all imperialism. It was the National Socialist way. The end of bank financing and slavery to interest, land reform and settlements, social policy and large-scale socialization measures."

"But on the other side, he was offered the immediate reconstruction of the *Wehrmacht* in accordance with the tested and true manner of the Prussian General Staff and, with it, the chance of grabbing the territory his *Volk ohne Raum*[70] needed so badly. And, as a result, two vast ideas faced each other in the soul of the man who'd seized greater power than any monarch had ever had. The revolutionary way promised a slow approach to the ultimate goal, although over a broad front. It was an experiment, fraught with great danger and involving methods hitherto untried in Germany. It was breaking new

---

70   Translator's note" = "Nation without space". One of the National Socialist basic tenants that the German peoples needed more territory in order to realize their potential.

ground both in theory and practice. The way of the generals was the traditional one, well tried, and highly successful in 1812/13, in 1864, 1866 and again in 1871. The General Staff, with its burning desire to avenge the 1918 defeat, were ready to put up with Corporal Hitler and to swallow National Socialism and its social reforms, if only it gave them the chance to fight another war. The *Führer*, on the other hand, was ready to tolerate the generals, however ill-disposed they were towards him, and was content to swallow their conservatism and leave capitalism unharmed, so long as they'd help him to his final goal—the conquest of vast territories for his *Volk ohne Raum*."

"So both parties went into business firmly determined to get the better of each other. And the real tragedy for Germany is that they both succeeded."

"In this conflict of ideas in Hitler's mind, the experiment of revolutionary National Socialism had nothing to offer which could equal the attractions of either the conquest of territory or of becoming a figure in world history. It offered only the long and arduous progress of one of the greatest of all national experiments."

"It was as though the Devil himself had taken Hitler to the top of a high mountain and shown him the world below: 'You see that...it's all yours if only you'll sell me your soul.'"

"On the other side, there were the masses whose blood had paved and guarded the road up to the mountain, who had nothing to offer but their faith, their loyalty and their militant revolutionary pride. It was because of this pride that the pistols and submachine guns had to bark once Hitler had chosen the way of the generals. And in front of those pistols and submachine guns died the elite of the old *avant-garde,* big men who couldn't be pushed around like the people who climbed on the bandwagon later. The leaders of the organization that could claim all the credit for the victories in the streets and meeting places over communism—the *SA*. For the sake of appearances, of course, a few shady characters and corrupt people, plus a *General* Schleicher, together with wife and housemaid, had their brains blown out at the same time. But at that moment, my friends, the idea died. What came afterwards was National Socialism without the socialism. It might have been Fascism, perhaps, but it certainly wasn't National Socialism. What came was the beat of the drum and the marching columns, the waving flags and the fanfares. But it no longer had the spirit of men ready to blaze a new trail with all the hardships and conflict it involved. That spirit was gone."

A storm of voices broke loose and fierce arguments, both for and against, flew backwards and forwards. It was some time before the heat died down.

"But, you know, it must have been like that," a young *Waffen-SS officer*, recipient of the Knight's Cross, said passionately. "There must have been something wrong at the roots, otherwise the moral collapse wouldn't have been so frightful. Look at what happened in other wars we lost, even in 1918, when at least the officers kept face. Look at the generals. Even in this war, 231 of them died in action in this war, as a soldier's code demands. We know that 58 committed suicide. But we also know that 22 were shot for resistance, treason and cowardice in face of the enemy. And we know that Seydlitz, von Daniels, and even, God damn him, Paulus stuck a knife in our back. God almighty! I don't know who in God's name I can look to at this moment. Such a thing has never happened before in our lives. Of course, there's always one Judas somewhere. But this is a mass movement. Generals who desert? Don't you see, all of you, there's a world in collapse far more terrible than the ruined cities of the *Reich*? Don't you see that there's simply no air left for us to breathe?"

He was silent a moment, then he went on more quietly: "My *Reichsführer* refused a military funeral to one of my closest friends who'd committed suicide because his fiancée had cheated on him. After his death, he had my friend's name struck off the rolls of the *SS* with ignominy; he refused him a burial with military honors. And then, after the collapse, he himself goes about the country in disguise like a character in a cheap detective novel, gets himself caught and swallows cyanide. Why didn't he take his responsibility before the victors' tribunal and save hundreds of poor bastards from the gallows, people who'd done no more than carry out his orders? It's not so simple, these matters concerning traitors and saboteurs. The real trouble lies deeper. So deep that I for one have no more desire to go on living in such a world."

"But wait a minute," I said, "don't talk such damned nonsense. Don't you see that we've got to carry on, for the sake of our children, if for nothing else ? We've got to go on so that we can tell the next generation how not to do things. And because we're soldiers, we know that it isn't the flag that matters but the spirit behind it."

"Oh, God!" another cried, "I'm sick of it all, sick and tired. Sick of the whole bloody war, of all this blasted National Socialism and all your damned stupid talk. You won't change anything by it, we played and we lost. Let the dead rest in peace and, for Christ's sake, stop fouling your own nest."

"Excuse me for butting in," the old *Major* answered him, "but I just don't think we can afford that sort of bourgeois decency, however honestly it may be meant. It's only by realizing our mistakes that we can preserve future generations from a similar fate. If our way was wrong, then we've got to say so outright. Come what may. And if a lot of what we did was good and right, then we'll say that too, out loud, in front of and despite the entire world. As long as we remain alive, faith will remain alive in the continued existence of our people. Or are you sick and tired of that as well?"

The young *Oberleutnant* said nothing and walked off. Gradually, the last men of the group made their way off to their tents for the night.

The next morning, we found the young Knight's Cross recipient hanged in the latrine. In his pocket was a slip of paper that said: "I know what I'm doing is wrong, but I've got no more strength left. I'm off back to the boys of my old company who were happy to go before me and also set up camp for me!"

When the *Standartenführer* woke me up and showed me the piece of paper, I was also overcome by the wild longing for death that I had felt so often since 8 May. Nothing throughout the war, not even its end, had oppressed me so heavily as this desire for death.

Again and again I had to force myself to call up a picture of the only two human beings who formed my link with life: My mother and my wife. And, again and again, I had to tell myself that somebody had to remain who would one day raise a voice for truth.

***

So the time passed. Soon it was weeks, then months. No end and no hope. Twenty years for the *Waffen-SS*. All officers to be declared war criminals. Deportation to the colonies.

Nevertheless, the food and the treatment suddenly became much better. For a time, we had plenty to eat and good food: Chocolate, real coffee, canned goods. Later it deteriorated again, but it remained tolerable.

Late autumn came without our noticing it. Not a line from home, I had no idea whether my next-of-kin were still alive or not. I did not even know whether my mother was in the Russian or the British zone. But the ignorance that tortured me also kept me alive. I had to hear what had happened to them; after that, who cared. It would have come as a relief.

Small fires flickered in empty American cans in the frozen tents. The interior of our 16-man tent was covered with soot. But it was tolerably warm.

"Nine years," the *Standartenführer* said quietly, "nine years I sacrificed to Himmler, nine wasted years, fool that I am."

The recipient of the golden party badge clenched his fist. "Himmler and Göring, crap. Why talk about them? It was that man we gave the power to, that man alone. He was lord over life and death, and by God he made full use of it. We kept faith till the end. Did he do the same?"

A young *Untersturmführer*, who had been transplanted straight from school into the inferno of the invasion front and had twice been severely wounded, looked at me expectantly. I understood, but did not as yet say anything. A white-haired *Oberstleutnant* spoke up instead: "I never belonged to the party, but just because we had the worst of it, that's no reason to blindly repeat what our victors tell us."

"We've had total war," the *Standartenführer* scoffed again, " and now we've got total defeat..."

I could no longer keep quiet.

"What do you mean, total war? To say that we've waged total war is total nonsense. We aren't even capable of it. We started big and finished half-stepping. It takes the Russians to wage total war. But from what I've heard here, I have no doubt that our defeat has been total."

"Are you going to defend that man after all the misery that's befallen our people?" a police lieutenant asked me sharply. "Did you see the children dying on the treks from East Prussia? Did you see the slaughter of our women and old men in East and West Prussia, in Yugoslavia, Hungary and, worst of all, in the *Sudetenland*, where the Czechs covered themselves with everlasting disgrace...those Czechs," he groaned. We said nothing; we knew that his wife and three small children had been clubbed to death in Prague.

"The Sudeten Germans fought at the front, and they've paid their account in full in their own blood. But the Czechs? They stayed at home all through the war and had all the work and bread they wanted. Not a hair on their heads was mussed up, except where they sabotaged or assassinated, and there was precious little of that. The Czechs of all people! That tall, blond people, the most intelligent of all the Slavs! I can understand the Ukrainians or the Serbs having an account to settle, but the Czechs?"

"I'm not trying to defend anyone," I began quietly. "I've already said, some time ago, that Hitler was the voice and herald of the Germany we all dreamed of. We can leave history to judge his acts one way or the other. But we're among ourselves here now...far away from the emigrants who've come back in American uniforms to take their revenge on us...a long way from the self-styled resisters...those people, 90 per cent of whom waited until the Allied troops were approaching, before they discovered their anti-*Nazi* feelings and then quickly used them to cover up the lucrative business deals they had done with Hitler's Germany. No, we're alone here, amongst ourselves, in all our wretchedness. We don't need to justify ourselves before anybody. Well, then, what about asking ourselves whether we ourselves are not to blame for the disaster that has befallen us and the whole world?"

The *Standartenführer* exploded: "Us?"

They all started shouting at once. "Where the hell have you been all these years? If you'd as much as hinted at anything like tat before, you'd have been put up against the wall."

"A man, no matter how clever or ambitious may be, is only that which his people entrust in him," I continued, unperturbed.

"Did any of us say no, even inwardly, when our troops marched into Czechoslovakia after Munich? That, my friends, was the moment when we left the road of true National Socialism, and it was for the world to see. That was the moment, when, as a people, we broke the word that Hitler had given on behalf of all of us: One *Reich* of the German people. The Czechs are not and never have been Germans. We raised our hand against another people with no motive other than sheer imperialism. True, this particular people happened to be the most conveniently situated for our economic and geographical aims, but they weren't German. At that moment, the last spark of our socialist ideals was quenched beneath the beating drums of our invading armies. At that moment, we became imperialists before our own consciences and before the whole world. Did we say no that day, even inside ourselves? We did not, not one of us, and anybody who says he did is only lying to save his skin. We were drunk with the dream of power: the world, the whole world! We thought it was something new, but it was as old as the world itself: Thy neighbor's goods, thy neighbor's wife. Look back in history and you'll see that it's a road that all great peoples have taken before us, the Romans, the Greeks, the Asiatics under Genghis Khan, the French, the British. And now it's the Russian's turn. It seizes a people like a great delirium. The delirium of power."

"All very fine and good," one of the highly decorated ones interjected angrily. "But my wife's got three children to feed, and I don't know what they're living on or whether they've got a roof over their heads."

"Just a minute," the young *Untersturmführer* answered him. "You think of that now, but didn't you once preach to us that everything had to be subordinated to the great cause?"

He turned to me: "Our desires, our will, even life and death? I think you're right, only too right. But does it follow that we soldiers who've had to pay the bill for this with our blood and now apparently with our lives, have suddenly all become criminals and gangsters? That's what the clever ones, those who were quicker on their feet than we were, and the emigrants are saying. Didn't we simply fight, attack, defend and even die if we had to, the same as all soldiers anywhere on this earth? Is it true that we've slaughtered children, raped women and massacred the defenseless? Are we to live the rest of our lives in the odium of disgrace, just because we believed, just because we fought bravely and because, damn it all, we were in a delirium?"

"I want to ask you a few questions," I began again, "a few questions that have been plaguing me ever since we've been here, deeply humiliated. If you can find the answers then I'm wrong and will say no more.

"Never in my life did I have a chance of talking to Hitler. And even if I had, it wouldn't have meant anything. I was the little guy, he the *Führer*. The master, as one of you so rightly put it, over life and death. I don't, or rather didn't, know him any better than all the other millions. But I do know Germany and I know that we're all the same, we Germans: All suffering from the same hereditary disease, which God must have given us as a nation as our own particular cross. We, the people who produced the great thinker and critic of pure reason, we, the nation of philosophers, have all become romantics and visionaries as soon as it's a question of politics. In initiative and drive, in the power to invent and produce, we're as good as any other nation in the world. But whenever we enter the slippery ground of politics, we lose all power of criticism. In our thoughts and lives, politics leads a separate existence of its own. We ought to be realists like the other Germanic peoples who see politics only as the business of the nation, as something that must always be subordinated to the nation's interests and not be the master of it, as it is with us. Other people don't wage war for a principle or for the sake of a *Weltanschauung* or some idea or other, but for national advantage. And what a man does for his own advantage, he does soberly and with a clear head. He's careful to make the best use of his chances and to avoid weaknesses, the same as any small merchant in his daily life. But not so with us. We're the slave, not the master of politics. Hitler couldn't do anything different. In spite of his imperialism he was a true son of his people, whose interests he sacrificed to principles, perhaps without even knowing it. So, despite his mistakes, which we will probably never acknowledge as our own, he was actually a personification of the German people. That's why we've lost this game so thoroughly. Not just because of our mistakes; others made those too, but they never stopped calculating at the same time. That's something we've often tried to do in politics, but have never learnt how."

I continued: "What did the world know of the State behind the frontier posts of the Soviet Union? What did it know of the danger brewing behind the barbed-wire boundaries and the watchtowers of the secret police? The White Russian refugees knew nothing about it. They knew about as much of the Soviet Union as the refugees who left Germany and Austria in 1933 and 1938 knew of their own countries; all they could give was a distorted and untrue picture of the true situation. But we did the reconnaissance-in-force for the whole world. Today, the aims of the Kremlin lie open for all to see. We know the fighting power of the Soviet armored troops and cavalry; we know the weaknesses of the Soviet Air Force and the strength of their infantry. We know the good and bad points of their fighting methods and the outlook and state of morale of most of the different Russian nationalities. We also know great parts of Russia's industry. The lid is off the political preserve; the great secret of the east has been prized open. And there's something more. The people inside this preserve have had their chance to see beyond the Iron Curtain, a fact that bodes no good for their masters. Nothing in this world is completely without meaning, even if it is not apparent at the time. We've given the whole world a look at the Soviet Union, its aims and dangers. At this moment, in our hour of collapse and of the most shameful defeat of all time, we Germans, prostrate and crushed as we are, have played our last and greatest trump to the gentlemen in London and Washington, Paris and Nanking: Soviet Russia with the mask off. And there's more yet...our defeat has created a vacuum, which will force the whole world to make its greatest decision. The great nations will now have to decide. And it is we who have forced them to it. That's something worth dying for, even if we won't be there to benefit from it, and that's not yet certain. For the whole of mankind will be heir to our sacrifice."

Silence hung over the tent, and we settled down to sleep in silence. Hours later I awoke and saw the *Standartenführer* standing by the entrance to the tent and staring out into the night. I got up quietly: "Are you feeling bad?"

"I can't sleep," he muttered. "You've driven us all crazy with your talk." He turned, and I saw in the flickering glow of the fire that his face was wet with tears.

Chapter Thirteen:
The Reckoning Of Stalingrad

A short while later, we were split up and sent off to different camps. The wanderings of our barbed-wire Golgotha began.

All this time I had had no word from either my mother or my wife, and the uncertainty about their fate was a worse torture than all the imprisonment. When, at last, I received my first mail in January 1946, it was a deliverance.

At about that time the first stories began to reach us from comrades who had been prisoners in Russian hands. In accordance with the American "automatic detention" policy, every soldier or officer who returned from a Soviet prison camp, after he had escaped or been released for severe illness, was rearrested and put into our camp. The stories of these men took us back once again to the vastness of the east and the murderous war of the steppes.

Men who had been through the Focsani starvation camp told their stories. My friend Karl told us with horror in his eyes of the mass dying of our men; of the original 9,000, about 6,000 had died in nine moths. The picture we formed from these reports was far more horrible in its reality than our worst fears.

Many mistakes were committed in the east on the German side, mistakes that burn in our hearts and are indelibly written in the annals of history. But these mistakes have long been paid for and overshadowed by the torture and death of millions of defenseless German men, women and children in any territory that has come under the rule of the Red Star.

All other reports, however, were put in the shade by the story told by a *Major* who had managed to make his way back to Germany after a hazardous and adventurous flight right across Russia and Hungary, and who then found himself, via "automatic detention", inside the barbed-wire cages of the west.

He had been through the Stalingrad holocaust as commander of a line antitank battalion, and he been taken prisoner at the same time as Paulus. He had lived through every phase of the drama, and his account was sober and matter-of-fact, containing neither false pathos nor heroics. He called it "The Reckoning of Stalingrad" and a heavy reckoning it was.

235,000 men had taken part in the defense of Stalingrad.

40,000 of them had been flown out as wounded.

90,000 men, among them 2,000 officers and civilian officials, had fallen into Russian hands as prisoners.

Thus, 105,000 officers and men had remained among the ruins of Stalingrad.

The tens of thousands of wounded whom the Russians found there were quickly dealt with. Explosive charges were simply tossed into the hospital shelters. On 3 February 1943, the Russians dynamited the entrances of the enormous Timoschenko bunker, thus burying alive the thousands of German wounded lying inside.

So died the wounded at Stalingrad.

And what of the living?

Of the 90,000 prisoners, between 40,000 and 50,000 died of starvation within the first six weeks in the Beketoffka Prison Camp on the Volga, some 60 kilometers miles south of Stalingrad.

Rations initially consisted of a little millet or fishwater soup and a small piece of bread twice a week.

The 2,000 officer and civilian officials taken prisoner were shortly afterwards moved to the officers' camp at Krassno-Armaisk on the Volga. Having been stripped of everything, not only the usual watches and rings, but also boots, sweaters and even pencils, many of them had to march through the bitter cold in their socks, which were soon reduced to rags. Any man who refused to give up his personal belongings was shot out of hand. As was to be expected in those conditions, illness and disease began to appear after a week—mainly dysentery, typhus and typhoid. The prisoners were completely helpless in the face of these epidemics, having been left without medical aid of any kind. The 200 battalion physicians among them had had all medicines and medical instruments taken from them. Even the field dressings had been cut out of the men's tunics.

A little more than a month later, 1,300 officers were transferred to Jelabuga on the Kama River, between Kazan and Ufa. The other 700 were already dead.

The transport was carried out in cattle cars, many of them badly damaged, with icy winds blowing in unchecked through every cranny. The trucks were rated for 8 horses or 40 men, but 70 men were crammed into each of them. They were forced to lie on top of each other to get in at all. The men o the bottom were often in danger of asphyxiation.

A crack in the wall served for the needs of nature and conditions in the trucks were indescribable, particularly where there was dysentery. Daily rations during the journey, which lasted two weeks, consisted of a bucket of watery soup among the 70 men plus two and a half ounces of bread per man, or one salted herring for 16 men. From the bucket of soup, each man received about one or two tablespoonfuls.

The bodies of those who died on the journey, between 15% and 20% in each rail car, had to stay with the living. Apparently, the commander's orders were to hand over the exact headcount, dead or alive. So the living slept on the corpses of their dead comrades. Sometimes they put the bodies, frozen stiff with the cold, up against the worst holes in the truck walls so as to provide themselves with some protection from the wind.

The officers were unloaded in Kissna, and a four days' march began. Three hundred were unable to make the effort and remained lying by the roadside. Many of them died from exhaustion, and the others were simply shot. Any man who still possessed a greatcoat, or had been able to salvage or conceal his haversack of underclothes, had it taken off him by the civil population, stirred up by the local communists. Anyone who resisted was beaten to death with wooden clubs or stones, without the guards lifting a hand to intervene. Apparently, the number of heads no longer mattered now that the train trip was over.

In the new camp at Jelabuga, where the prisoners were accommodated in a former Greek-Orthodox monastery that the Bolsheviks had converted into a prison, there were again no blankets, no clothing and no medical assistance. Soon the camp was one vast epidemic colony, but without drugs or medical care. Within a few weeks, another 600 had died. More and more batches of officer prisoners kept arriving from the various fronts, keeping the total population of the camp around 1,000 men. The others simply died off. The weight loss among the camp inmates was appalling; none of them, not even the tallest and strongest, weighed more than 50 kilograms, most only 42 to 45.[71]

Things improved in the summer of 1943, the result, rumor had it, of intervention by the American Military Mission in Moscow. Meals became regular and rose to 1,700 calories a day. On the other hand, heavy manual labor in the forests was introduced at about the same time. Prisoners were forced to haul sledges or carts piled high with timber, over a distance of 36 kilometers a day. Day after day, they dragged themselves across the country, harnessed to self-made raffia ropes. They were nicknamed by the local Russian civilians as "little Stalin ponies".

Any man who collapsed was allowed to rest on his wooden bunk for a few days, without medical aid or supplementary rations. But even that came as a welcome relief to those tortured men.

When, on one occasion, the prisoners refused to work in the pouring rain without coats or capes, the guards tied ropes round their necks and dragged them off to work. Faced with the choice of giving in or being strangled, our men had to yield.

Many a time the horrors of the German concentration camps had been discussed by the soldiers of the Eastern Front in all the merciless battles and rigors of their own lives and, with rare exceptions, this inhuman institution had been condemned. Every one of us condemned outright the infamous deeds that we heard of later and, although we had no direct responsibility for them, we nevertheless felt shame. But after hearing the stories of the men who came back from the Soviet hell, our feelings about the concentration camps became blunted. What difference was there? Many of the former concentration camp guards, whom we met for the first time in the internment camps, swore in fact that such horrors as we had heard of from Russia, had never been matched even in the worst of our concentration camps.

***

Once though, in the middle of the terrible news that ambushed us again and again, there was some good news.

We were sitting together one day beside the bunk of an old *Oberst* from Hamburg and were red-faced with the heat of argument.

---

71 Translator's note: 50 kilograms is approximately 110 pounds, with 42 kilograms about 92.5 pounds and 45 about 99 pounds.

"We ought to have taken England," said a young *Luftwaffe* officer, a recipient of the Knight's Cross. "We ought to have rubbed out that damned aircraft carrier, whatever the cost. That was our fatal mistake—not to have risked the hop across the Channel after Dunkirk. It would have been a risky operation, but it would have brought victory. Where could the American bomber squadrons have taken off from? In any case, would America have come into the war at all? England...that was the turning point, long before Stalingrad."

"My dear friends," said the old *Oberst* in a deadly serious voice, "let us raise our coffee cups and drink to the victorious Labour Party."

We looked at each other, speechless. The young pilot coughed: "Uh...perhaps the *Herr Oberst* would like to sleep? We'll go at once." The old gentleman laughed until he cried. "So you think I'm not right upstairs. That's not the case at all. Don't you see that nobody could have revenged us on Britain quite as thoroughly as the Labour Party? Everything Britain fought for is gone. Her powerful empire scattered, even after such a victory. Never in our wildest dreams could we have put our military objectives so high. India, Egypt, Palestine... with the Near East not far behind! And to whom does Britain owe it all? To whom do we owe this satisfaction in the face of our shattered Germany? To the Labour Party! I grant you it may be childish to gloat because we're none the better off for it, but please leave me this small satisfaction. And so raise your glasses...hip, hip hurray for the Labour Party."

The cheers and laughter filled the barracks.

"There's only one thing about that," I said at the end. "Things don't quite balance out. The fact is that anything that's lost to the empire nowadays is lost to Europe and to ourselves, whether we like it or not. Britain is in an apparent dead-end street. The Germany of yesterday can laugh itself sick about it, but the Germany of today must look with fear and trembling on the self-destructive development of British politics. And that is the honest-to-God truth."

The old *Oberst* muttered something. "When I see our devastated towns before me," he said smiling, as we left, "I suppose you're right, but I still can't help getting a kick out of it. We're finished, that's right, but we've dragged proud England down with us...and without lifting a finger. I know I shouldn't say it and you mustn't be angry with me, but it's given me such a kick that I can now bear to face our own downfall."

***

About the middle of that year, we began to notice a distinct change in our treatment. International politics began to throw their shadow even over the prisoners behind the barbed wire. Moscow's first emissaries were beginning to make their appearance. Previously, they had been unable to show their faces, but they had thrown caution aside and were busy making skilful use of American clumsiness to propagate their gospel among the prisoners. A group of my comrades turned to me in their anxiety. We held council and decided to act. Starting in a small way, we collected the most important news items from all the newspapers we could lay our hands on and organized a form of "news agency". We thus systematically defeated the Bolshevik propaganda and, at the same time, also dealt with the orthodox National Socialist, those who had learnt nothing and forgotten all.

The American occupation authorities viewed our activities with great distrust. Not only did they give us no help, but they actually tried to hinder the work. A number of refugee emigrants and a deserter who were employed in the American camp command made things very difficult. But we disregarded them and went on our way. Within a few months the, communist specter was laid to rest and even the most disheartened of our people had regained their faith in life and their confidence in the future. There was still much to overcome, and much yet remains to be endured. We who today stand in the forefront of great decisions, know the danger they involve.

Although there were many sensible and far-sighted Americans—Colonel Wooten, the well-known commander of Camp Markus W. Orr comes to mind—they did nothing to assist our inner realignment. At least they did not hinder it. There were also very many, especially amongst the emigrants, who continually subjected us to petty frustrations even during this period while we were struggling to get our bearings. They came, these people, in the uniform of the victorious US Army and confused their personal motives—in many cases derived from the appalling fate they had suffered at the hands of Hitler's Germany—with the interests of the United States.

But even in the places where we did find understanding and feeling for our situation, we frequently met with a complete lack of understanding of the problems of Europe.

The easily won invasion of a bomb-blasted Germany, which had already bled itself white on its Eastern Front, had had the same effect on the American mentality, as the easy defeat of France had once had on Hitler's Germany. In both cases, the victor gained a sense of security which almost bordered on arrogance.

Sometimes, when we had a chance to talk to American officers, we were left with the feeling that the ocean separating us from the American continent was infinite.

But we for our part also tried to understand our conquerors. It is an invariable rule that a conqueror, even the most fair-minded, is led to despise the people he has overthrown or at least to rate them very low. And how were we to make the American, with his infinite superiority over us in food, arms, equipment and all forms of military comfort, understand how we had fought our battles in the east and what we had been through?

We also tried to understand that there are deeds for which the victor can claim the right to sit in judgment over the vanquished. Individual acts of villainy and actual crime.

Such deeds would also have been condemned by a tribunal of German front-line soldiers.

But what we could not understand was how the victor powers could sit together in judgment on a political idea and its supporters. It was this that gave the Allied occupation its colonial character.

Furthermore, we completely failed to understand how the victors could judge and punish soldiers, officers and generals who had done nothing but their duty, who had done what is upheld to the soldier in every language as his highest virtue: The execution of his duty in accordance with his oath of allegiance. We had to suffer being labeled members of a criminal organization, even though in fact we were nothing other than soldiers of an army, which, as will be admitted, was not among the worst in the world.

Most of us were not even members of the *Nazi* party. Many had voluntarily joined the *Waffen-SS*, in the same way that in the United States the best and sharpest of the American troops went to the crack Marines—some of them even being recruited for the Marines.

We had no part in the concentration camps, in the blood baths and the war crimes, which would have been viewed by us with equal horror, had we known of them.

Our officers were among the most courageous of the German field armies; our Generals Gille, Hauser and Steiner among the most competent.

Our men were no less loyal and gallant than the British, Americans, French or Russians.

The judgment of the victors did not touch us; whether in the prison camps of the west or the east, we remained what we were— soldiers.

We laughed outright when we heard of Soviet judges and prosecutors declaring invalid the requirement for German soldiers to obey orders.

From talking to many thousands of Red Army officers and men, we had learned in Russia that there is no army in the world where failure to obey an order is punished as mercilessly as in the Red Army. Above all, we knew the Red Army regulations, written down in black and white, signed personally by *Generalissimo* Stalin and countersigned by Marshal Bulganin. Among other things, these stated literally: "To the subordinate, the order of his commander is the law. All orders are to be carried out unconditionally, exactly and punctually."

We were only sorry that those Soviet judges could not have been asked to say what would have happened to any Red Army man or officer who had refused to carry out an order because he thought it wrong or incompatible with his personal conscience.

No, the accusations and verdicts of those judges did not touch us.

But one thing did: That American judges should have given these verdicts without any protest from American officers or soldiers.

When, in fact, despite the bomb-shattered, war-torn Germany, despite the lost war—lost not through Stalin's divisions but solely and exclusively through the shattering hammer blows of the US Air Force—there lived, deep down in every German's soul, one great hope: The United States of America.

Then came collective guilt for the millions...

Then came hunger and distress...

But these too we overcame, and we tried to understand, even though by that time all understanding was practically gone.

We made great efforts, slowly but surely, to map out new roads. We found them. Not with a lot of fanfare but a quiet search into the inner self.

We found that a man has his foe chosen for him. The enemy is suddenly there, face to face, as if ordained by nature. There is no discussion with him, no negotiating. The most one can do is to submit, for better or for worse. But friends must be found. They must be weighed in the balance and put to the test and then the advantages and disadvantages soberly weighed against each other.

Bolshevism is our natural enemy—pre-ordained, on a national level, from the standpoint of the classes and culture—and there is nothing to be done about it. The truth of this has been proved beyond all doubt by the fate of the Baltic Germans, the ethnic Germans in Yugoslavia, Hungary and the Ukraine, the Sudeten Germans and the Germans from the Volga. And, not least, by that of the Germans in the eastern half of Germany itself.

At the end of every compromise with Bolshevism—whether garbed as a Leninist world revolution or wearing the uniform of a Stalinist world imperialist—is the shot in the back of the head or the *Gulag* in Siberia.

Bolshevism must level down, that is its nature. It must create a laboratory of the people whom it controls, within which it can conduct its experiments freely, without fear of criticism or opposition. No amount of shutting our eyes will change this fact, nor desperate wishful thinking that we alone will escape. Even if there weren't the examples of Yugoslavia, Bulgaria, Romania, Hungary and Czechoslovakia, the cup does not pass by. It must be drained and its effects overcome.

As long as we can find the inner strength for this, then nothing is yet lost, and the millions of our war dead in the east will not have died in vain. They can rest in their destroyed and desecrated burial spots. We Germans have done our share of atonement for the mistakes of yesterday.

We knew that. It was just that the Americans seemed to have heard none of it. That the Americans in 1945 transferred hundreds of thousands of German soldiers who had already crossed the demarcation line back to the Red Army cries out to heaven. That they delivered Slovakians, Croatians, Hungarians, Estonians, Latvians and Romanians to the Bolsheviks cries out to heaven. That the British forcibly turned over Cossacks, who had fought with the German Army for freedom and against Communism, to the Soviet executioners in the Kärnten region of Austria cries out to heaven. That the British handed over Croatians and ethnic Germans to the Tito murderers cries out to heaven. The fact that they transferred German and East European anticommunists over to the Bolsheviks, even within the shadows of rising conflicts with the Bolsheviks, was infuriating. The gallows on which those people died represented the only bond that had remained between East and West. Only in eliminating European anticommunists were East and West still of one accord. Otherwise, they were facing each other in increasing animosity.

Once again, good comrades—Sudeten Germans and Croatians—were being delivered up. Upset German translators told us that on 19 March 1947 in the internment camp at Glasenbach, where I had been transferred after being in the hunger camp at Bad Aibling and the internment camp at the light infantry garrison in Garmisch. All of us knew that anyone on that list was condemned to death.

Depressed, we sat together during our meager evening meal in our barracks. No one had any desire to speak, but no one wanted to be alone, either. Suddenly, someone threw open a door: "Revolt! They're revolting. What are you waiting for?"

His eyes were on fire. We didn't recognize the man any more, he had changed so much. I quietly continued to spoon down my beans.

"You shouldn't go walking by yourself so much," Karl said. He had been a *Flak* platoon leader in the Viking division.

"I'm not crazy," he cried out and threw a window open. From a distance, there was a loud roar; it grew in intensity like a hurricane. In a flash, we jumped up and ran outside.

There was a wild movement in all of the alleyways and roads of the camp. The interned soldiers stormed out of the barracks. Only the most careful of those among us remained demonstrably on their beds.

In the motor pool, the men who knew they were going to be turned over to the Soviets had conferred among themselves and decided to go down fighting rather than continue to be treated like cattle headed to slaughter any longer. It was mostly Sudeten Germans and Croatians that were supposed to be delivered to their executioners. A young *Untersturmführer* from the *Sudetenland*, Willi, had assumed command. In a flash, they had taken an American truck, which had been used for transporting rations. A tank driver from the *Leibstandarte* got behind the wheel. The others mounted up. There were almost three dozen of them. But the motor was not easy to get started. A few American infantry had already shown up, curious to see what was going on.

The Austrian guards, who were posted in the watchtowers, because that was too hard for the Americans to do, were dozing.

Finally, the truck started up. The former tank driver stepped on the gas pedal and the heavily loaded truck rumbled off in the direction of the electrified double row of barbed wire.

The internees, who were standing in front of their barracks, stiffened up. The engine howled in the darkness. One of the gendarmes began to fire. Rounds hit the radiator, and ricochets whistled through the air. At the barbed wire, there was an ear-deafening detonation and a flash of lightning, but the vehicle then began to move out slowly into the open. Keeping his wits about him, the driver did not aim for the street, where he would have received all of the fire on his flank. Instead, he raced across the 100 meters or so to the edge of the woods. In a flash, the men dismounted. Two wounded me, one of them quite badly wounded with a round in the upper thigh, were dragged along. One dead man remained behind.

At that point, the majority of those present had not stirred and had only breathlessly watched what was happening. The dead man and the blood freed us from our inactivity. A chorus of angry cries arose; a hail of stones thundered against the wooden watchtowers. The guards disappeared as quickly as possible. The firing died out, because the guards were lying flat on the floors of the guard positions. The vehicle was able t get through, however and, along with it, its occupants. Only a few were caught in the further course of events.

And the camp awoke. Around 10,000 internees stormed out of their barracks. Two years of imprisonment without proper interrogation...two years of being imprisoned without an investigation or a proper court judgment...above all, two years without any prospect of an end to this automatic arrest...all of that came to a head. In a flash, the fences of the camp were torn down; the guard shacks turned over and destroyed. Groups formed that marched through the camp singing; other sank into the arms of other comrades, crying and celebrating their newfound brotherhood. Nobody thought of everyone marching out of the camp as a single group, although no one would have been in a position to prevent us from doing so. In order to capture those masses of individuals, divisions would have been required to get them all.

For the Americans, the breakout and the rebellion came as a complete surprise. In the camp administrative building was only a young officer, who desperately called anyone and everyone. Most of the officers of the American units were at the press ball in Salzburg. Military police fetched the soldiers—almost the entire force was out on pass—from nightclubs, cafes and bordellos. Alert unit moved in from Bavaria; a reconnaissance battalion raced in. It was not until a half hour had passed that the first completely intimidated Americans showed themselves. They contented themselves with forming a thin line around the camp headquarters, pistols and rifles at the ready.

A completely superfluous undertaking, since it would have already been way too late if the internees had attacked the American barracks.

After an hour, the commanding general officer came racing up in an armored car and attempted to summon the internees back into order by exerting self-confident demeanor. "You need to be back in the barracks in 10 minutes!" He thundered from the armored car. "That is all." The internees, primarily younger solders of the *Waffen-SS*, laughed resoundingly. In a completely unrefined manner, the pulled down their ratty and tattered uniform trousers and showed the American general their backsides.

The Americans were trembling. The individual soldiers, who had taken up position around the headquarters, were so spit upon by the raging demonstrators that they had difficulty keeping their eye cleared off.

One group of *Waffen-SS* soldiers yelled out to the general: "Are to trying to force us to be Communists?"

I was also wedged in with the mass of humanity. When the guns of the armored cars swung on us, I told the person next to me in a flat

266

tone: "If we don't get everyone moving now, there'll be a bloodbath like you've never seen before." Even a single volley of rifle fire in those tightly concentrated masses would have had a devastating effect.

But any appeal to reason was in vain. These people had been stepped on and humiliated for too long. Now they could care less. The first few armed themselves with wooden boards, with hatchets and crowbars that they had looted in the prison workshops and with knives.

But the Americans did not shoot. They behaved in exactly the opposite fashion that we had expected. If a similar revolution had broken out in a German prison camp and our officers and soldiers had been so mocked, any noncommissioned officer would have opened fire after a short unheeded demand for the rioters to break up.

Whether it was that they feared that the salvoes in this internment camp would not only be heard in Salzburg, but also in Berlin, Vienna and Moscow or whether it was that Colonel Wooten, who had been a camp commander earlier had made a lasting impression, the Americans remained at figurative shoulder arms.

Colonel Wooten, who was fetched at this hour of need, elaborately undid his pistol belt and gave it to the closest American infantryman, who promptly dropped it in his excitement. But no one laughed, when the pistol fell to the ground. The masses had turned silent.

Colonel Wooten advanced into the middle of the massed humanity. "What do you want, my friends?" he asked, calmly.

The rifle of the American soldier, who was not five steps in front of me, was shaking.

Everyone yelled at cross-purposes: "Release...Investigations... Stop the automatic detentions...Proper treatment!"

Colonel Wooten proposed forming a commission, and that actually happened. The former division surgeon of the "Viking" Division, *Dr. Felix Rinner*, was chosen as the camp representative.

It did not become general knowledge until the next day that a few camp informants and spies for the Americans had been severely beaten. In the case of one of them, an academic, the beating turned into high drama. Without anyone knowing it, he had suffered for years from a brain tumor. A fist to the face had caused it to burst, and he died.

Other than that, the uprising at Glasenbach had been a complete success. At least one camp had rebelled and not taken everything lying down. In their hour of darkest need, courage and comradeship had once more attained victory: Not a single person was turned over to the Russians from that point forward.

The camp started to be closed down. Fourteen internees had been denounced to the Americans by informants as the "general staff" of the rebellion, and they had been turned over immediately to Austrian courts by a gigantic assemblage of armed-to-the-teeth guards. I was among them. In actual fact, there had been no staff. Our disappointment and bitterness had only vented itself.

For all of us, a new chapter in our lives began. We attacked life the same way we had attacked death for years. Those who had been kept back the longest by the power of the victors, had a more difficult time of it than those who were able to resume their battle for existence earlier.

Even so, the time spent behind the barbed wire was not lost time.

The great Russian Marxist revolutionary, Wladimir Illjitsch Ulyanow, the man known as Lenin, whose glass sarcophagus stands in the Red Square in Moscow, once said: "Mistakes are there for us to learn from." Let us take this deep to heart.

Anyone who emerged alive from the horror of those five bloody years and still has learned nothing or has forgotten all he has learned deserves to be beaten to death.

The German people did not die on 1 May 1945. But because they survived, we, who today are life's outsiders, derive a duty and also a right. For we were not gangsters and murderers, but soldiers and fighters, such as exist the world over, wherever flags fly.

Let us bury this treacherous romanticism and the false arrogance and, with them, the fraudulent self-accusations and spineless cowardice.

Let us live the life of true reality.

Epilogue

Many on both sides of the intellectual barricades will arise and attack this book. Some will find our own mistakes overemphasized, other not enough. Gentlemen on the other side will pronounce it a provocation.

Nevertheless, it has been written with one object only—the truth—by one who lived through the fiercest of fighting, both of arms and of the heart.

Whatever may be said for or against it, one thing is certain: That is the way it was.

If the dead could rise—the men who lie on the Northern Highway, at Rostov, on the Mius, by the tank trench at Malgobek, at Kharkov, along the Narva, on the Wolchow, at Stalingrad, at Lemberg, at Budapest and Stuhlweißenburg, even to those last ones in the Vienna Woods—they would all bear witness to my story.

The German poet, Hans von Schwarz, in one of his plays said: "Nothing is more revolutionary than duty."

Let us live up to this. There is nothing greater that life has to say to us. And our duty is to the shattered Fatherland, whether Germany or Austria, and to the reeling and bleeding German people.

The great delirium is over for good. From now on, a hard and rational sobriety must be our watchword.

Rank Comparison Table

US Army	German Army	Waffen-SS	Commonwealth Forces
Enlisted			
Private	*Schütze*	*SS-Schütze*[1]	Private
Private First Class	*Oberschütze*	*SS-Oberschütze*[2]	(None)
Corporal	*Gefreiter*	*SS-Sturmmann*	Lance Corporal
(Senior Corporal)	*Obergefreiter*	*SS-Rottenführer*	Corporal
(Staff Corporal)	*Stabsgefreiter*	*SS-Stabsrottenführer*[3]	(None)
Noncommissioned Officers			
Sergeant	*Unteroffizier*	*SS-Unterscharführer*	Sergeant
(None)	*Unterfeldwebel*	*SS-Scharführer*	(None)
Staff Sergeant	*Feldwebel*	*SS-Oberscharführer*	Color Sergeant
Sergeant First Class	*Oberfeldwebel*	*SS-Hauptscharführer*	(None)
Master Sergeant	*Hauptfeldwebel*	*SS-Sturmscharführer*	Sergeant Major
Sergeant Major	*Stabsfeldwebel*	(None)	Regimetal. Sergeant Major (RSM)
Officers			
Second Lieutenant	*Leutnant*	*SS-Untersturmführer*	2nd Lieutenant
First Lieutenant	*Oberleutnant*	*SS-Obersturmführer*	Lieutenant
Captain	*Hauptmann*	*SS-Hauptsturmführer*	Captain
Major	*Major*	*SS-Sturmbannführer*	Major
Lieutenant Colonel	*Oberstleutnant*	*SS-Obersturmbannführer*	Lt. Colonel
Colonel	*Oberst*	*SS-Standartenführer*	Colonel
(None)	(None)	*SS-Oberführer*	(None)
Brigadier General	*Generalmajor*	*SS-Brigadeführer*	Brigadier
Major General	*Generalleutnant*	*SS-Gruppenführer*	Major General
Lieutenant General	*General der Panzertruppen etc.*	*SS-Obergruppenführer*	Lieutenant General
General	*Generaloberst*	*SS-Oberstgruppenführer*	General
General of the Army	*Feldmarschall*	*Reichsführer-SS*	Field Marshal

[1] *SS-Mann* used as the rank designation prior to 1942.

[2] Rank not used prior to 1942.

[3] This rank did not exist officially, but it has been seen in written records.

KIEV
KHARKOV
Poltava
R. Dnieper
R. Donets
Novo Archangelsk
Dnepropetrovsk
Voroshilovgrad
Bobrinets
U.
S.
Zaporozhe
R. Mius
Novo Danzia
Taganrog
Sambek
Mariupol
Kherson
Berislavl
Melitopol
ROSTOV
Bolshe Kopani
Chulakovka
Perekop
SEA OF AZOV
CRIMEA
R. Kuban
Sevastopol
Krasnodar
Armavir
Maikop
Tuapse
BLACK SEA
CA
Ba
TURKE